S0-BRZ-036

West Nipissing Public Library

PRUNING
PLANT
BY
PLANT

Andrew Mikolajski

LONDON, NEW YORK, MUNICH, MELBOURNE, DELHI

DK London
Project Editor Becky Shackleton **Project Art Editor** Rebecca Tennant
Senior Editor Helen Fewster **Senior Art Editor** Joanne Doran
Managing Editor Penny Warren **Managing Art Editor** Alison Donovan
Illustrations Debbie Maizels, Peter Bull Art Studio, Martine Collings
Jacket Designer Mark Cavanagh **Database Manager** David Roberts
DK Images Claire Bowers, Lucy Claxton, Claire Cordier
Senior Production Editor Jennifer Murray **Senior Production Controller** Jen Lockwood
Publisher Mary Ling **Art Director** Peter Luff

DK Inc
North American Consultant Lori Spencer **Editor** Kate Johnsen
Senior Editor Rebecca Warren

DK India
Senior Editor Nidhilekha Mathur **Editors** Janashree Singha, Manasvi Vohra
Assistant Art Editor Pooja Verma **Picture researcher** Nivisha Sinha
Senior DTP Designer Tarun Sharma **CTS Manager** Sunil Sharma
Senior Managing Editor Glenda Fernandes **Managing Art Editor** Navidita Thapa

First American Edition, 2012

Published in the United States by DK Publishing
375 Hudson Street, New York, New York 10014

13 14 15 16   10 9 8 7 6 5 4 3 2 1
001—181299–Aug/2012

Published in Great Britain by Dorling Kindersley Limited
in association with the Royal Horticultural Society

A catalog record for this book is available from the Library of Congress.

ISBN 978 0 7566 9272 8

DK books are available at special discounts when purchased in bulk for sales
promotions, premiums, fund-raising, or educational use. For details, contact:
DK Publishing Special Markets, 375 Hudson Street, New York, New York 10014
or SpecialSales@dk.com.

Printed and bound by South China Printing Company, China

Discover more at
www.dk.com

Contents

Using the guide

This guide provides illustrated advice on pruning over 200 of the most popular garden plants and fruit crops. Ornamental plants are listed in alphabetical order by botanical name, with tree fruit and soft fruit described in a separate section.

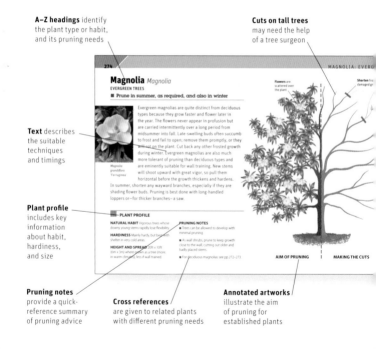

A–Z headings identify the plant type or habit, and its pruning needs

Cuts on tall trees may need the help of a tree surgeon

Text describes the suitable techniques and timings

Plant profile includes key information about habit, hardiness, and size

Pruning notes provide a quick-reference summary of pruning advice

Cross references are given to related plants with different pruning needs

Annotated artworks illustrate the aim of pruning for established plants

Popular fruit crops appear under their common names

Artworks show how to prune for the most productive plants, with advice on wire-training where appropriate

464

Black currants
Ribes nigrum

■ Prune in mid- to late winter

An excellent source of vitamin C, black currants are round, dull black fruit with a very tart flavor. The plants are neat-growing, twiggy, deciduous shrubs that benefit from annual pruning. They like fertile soil but are tough plants and will tolerate a range of conditions.

Plant new plants slightly deeper than they were in the pot to encourage a multi-stemmed form, and cut all stems down to within 4in (10cm) of the base. Growth produced in the first year will not fruit. The following winter, remove straggly stems and others as necessary to create an open-centered bush—the unpruned stems will flower and fruit the following year. From then on, in mid- to late winter, remove up to one-third of the fruited stems. Old bushes can be renovated by hard pruning, but this will be at the expense of the following year's fruit.

FRUIT PROFILE

FLOWERING TIME Mid-spring

HARVEST When ripe, in summer

HARDINESS Fully hardy

HEIGHT AND SPREAD Plants grow to around 4ft x 5ft (1.2m x 1.5m).

FORMATIVE PRUNING Cut back all stems to a low framework on planting. Prune to create an open-centered bush.

ESTABLISHED PRUNING Cut out some of the older stems annually.

Well-spaced branches with an open shape

Ripe fruit hangs down in long clusters

Cut out a proportion of older stems that have fruited

Remove any twiggy growth that will not fruit

AIM OF PRUNING

MAKING THE CUTS

Prune out wayward shoots

Fruit profile details flowering and harvesting times, and advice on establishing young crops

Stripped down branches show exactly where to cut

What is pruning?

Many gardeners approach pruning—the regular cutting and trimming of plants—with trepidation if not downright fear. But in essence, it is no more than a means of keeping woody plants—trees, shrubs, and climbers—healthy and productive so they give the best possible performance throughout their lives.

BENEFITS OF PRUNING

Pruning should always be a positive act. Essentially it is a matter of encouraging plants to do what you want them to. Pruning young plants in the early years establishes good habits, and once they are mature, pruning refreshes them, encouraging vigorous new growth. Although it's possible to reduce the size of a plant and restrict its spread, this is seldom the principal goal of pruning.

We grow plants for particular reasons: usually for their flowers or berries—or occasionally both—but sometimes for another ornamental feature, such as colorful stems or leaves. Correct pruning ensures that plants direct their energy into producing these. Plants grown for edible fruit have their own particular needs.

HEALTH AND EFFICIENCY

Plants exist in a state of permanent adolescence: they never stop growing throughout their lives. Pruning exploits this, encouraging them to push out new stems that are always more productive and disease-resistant than the old. Routinely cutting out dead or damaged material, which may itself harbor disease, keeps them healthy. You can even restore vigor to old, neglected plants—pruning can give them a new lease on life.

TIMING

Successful pruning is a matter of removing the correct amount of material at the appropriate point in the year. While some plants benefit from pruning annually, there are many that need little attention. Always remember—it is difficult to kill a plant outright through pruning, and with a considered assessment of a plant's needs a positive outcome is virtually guaranteed.

Forsythia is a deciduous shrub that can become untidy if neglected. Regular pruning ensures a reliable display of cheery, vivid yellow flowers that wreathe the bare stems from early to mid-spring (see pp.192–193).

Reasons to prune

Plants will grow naturally perfectly well with minimum intervention, but in the garden it often becomes necessary to impose your will. Left to their own devices, plants may lose their shape or succumb to disease, particularly if they are damaged. Fortunately, most plants are very forgiving of pruning when it is done correctly.

A RANGE OF HABITS

When we talk about "habit," we mean the way a plant grows and the overall shape of it. Pruning develops and maintains the habit but can occasionally be used to thwart the plant's natural tendencies. For example, most trees are strongly upright, with a single main stem that thickens to form a trunk supporting a canopy of side branches—rounded, spreading, teardrop-

Plants with upright habits have branches that turn upward, producing an elegant crown that tapers toward the tip. Remove any wayward growth that spoils the outline.

Plants with a weeping habit have flexible stems that cascade downward. Cut back any that grow upright back to downward facing buds, and trim those that drag on the ground.

shaped, severely upright, or weeping. You can cut back this main stem to stimulate branching from lower down; alternatively you could allow the tree grow naturally, pruning merely to maintain the outline.

Shrubs are much smaller. Some are very compact and slow-growing, making dense domes; others are more open and rangy, even becoming treelike with age and developing thick main stems. A number produce quantities of arching, whippy stems annually from the base. In all cases pruning is usually a matter of clearing away old stems to make way for the new.

Remove faded flowers to encourage fresh growth and further flowering.

Climbers are generally plants of great vigor; left alone they tend to accumulate a mass of bare stems with flowers and leaves only appearing above eye level. Pruning and training ensures they are covered in flowers from the base upward.

ROUTINE TASKS

Pruning for habit is done at specific points in the growth cycle (see p.14), but some jobs are more routine and contribute to the plant's upkeep. If they start to rot, dead petals can introduce disease. Deadheading a tree is unnecessary and impractical, but shrubs valued for flowers benefit greatly if faded blooms are removed since it prevents plants from expending energy in seed production. Instead they put on fresh growth—and bloom the next year. If you remove spent blooms on repeat-flowering

Cut out growth that is not typical, such as plain shoots on variegated forms.

Remove suckers from the base of trees—they spoil the outline and sap their energy.

Remove dead growth; it looks unattractive and can be susceptible to disease.

Broken or damaged branches should be cut back cleanly, beyond the break.

Gumming can be a sign of, or precursor to, disease. Cut out badly affected branches.

plants like roses, it stimulates production of more flowers; from the plant's viewpoint, this is the first stage in seed formation.

Variegated plants sometimes develop patches of plain green shoots, which are always more vigorous than the patterned ones. Left unattended, they tend to shoot outward, dominating the plant. Cut them back promptly to their point of origin, otherwise the entire plant may revert to green. Plain cream shoots on variegated hollies (*Ilex*) are probably a response to a sudden change in the temperature. Since they cannot grow much—because they lack green pigment—remove these shoots before they die back to leave a dead patch.

Many ornamental trees and a few shrubs and climbers are grafted: the parts above ground grow on the roots ("rootstock") of a related, usually very vigorous plant. The rootstock itself can produce shoots, either from the base of the trunk or from below the soil surface. Such shoots ("suckers") have a tendency to take over the plant, so cut them back as soon as you see them.

Shapely plants occasionally throw out a stem that is not typical. Upright conifers often produce a strongly horizontal branch, and overlong shoots can appear on normally neat-growing plants, spoiling their outline. To remove them, reach into the plant and sever these shoots from the main stem; if you cut them off flush with the foliage, they will rapidly grow back.

GOOD HEALTH AND VIGOR

To keep plants healthy and productive, you should routinely remove all dead, diseased, or damaged material as soon as you spot it. Dead stems are easily identified in summer when plants are in full growth. Weak stems are unlikely to flower well and may be cut back at the same time. Also remove diseased growth, such as stems showing discolored blotches and those with heavily spotted or distorted leaves, before the problem spreads to other parts of the plant or other plants in the garden. Cut clear back into healthy wood.

Pruning is sometimes a matter of damage limitation. Plants occasionally suffer harm in fall or winter as a result of hard frost, strong winds, or heavy snowfall.

Damage may also be caused by insect pests, birds, and small mammals at any time of year—and sometimes by gardeners themselves if weedkillers are splashed onto leaves, growth is scorched by a bonfire, or stray stems get caught in lawnmower blades. Wounded growth is likely to rot, and the break can provide an entry point for viruses or diseases.

Stems that cross will rub against each other. Where they touch, bark may wear away or fail to thicken properly, weakening the stems and making them vulnerable to disease. If stems become very congested—as often happens with climbers—air will not flow freely among them, and fungal diseases can take hold. Clematis commonly show signs of mildew in late summer as a

If two branches rub, neither will grow well and the wounds may become vulnerable to infection. Remove or shorten the weaker one.

Pruning congested growth to let in light and improve ventilation greatly benefits the stems that are retained.

result of cool stagnant air carrying fungal spores settling around the stems. Thinning the growth significantly lowers the risk of potential problems.

REGENERATION

Pruning can give a fresh lease on life to plants that have been neglected, those that have outgrown their allotted space, or to shrubs that have become very leggy. Climbers with an accumulated mass of tangled stems that are thick and woody at the base may be brought back into line through hard pruning. It may also be suitable for plants that have been severely affected by pests or diseases and to even up growth on damaged plants.

Tame overgrown shrubs by cutting all the stems back to a framework at the end of the dormant period. Recovery is usually brisk.

Cut stems back to a low framework. If there are live buds low down on the stems, cut to just above them. However it is often necessary to cut into bare wood in order to encourage dormant buds to break through the bark. This type of pruning is always best done in late winter to early spring, just before growth is about to start.

Slow-growing plants may take several years to recover fully. Always feed plants well after regenerative pruning, and keep them well-watered during the first growing season. Spread a mulch of organic matter around the base of the plant to improve the soil.

Unfortunately some plants are extremely reluctant to regenerate if treated in this way. Scrubby plants such as heathers (*Calluna* and *Erica*) will not produce new growth if shortened back into bare wood. While older stems of some Mediterranean

plants such as sages (*Salvia*) and lavenders (*Lavandula*) can be cut back hard, this treatment is seldom successful on the whole plant, and old, straggly specimens are often best replaced. Apart from yew (*Taxus*) and cryptomerias, conifers need a cosmetic approach. Cut out patches of dead foliage, then fold live growth around the area, tying the stems in position to conceal the bare patch. Plants that are very bare at the base or are carrying a lot of dead material are best replaced.

Mature trees can be difficult to renovate, and work often has to be done in stages to preserve the balance of the tree. Tasks that involve working at height and the use of powered cutting equipment are best left to certified tree surgeons.

Minimal pruning needed. Some plants are naturally shapely, and pruning is needed only to maintain a clear outline.

RESTRICTING SIZE

Use pruning to restrict the size of plants that might otherwise grow too big. This involves annual shortening of all or some of the growth and removal of any over-vigorous shoots. Some plants respond particularly well to this treatment and can be cut to precise shapes. These plants are often used for topiary and hedges. However, regular pruning to neaten plants can come at a cost: depending on when you prune, you may be removing stems that are capable of flowering and fruiting.

A few plants are best with no pruning at all. They are often slow-growing and flower only when well established.

PLANTS THAT DISLIKE REGULAR OR EXTENSIVE PRUNING

- *Abeliophyllum*
- *Acer* (Japanese maples)
- *Cistus*
- *Cytisus*

- *Daphne*
- *Hamamelis*
- *Juglans*
- *Lapageria*

- *Liquidambar*
- *Magnolia* (deciduous)
- *Prunus* (deciduous)
- *Rhodochiton*

When to prune

Knowing the best time to prune a specific plant can be critical. While pruning at other times may do no long-term damage, it may affect performance in the following year—and sometimes the one after.

HOW PLANTS GROW

Plants have an annual growth cycle that is dictated by seasonal changes. They are mainly dormant in winter, when days are short and temperatures are low, but some will flower at this time. Longer days, higher temperatures, and gentle rain encourage a burst of vigorous new growth in spring. In hot, dry conditions in summer, plants experience a second dormancy. Stems thicken and harden, becoming more frost resistant. Fall storms strip the leaves off deciduous plants, and although little happens above ground at this time, plants experience a surge of root growth.

TIMING PRUNING

Many hardy plants flower in late winter to spring on stems that grew the previous year. Prune right after flowering to give them enough time to develop fresh growth for flowering the next year. Plants that bloom in summer and into fall do so on wood they produced in spring. Prune these in late winter to early spring. A few plants, like *Chaenomeles* and some roses, flower on both old and new wood; see specific entries for how to prune these.

Some plants have copious amounts of sap when in active growth and are best pruned during a dormant period, either in late winter or from mid- to late summer, to prevent "bleeding." Fall weather is often springlike, with short, mild days and cool nights. Prune at this time only if it is essential: it can encourage a flush of new growth that will be susceptible to frost.

The stems of new growth are brighter in color and more flexible than older wood.

SEASONAL TASKS

The following is a season-by-season guide to annual pruning jobs. See individual entries for details on specific plants.

SPRING
- Prune winter-flowering shrubs and climbers
- Prune summer-flowering shrubs and roses
- Remove frosted growth from all plants
- Trim hedges

SUMMER
- Prune spring-flowering shrubs and climbers
- Prune overgrown *Clematis montana*
- Shorten any whippy extension shoots on climbing plants
- Tie in suitably placed new shoots on wall-trained plants
- Deadhead repeat-flowering roses—leave some behind if hips are desired
- Cut out green shoots on variegated plants
- Prune ornamental cherries and other *Prunus*
- Cut back unwanted leafy growth on plants that are grown for fall berries
- Trim hedges

FALL
- Prune only to stabilize plants against fall and winter storms
- Shear over climbers on walls to neaten

WINTER
- Prune plants that bleed copious amounts of sap when in active growth
- Cut back bare, under-performing, or overgrown shrubs and climbers to renovate
- Cut back the previous year's growth on coppices and pollards in late winter
- Shorten sideshoots on wisterias

Tools and tool care

Using the appropriate tools makes pruning an easy and enjoyable task and reduces the risk of long-term damage to the plant. Pruning wounds heal most rapidly if they are made with clean, sharp blades. Take care of your tools: blunt, rusty blades can tear or crush stems, making the plant more vulnerable to fungal infections.

PRUNING TOOLS

Always select the correct tool for the job. For thin stems or shoots, use pruners. Bypass pruners have curved blades that cut like scissors; anvil pruners have a straight blade that cuts against a flat anvil—excellent for cutting material that is firm and woody. To reach down to the base of a plant, or for pruning above eye level, use loppers. Many models have adjustable handles to extend their reach, and most will cut thick stems. To tackle older branches or trunks, use a pruning saw. Depending on the arrangement of the teeth, these will cut either on the push or pull stroke, although some cut in both directions. There are also models available with folding blades. If you need to cut back a hedge or neaten the growth on a climber or groundcover plant, use shears with straight blades. Models with wavy-edged blades are intended for use on thick stems. Clean your tools after use, and store with the blades closed or folded away.

HEALTH AND SAFETY

Pruning can be hazardous, and not just because you are using sharp tools. The cut edges of firm stalks can also be sharp, and plant stems may be thorny. Contact with some plants and sap that bleeds from the cuts can cause allergic reactions. Wear protective gloves as necessary.

When dealing with a tall plant such as a tree or a hedge, make sure that your ladder is stable and firmly anchored to the ground.

Pruners are the quintessential pruning tool and should be used for cutting stems of pencil thickness or thinner.

Pruning saws with serrated blades are used for cutting back older stems that are too thick for pruners.

Loppers are the ideal tool for cutting stems back to near ground level due to their strong blades and extending handles.

Shears are for clipping hedges to shape; they are also used to neaten established climbers and groundcover plants.

Thick gloves are essential; they not only protect your hands from unwanted cuts and scratches, but also against irritant sap.

An oily rag should be used to wipe down blades after pruning to keep them clean and extend the life of the tool.

Where to start

When pruning, you need to have your eye on the plant's future performance rather than the immediate result. Your pruning method will depend on its existing structure and the desired habit, and the types of cuts you need to use will depend on the position of its buds. A careful appraisal of the plant will ensure a successful outcome.

BASIC PRINCIPLES

Pruning stimulates new vigorous growth, which will appear from a bud, or pair of buds, just below the point where you make the cut. In other words, to stimulate fresh growth from near the base of a plant, you will need to cut stems back hard. When you prune a plant, you are effectively wounding it. Cuts made with sharp, sterile blades heal rapidly, especially if they are made during still, dry weather, so ensure that tools are kept clean and rust-free. If the weather is wet or if rain is forecast, delay pruning. Certain fungal diseases are carried in rainwater and may enter plants through pruning cuts.

New shoot buds—here on a rose—are clearly visible in early spring, often breaking out of bare stems.

Opposite buds are produced by the plant in pairs at the same height on both sides of the stem.

Alternate buds will appear singly at different heights and at alternating points along the plant stem.

IDENTIFYING BUDS

Plants produce fresh new growth annually in spring. Growth buds appear singly at stem tips and also lower down the stem, either in pairs on opposite sides or alternately (see left). The bud at the stem tip is always the strongest; cut back to other strong buds for vigorous growth.

ASSESS YOUR PLANT

Before you make a cut, take a good look at the plant overall, taking into account its natural habit and how you want it to grow. Remove all dead, diseased, and damaged material, cutting back to healthy growth. Shorten stems that are already very vigorous and healthy only lightly, or leave them unpruned. Weak-growing stems can be pruned harder to stimulate strong growth. Remove any crossing or crowded stems in the body of the plant. Resist the temptation to cut all stems to the same height—only in the case of renovative pruning (see p.26) or coppicing (p.28) is this likely to yield a good result. The plant may look lop-sided after you have finished, but fresh growth will restore the balance.

MAKING THE CUTS

Always cut just above a bud, or pair of buds. Cut too far above the bud and the stub of wood remaining will blacken and start to die back, possibly killing the whole stem. Cut too close and you risk crushing it. On stems

Pinch prune plants by nipping off shoot tips while stems are still young and soft.

Cut stems back just above a new shoot that is pointing in the desired direction.

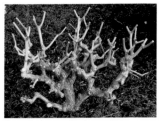
Some plants are cut back annually to a permanent low framework (see pp.28–29).

with opposite buds, cut straight across the stem. This will cause two new shoots to appear from just below the cut, growing outward in a V-shape. Pruning promotes a bushy, dense, compact habit.

If the buds are alternate, angle the cut away from the bud—this prevents raindrops from collecting on the bud, which could cause it to rot. Cut to a healthy bud pointing in the direction you wish the new stem to grow. Cutting just above a bud facing outward encourages a plant with a vaselike shape and an open center.

PINCH PRUNING

To encourage a bushy habit on young plants, repeatedly remove the shoot tips so that the stems branch rather than lengthen. Since the developing growth is very soft, it is simplest just to pinch it off with your finger and thumb. This technique may be also be used to prevent flower formation on soft-stemmed plants that are grown principally for their foliage, such as brachyglottis.

SUCKERS AND WATERSHOOTS

Suckers often appear from the base of a tree or shrub that has been grafted onto the rootstock of a related plant. They are usually very vigorous and will not be similar to the grafted plant. If they are found at the base of the main stem or trunk, cut them back with pruners.

If they emerge some distance away, it is best to dig down and sever them back at their point of origin on the root. If the tree is growing in a lawn, regularly mowing over the suckers when you cut the grass can be sufficient to keep them under control.

Watershoots are very vigorous stems that appear on the trunks of established trees, sometimes in clusters. They are particularly common on pollards (see p.29). Not only do they spoil the clear line of the trunk, but they also attract insect pests that then move to other plants once this food source is exhausted. Ideally, rub off the shoots with your finger and thumb while they are still at the bud stage and

Unwanted watershoots can appear around an existing pruning wound on the trunk of an established tree. Cut them back promptly— they look unsightly and may attract pests.

very soft. Longer shoots can be trimmed back with pruners, although this can leave a visible wound on the trunk.

REMOVING BRANCHES

It may sometimes be necessary to remove a branch from a mature tree, perhaps due to disease or damage. It is tempting to saw straight down through the branch from above, but this is risky. Once you have cut halfway through, the weight of the branch may tear it from the tree, potentially ripping bark from the main trunk and leaving an ugly wound that will not heal properly. To avoid this, first make an upward cut on the underside of the branch, slightly angled toward the trunk to allow rainwater to run off it. Then make a downward cut to meet it. This will allow you to remove the branch neatly. Shave off any jagged or torn pieces of bark from around the wound on the trunk with a sharp knife. The cut surface should be allowed to heal naturally—wound paints are not necessary. If the branch is very long and heavy, cut it back in sections. Often, new shoots appear around the cut, and these are often strongly upright, spoiling the outline of the tree unless removed. They can be rubbed off at the bud stage or trimmed back as shoots. If heavy branches are out of reach on tall trees, or you are concerned about doing the job yourself, employ a professional tree surgeon.

To remove a branch, make a preliminary cut on the underside of the unwanted branch, then make a downward cut to meet it. You will be able to remove the branch cleanly.

Formative pruning

Nearly all woody plants benefit from pruning on planting and in the early stages of growth. The aim is to establish the form: shrubs should develop an even, balanced shape while trees will form a single trunk or several slimmer trunks. Climbers should be encouraged to cover the chosen support. Generally only conifers are planted without pruning.

A HEALTHY START

Plants are usually sold in containers ready for planting in the ground at any time of year. But many deciduous trees and some shrubs, such as roses and hedging plants, are sold "bare-root" during fall and winter

Young shrubs should be pruned on planting since this ensures that they will grow as you want them to. Lightly firm the soil around the plant, and then shorten the stems to create a balanced framework.

when dormant. Bare-root plants are grown in fields then lifted just before sale and sold as they are. They are often available by mail order. Cut any damaged stems back to visible buds, and remove obviously dead roots. Light trimming of the remaining roots encourages fibrous feeder roots to form from the cut edges. These new roots are very efficient at absorbing moisture and nutrients from the soil, speeding up establishment.

PLANTING

Prepare the soil before planting by turning it over, removing any weeds, and adding garden compost or other soil enhancer. Dig a planting hole that is large enough to accommodate the roots. Slide the plant from its pot, and place it in the hole. Check the planting depth—the compost surface should be level with the surrounding soil. Soak the roots of bare-root plants for about an hour before planting. The soil mark toward the base of the stem, or stems, indicates the soil level in the field and marks the appropriate planting depth.

SHRUBS

Check over plants carefully, and remove any dead, diseased, or damaged material. Depending on how the plants were treated at the garden center, growth may be straggly or uneven: shorten overlong stems. Trimming back the remainder may

If the stems of a newly planted climber do not reach the support, insert short canes as a "bridge" to which you can attach the young shoots until the plant becomes more established. Water plants well after planting.

result in a bushier plant. Plants are often sold in full flower so formative pruning can be delayed until after flowering.

CLIMBERS

Climbers are normally grown against a support, such as a wall or fence, or trained to ascend the uprights of a pergola, or an obelisk, wigwam, or pillar in a border. On planting, fan out the stems, and angle them toward the support. Cut back any weak or damaged material. As they grow, train the stems in horizontally to achieve good coverage. Against a wall or fence, plant at a distance of 12–18in (30–45cm) from the base so that rainfall is not unduly screened from the plant roots.

Cut back with pruners any strongly upright shoots that compete with the leader and spoil the natural habit of the plant.

To produce a clear trunk, remove the plant's lower side branches the third year after planting if they are not shed naturally.

TREES

While many trees are sold in containers for planting all year round, deciduous trees are also available as "whips" when dormant during fall to winter. These have a single flexible stem of up to 6ft (2m) in height. Sometimes, short side branches are scattered evenly up the stem, or there may already be an established crown of upper side branches. All the side branches should be left unpruned when planting—unless they are damaged. If the tree has a crown, remove any crossing branches, and shorten any overlong growth to create a balanced, even framework. Trees should be staked on planting; the stake should be a third of the height of the whip, or if there is a crown it should reach just below the lowest strong side branch. Ensure that you do not damage the roots when inserting it.

Lower branches are normally shed naturally, over a three- to five-year period as the tree establishes. Alternatively, cut them back progressively starting from the base, from the third year after planting.

MAINTAINING THE LEADER

Most trees naturally produce a strong leading shoot, or leader, that thickens to form a solid central trunk, with a branching, sometimes spreading crown of side branches. Occasionally however, a tree will produce a second leader within the crown. This should be removed at an early stage: trees with two leaders are unstable and prone to wind damage. Cut the shoot back to the base with pruners.

If a leader is damaged in the early years, you will need to train a replacement. Find a strong-growing but flexible sideshoot just below the break, and cut the leader back to just above it. Tie an upright cane to the main stem, then bend the sideshoot upward, and attach it to the cane. The new shoot will soon function as a leader.

MULTI-STEMMED TREES

A multi-stemmed habit with several strong stems from near the base can look very attractive and will give plants stability,

especially if they are in an exposed location. Often a leader is lost naturally, and the tree will develop a shrubby habit, but you can also encourage this to occur by shortening the leader after planting.

Some trees, such as birches (*Betula*), eucalyptus, and amelanchiers naturally produce strong stems from ground level. If there are too many stems, reduce their number to about three to five. If you want a single trunk instead, select the strongest, and cut the remainder to the base.

Multi-stemmed birches are shorter and more stable than single-trunk trees. Use this shape to restrict size or for a windy situation.

Renovative pruning

While some plants remain vigorous and healthy even at an advanced age, others may gradually become less productive. Quantities of old stems can accumulate, which become progressively bare at the base. Renovative pruning involves cutting all the stems back to near ground level to stimulate new growth and revitalize the plant.

MAKING A START

If plants are bare or unproductive in places but are still producing other healthy new growth each year, there is a good chance they can be improved with renovative pruning. It can also be used to restore balance to plants that have grown out of

Winter-flowering mahonias often become gaunt and leggy over time. Cutting all stems down to near the ground in late winter or early spring results in healthy new growth—pruning can be staggered over several years.

shape, perhaps because they have been crowded out by another plant that has recently been removed. Many gray-leaved plants such as lavenders and sages do not respond well to renovation. It is often best to replace old, straggly plants.

Since renovative pruning involves cutting into old, often thick wood, it is usually necessary to use loppers or a saw. You may find it easiest to shorten some of the top-growth with shears or pruners first before tackling the base.

TIMING

Renovate just before the plant comes into growth, in late winter to early spring. On deciduous plants this is the most practical time since it is easy to gain access to the base of the plant. Hard pruning in summer to fall is not recommended. Cut all stems back to near the ground. Not all plants respond to such drastic treatment however, and often the job is best staggered over two to three years. In the first year, cut back only half of the stems, leaving the rest unpruned. If there is plenty of fresh vigorous new growth in spring, it will be safe to cut back the remainder at the same time next year, or over the next two years.

AFTERCARE

To boost recovery, fork in a general garden fertilizer around the base of the plant, and water it in well. Spread a mulch of organic material such as garden compost or well-rotted manure around the lower stems in a ring. As this breaks down, it will improve the soil structure and increase the nutrient content, as well as keeping the roots cool

Climbers that have accumulated a lot of dead stems like this honeysuckle can often be renovated by shearing the growth back hard. This will stimulate new flowering growth.

and reducing the need for further watering. If the mulch is wet, make sure that it does not touch the stems—this could lead to rotting. It can take a couple of years for plants to recover fully. They may not flower successfully until two or three years after renovative pruning.

PLANTS THAT RESPOND WELL TO HARD PRUNING

- *Berberis*
- *Buxus*
- *Camellia*
- *Cryptomeria*

- *Deutzia*
- *Forsythia*
- *Lonicera*
- *Philadelphus*

- *Ribes*
- *Rosa*
- *Spiraea*
- *Taxus*

Pruning for special effects

Pruning can be used to enhance a particular ornamental feature of a plant such as its stems or leaves, or to show off the flowers. Cut to geometric shapes, topiary plants can play a part in garden design. Hedges may often be little more than boundaries in a design, but they can be kept sharp with regular attention.

COPPICING

This traditional technique was used historically to encourage certain trees and shrubs to produce an abundance of whippy shoots that would be suitable for basketry and fence making. In practice it is a form of renewal pruning. In gardens coppicing is most commonly used on plants that have brightly colored stems such as salix and cornus, which make a striking addition to a winter garden, or to encourage the production of large, exotic-looking leaves.

Each year, in late winter to early spring, shorten all the previous year's growth to within one or two buds from the base, leaving a short stub. Each stub will then produce one or two vigorous upright

Regular hard pruning, or coppicing, of all the stems results in a woody framework that produces whippy shoots each year. Some colorful stems are particularly attractive.

shoots. Over time the base of the plant thickens to form a "stool." Cut out woodier, older parts as necessary using a saw. To develop a larger plant, cut stems back in alternate years, or shorten some stems by just a third to a half of their length.

While coppicing is usually at the expense of flowers, a few late-flowering shrubs are regularly treated this way. Unless cut back hard annually, *Buddleja davidii* is apt to become ungainly; hard pruning *Hydrangea paniculata* will result in larger flowers.

POLLARDING

This technique is related to coppicing but can only be used on trees since it requires a central trunk. Apart from the decorative benefits, it is useful to control the size of what could otherwise be an overlarge tree. Allow the tree to develop a single trunk as normal for a central leader tree. Once the trunk reaches the desired height, cut all the branching stems in the head back to their point of origin in late winter to early spring. Repeat the process every year—or every two or three years for a larger plant.

A pollarded tree typically has a rounded head of foliage on whippy stems, either at the top of a single stem or one that has been allowed to retain a few branches.

PLANTS FOR COPPICING AND POLLARDING

■ **Plants suitable for coppicing**:
Ailanthus, Berberis, Catalpa, Cercis, Cornus, Corylus, Cotinus, Eucalyptus, Paulownia, Rubus, Salix, Sambucus

■ **Plants suitable for pollarding:**
Catalpa, Eucalyptus, Paulownia, Platanus, Populus, Quercus, Robinia, Salix , Tilia, Ulmus

TRAINING CLIMBERS

Some shrubs, such as winter jasmine and garrya, are particularly suitable for wall training—usually on a system of wires. This technique is mainly used to shelter vulnerable plants from the worst of the cold winter weather but can also be used purely for decorative effect. Some plants can be be trained into striking formal espaliers and fans, forms developed for fruiting plants (see pp.428–430).

Climbing plants are often trained against walls or fences that act as supports, or over arches and pergolas for decorative effect (see below). In the wild climbing plants can use host trees for support, so consider training a climbing plant through a mature deciduous tree. Against a wall or a fence, train stems in horizontally as they grow, or in a loose fan formation. Attach them loosely to the wires with wire ties or horticultural twine to allow stems to thicken as they age. Less formally, simply hammer in vine eyes or nails to the wall at suitable points, and attach the stems to these as they grow. Once established, shorten overlong stems in summer, and cut back any shoots growing out from the wall. Tie in other stems to maintain even coverage. Cut back older, less productive stems entirely, and replace them with vigorous younger shoots.

COVERING ARCHES

Climbers are vigorous plants that can gallop up their supports, producing quantities of whippy stems but bearing all the flowers in a cluster at the top. To ensure that the whole plant is evenly covered with flowers, wrap the flexible stems in a spiral around the uprights as they grow. This will encourage flower-bearing sideshoots to form from even low down on the plant.

CREATING STANDARDS

Standards look a lot like pollards—with a rounded crown of foliage and occasionally flowers on top of a clear stem—but are

Vigorous climbers such as this clematis can be trained over arches, pergolas, and other garden structures to give color and texture.

Suckers or unwanted shoots sometimes appear on the stems of grafted standards. Rub them out at the bud stage, or trim them back with pruners.

much smaller. They can be produced either artificially by grafting a small plant onto a rootstock with a tall stem that acts as a trunk, or they are trained. Weeping standards are usually grafted trailing plants. Keep in mind that rootstocks are available only within the nursery trade and are not sold to amateur gardeners.

The simplest way to create a standard on its own roots is to select a young tree with a strong central stem that is already of the desired height. Cut back all the lower sideshoots to clear the trunk, leaving a cluster of sideshoots at the top. To encourage bushiness, shorten them to suitably placed buds. Once new shoots begin to develop, tip prune them to develop a dense crown. When this is established, clip them over to neaten in mid-spring and summer, and at other times as required.

Standards can also be created from soft-stemmed plants such as fuchsias and lavenders (*Lavandula*) using pinch pruning (see p.20). Start with a vigorous, well-rooted cutting. Attach the stem to an upright cane, which is essential both to guide and support the growth. Pinch off all the sideshoots that form on the stem, apart from two or three at the tip. As the main stem extends, lower leaves are usually shed naturally.

Once the main stem has reached the desired height, pinch off the growing tip. This will encourage the sideshoots just below to lengthen. As they grow, keep pinching off the shoot tips after they have produced two or three leaves to develop a dense head. Once the head is established, clip over in early spring, and then again after flowering.

SIMPLE TOPIARY SHAPES

Geometric topiary shapes can look very attractive and are well within the reach of the average gardener. Whichever you choose, shorten all the stems on the selected plant in the first spring after planting to encourage dense, bushy growth, cutting back hard if necessary. Subsequent trimming is best done with pruners or ideally topiary shears. Clip over the new growth in late summer.

Domes and balls can be cut by eye: once the shape is established, clip over three or four times a year—but no later than late summer—to maintain a firm, even surface. For a cube, make an structure comprising four straight canes driven into the soil

To create a topiary spiral, clip to a cone shape, then finish off with topiary shears. Mark the spiral by wrapping a cord around the plant as a guide.

around the plant to mark the edges of the cube. Join them at the top with horizontal canes, tied in position with wire or twine. Stretch chicken wire over the frame to create the faces of the cube. Cut back any stems that grow beyond this. Once the shape is established, remove the structure, and clip over three or four times a year. For a pyramid, make the frame with three or four canes attached at the top. Use five or more in a wigwam arrangement for a cone.

HEDGES

Hedges are described as either formal or informal, depending on the severity of the pruning. Formal hedges are cut to produce a neat, wall-like finish. Informal hedges have a more relaxed outline and usually have an ornamental feature, such as flowers or fruit. Wildlife hedges comprise a mix of different plants that function as a

Boxwood hedges should be trimmed with geometric precision several times a year for a strictly formal design.

Informal hedges will flower and fruit like freestanding plants since they require less frequent pruning than formal types.

habitat or food source for birds, small mammals, and invertebrates.

All hedging plants should be pruned when planting—hard, if necessary—to encourage plenty of new growth near the base. Once established, cut twice a year, in mid-spring and in late summer. Formal hedges can also be cut at other times during the growing season to neaten. Fast-growing hedges, such as Leylandii cypress, should be cut at least

four times a year. Most trimming can be done with hand shears. Ornamental hedges should be pruned more selectively immediately after flowering. If fall fruit is required, such as the decorative hips of *Rosa rugosa* or berries of pyracantha, leave a proportion of the flowered stems unpruned. Cut back unwanted leafy growth once the fruit has started to form. All hedges should be fed and mulched after cutting, as for other plants.

PLANTS FOR HEDGES AND TOPIARY

■ **Plants suitable for hedging:**
Berberis, Carpinus, Crataegus, Cupressocyparis leylandii, Fagus, Laurus, Lavandula, Pyracantha, Rosa, Rosmarinus, Thuja, Santolina

■ **Plants suitable for hedging and topiary:**
Buxus, Ilex, Laurus, Lavandula, Ligustrum, Lonicera nitida, Prunus, Taxus

PRUNING A–Z

Ornamental plants

Abelia

DECIDUOUS AND EVERGREEN SHRUBS

■ **Prune from late winter to early spring**

Abelia x grandiflora

This valuable group of shrubs contains both evergreen and deciduous types. Dainty, white or pink trumpetlike flowers appear mainly throughout summer and fall; the first flowers form on older wood, while the new season's growth flowers later on. In very cold areas plants will benefit from wall protection.

Between late winter and early spring, cut out all obviously dead and damaged stems. If necessary prune the plants again in summer, shortening overlong shoots that have flowered to make way for new strong shoots that will flower later on. Abelias are suitable for informal wall training—remove any awkwardly placed shoots in spring and summer. Generally the plants respond well to hard pruning between late winter and early spring, although this may result in the loss of most of that year's flowers.

PLANT PROFILE

NATURAL HABIT Plants usually form compact, neat-growing shrubs.

HARDINESS Generally hardy, although evergreen types are more vulnerable to cold.

HEIGHT AND SPREAD Usually within 5ft x 5ft (1.5m x 1.5m) when pruned.

PRUNING NOTES
■ Prune to refresh the plant—removing older branches will maximize the production of new flowering stems for the following year.

■ Trimming to neaten in summer after flowering may result in the loss of the following spring's flowers.

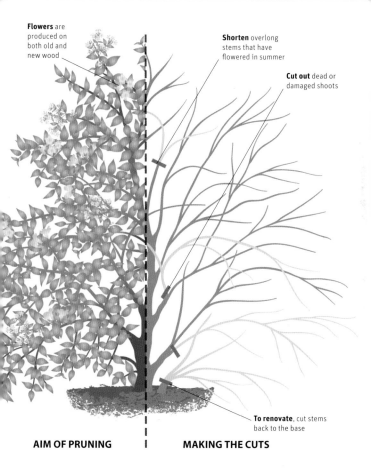

Flowers are produced on both old and new wood

Shorten overlong stems that have flowered in summer

Cut out dead or damaged shoots

To renovate, cut stems back to the base

AIM OF PRUNING

MAKING THE CUTS

Abeliophyllum
DECIDUOUS SHRUBS
■ **Prune from late winter to early spring, after flowering**

Abeliophyllum distichum

A. distichum is the sole member of this group and is a deciduous shrub that produces its dainty white flowers in the middle of winter. While perfectly hardy, it needs summer heat to ripen the wood fully in order to flower successfully. The protection of a warm wall is advisable in cold areas, although formal wall training is not possible—attach the stems loosely as they grow.

The plants are slow growing, so pruning should be kept to a minimum. Assess the plant after flowering and cut out any thin shoots that did not flower, crossing stems, and also any dead or damaged growth. Remove any awkwardly placed branches to improve the shape of the plant. Abeliophyllums are apt to be twiggy and grow unevenly, so pruning should be a matter of balancing the framework.

PLANT PROFILE

NATURAL HABIT Somewhat untidy plants that are fairly slow growing.

HARDINESS Fully hardy, but in cold areas a sheltered spot is needed in order for the flowers to develop.

HEIGHT AND SPREAD 4ft x 4ft (1.2m x 1.2m), with a wider spread if wall trained.

PRUNING NOTES
■ Pruning is best kept to a minimum.

■ Remove only obviously dead or damaged growth as well as any crossing branches.

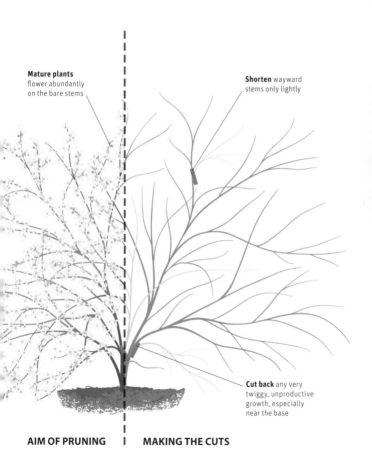

Mature plants flower abundantly on the bare stems

Shorten wayward stems only lightly

Cut back any very twiggy, unproductive growth, especially near the base

AIM OF PRUNING | **MAKING THE CUTS**

Abies *Silver fir*
EVERGREEN CONIFERS
■ **Prune in mid-spring, or at other times, if necessary**

Abies koreana

The silver firs are mainly strongly upright conifers with a firm, triangular outline—specimens often become more columnar as they mature. Dwarf varieties are more compact and dense-growing, a few spreading wider than they are tall. Varieties with bluish gray or silver leaves are popular, and some, such as the Korean fir (*A. koreana*), are grown for their violet-blue cones.

Pruning is seldom necessary, although it is important that plants have a single dominant leader on upright types. Cut back any competing leaders at their point of origin while the plant is young—if a double leader becomes established, it will cause a kink in the trunk. If the remaining branch is not pointing directly upright, attach a cane to the main trunk, then tie the branch to the cane to encourage vertical growth. Cut out any upright shoots on more prostrate varieties.

PLANT PROFILE

NATURAL HABIT Mainly upright conifers with a distinctive conical shape.

HARDINESS Fully hardy.

HEIGHT AND SPREAD Plants grow to around 52ft x 20ft (16m x 6m), depending on the type. Dwarf forms are more compact.

PRUNING NOTES
■ Keep pruning to a minimum.

■ Remove competing leaders.

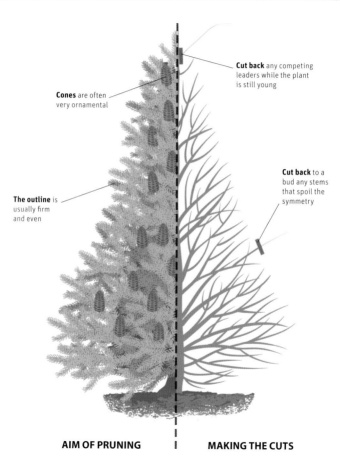

Cut back any competing leaders while the plant is still young

Cones are often very ornamental

Cut back to a bud any stems that spoil the symmetry

The outline is usually firm and even

AIM OF PRUNING

MAKING THE CUTS

Abutilon *Flowering maple*
DECIDUOUS AND EVERGREEN SHRUBS
■ Prune in early to mid-spring, as new growth begins

Abutilon vitifolium 'Veronica Tennant'

Not all abutilons are hardy enough for growing outdoors in cold climates, and those that are will need a sheltered spot. *A. vitifolium*, the hardiest, can be grown with minimal pruning—simply remove any dead or frost-damaged growth in spring. Other varieties respond well to annual pruning in early to mid-spring, which encourages fresh new growth and good flowering. Shorten the previous year's stems by up to one-third. Any bare stems can be cut back harder to strong shoots nearer the base. Variegated types can be cut back hard annually to stimulate the production of larger leaves. Types with arching stems can be trained against a warm wall. Aim to develop a fanlike framework of main branches; shorten sideshoots annually, and cut out older branches, training in suitably placed new stems as replacements.

▍ **PLANT PROFILE**

NATURAL HABIT Upright or arching, mainly evergreen shrubs. Some evergreens may lose their leaves during a cold winter.

HARDINESS Most are vulnerable to frost and need a sheltered spot in cold areas.

HEIGHT AND SPREAD 10ft x 6ft (3m x 2m). Some can be kept smaller with pruning.

PRUNING NOTES
■ For larger than usual leaves, cut all the stems back hard annually.

■ Although some types respond well to renovative pruning, none is long lived, and old specimens may be best replaced.

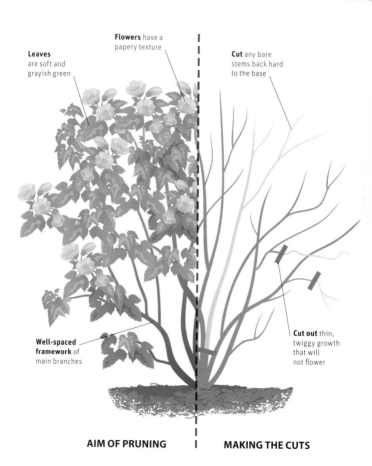

Flowers have a papery texture

Leaves are soft and grayish green

Cut any bare stems back hard to the base

Well-spaced framework of main branches

Cut out thin, twiggy growth that will not flower

AIM OF PRUNING

MAKING THE CUTS

Acacia *Wattle*

DECIDUOUS AND EVERGREEN TREES AND SHRUBS

■ **Prune in late spring, after flowering**

Acacia pravissima

Mimosas produce an abundance of fragrant, fluffy yellow flowers from late winter to early spring. Their delicate, airy appearance belies their vigorous growth—*A. dealbata* can become a large tree. Most will not tolerate hard frost, but some will survive in cold areas if given the shelter of a warm wall. Established specimens can survive a hard winter, although recovery may be slow. The plants can be grown without extensive training; alternatively if they are growing against a wall, the branches can be tied in informally.

Any pruning should be delayed until late spring to prevent new replacement growth from being damaged by frost. Trim or lightly cut back flowered shoots since acacias do not generally respond well to hard pruning. On wall-trained specimens, shorten awkwardly placed stems and overlong shoots.

PLANT PROFILE

NATURAL HABIT Vigorous but airy plants.

HARDINESS Vulnerable to frost, but some can survive low temperatures if given shelter.

HEIGHT AND SPREAD 10ft (3m) in both directions. Freestanding plants will grow taller in favourable climates. Growth can generally be restricted by pruning.

PRUNING NOTES

■ Prune out flowered shoots.

■ Shorten or cut out awkwardly placed stems on wall-trained plants.

■ Avoid extensive pruning.

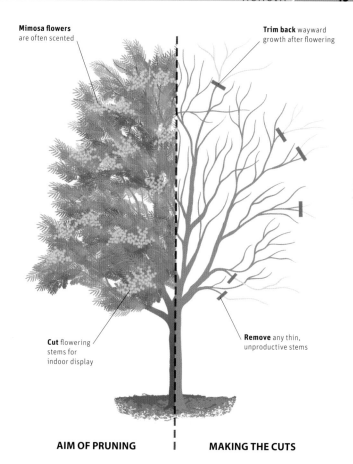

Mimosa flowers are often scented

Trim back wayward growth after flowering

Cut flowering stems for indoor display

Remove any thin, unproductive stems

AIM OF PRUNING

MAKING THE CUTS

Acer *Maple*
DECIDUOUS TREES AND SHRUBS
■ Prune in winter when the plants are fully dormant

Acer japonicum 'Aconitifolium'

Maples are valued for their hand-shaped leaves that turn yellow, orange, and red in the fall. Even though many are—ultimately—large trees, pruning is best kept to a minimum, and even then tackled only in winter when the plants are fully dormant, otherwise stems "bleed" sap when cut.

Commonly grown Japanese maples (varieties of *A. japonicum* and *A. palmatum*) are dainty, airy trees suitable for smaller gardens and ideal for growing in containers, especially in a sheltered, partially shaded courtyard. The leaves are often finely cut and are of interest both in early spring, when they unfurl with great elegance, and just before they drop. The plants are as delicate as they look, so restrict pruning to the shortening of twiggy growth and removal of anything that spoils the graceful outline.

■ PLANT PROFILE

NATURAL HABIT Graceful trees, either spreading or more upright.

HARDINESS Mainly fully hardy.

HEIGHT AND SPREAD Normally within 6ft (2m) in both directions. Plants grown in containers are generally smaller. Variegated forms are less vigorous.

PRUNING NOTES
■ Types with variegated leaves have a tendency to revert to plain green. Cut these stems out as soon as you see them.

■ Healing will be most rapid in dry, settled weather.

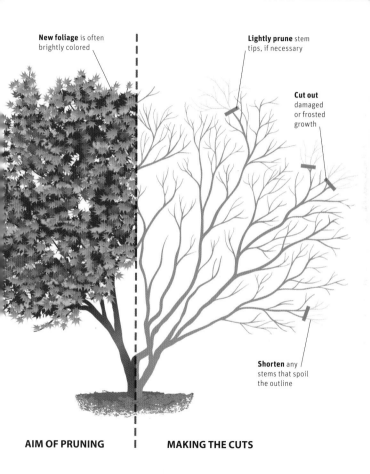

New foliage is often brightly colored

Lightly prune stem tips, if necessary

Cut out damaged or frosted growth

Shorten any stems that spoil the outline

AIM OF PRUNING

MAKING THE CUTS

Actinidia *Kiwi*
DECIDUOUS CLIMBERS
■ **Prune in winter and again in summer, if necessary**

Actinidia kolomikta

These deciduous climbers are grown for their leaves, and in some cases fruits. Plants within the genus grow with differing degrees of vigor, so pruning should be adjusted accordingly.

The most commonly grown, *A. kolomikta*, is a beautiful plant bearing pointed leaves that are either plain green or generously splashed with pink and cream. Since it is not very vigorous, pruning is straightforward. In winter, when the stems are bare, assess the framework and take out any older stems, thinning the remainder to even up the growth. In summer, shorten any wayward stems as you tie in new growth. If necessary, trim the plants for a neater shape. The kiwi fruit, *A. deliciosa*, often grown as an ornamental, is far more vigorous and will need regular pruning.

PLANT PROFILE

NATURAL HABIT Twiggy climbers with thin, twining stems.

HARDINESS Fully hardy.

HEIGHT AND SPREAD 10ft (3m) in both directions. With training, plants can achieve a greater width than height.

PRUNING NOTES
■ Good coverage of the support is best achieved by the removal of older, unproductive stems.

■ Train in strong new shoots to balance the framework.

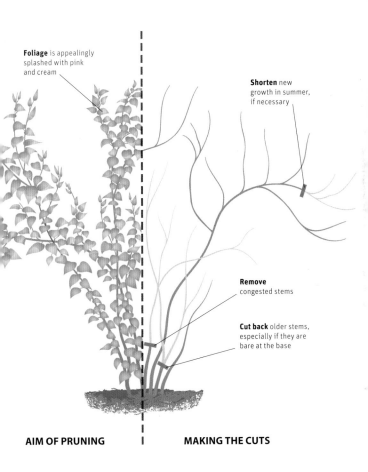

Foliage is appealingly splashed with pink and cream

Shorten new growth in summer, if necessary

Remove congested stems

Cut back older stems, especially if they are bare at the base

AIM OF PRUNING

MAKING THE CUTS

Aesculus *Buckeye*
DECIDUOUS TREES AND SHRUBS
■ Prune in late winter to early spring

Aesculus hippocastanum

These stately trees are grown for their overall presence and striking early summer flowers. When young they make fine specimens for smaller gardens, with their pleasing conical shape, but in time they can outgrow the available space and need replacing.

Pruning is best kept to a minimum in the early years when shoots low down the main trunk are needed to fuel the plant's growth. Start clearing the trunk three to five years after planting, cutting off unwanted thin shoots flush with the bark in late winter to early spring.

Leaf miners can damage trees, particularly from mid- to late summer. Affected parts of the tree need not be pruned out—health in future years is not necessarily adversely affected. Mature trees affected by bleeding canker, which causes dieback, are often best destroyed, though sometimes the problem can be managed through tree surgery.

PLANT PROFILE

NATURAL HABIT Stately trees, often symmetrical when young, becoming more open as they age.

HARDINESS Mostly fully hardy.

HEIGHT AND SPREAD Plants grow to around 80ft x 70ft (25m x 20m) when mature.

PRUNING NOTES
■ Keep pruning to a minimum.

■ The removal of older branches on mature trees is best done by a tree surgeon.

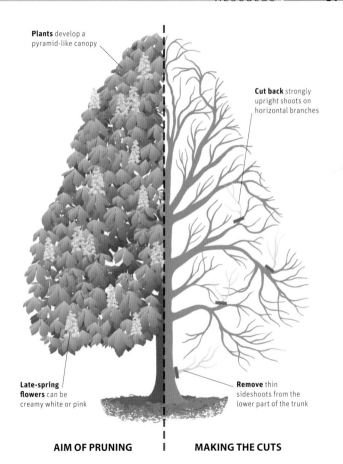

Plants develop a pyramid-like canopy

Cut back strongly upright shoots on horizontal branches

Late-spring flowers can be creamy white or pink

Remove thin sideshoots from the lower part of the trunk

AIM OF PRUNING

MAKING THE CUTS

Akebia *Chocolate vine*

DECIDUOUS CLIMBERS

■ **Prune in late spring to early summer, after flowering**

Akebia quinata

Akebias are vigorous climbers that are usually deciduous in cold climates. If the spoon-shaped leaves are not shed, they often take on bronze tints during cold winter weather. The small spring flowers—for which the plants are principally grown—are dark maroon-purple, and chocolate scented.

In the early years, establish a framework of main stems in a fan shape; shorten sideshoots once the stems have been tied in. In later years, prune annually after flowering, shortening all flowered stems, cutting back older long shoots, and tying in vigorous replacements. As with most twining climbers the stems tend to wrap around each other, leading to congestion within the body of the plant. Cut out older woody stems at the base, and untwine them from the younger ones, working from the base and cutting them in sections as you go.

PLANT PROFILE

NATURAL HABIT Vigorous climbers with twining stems.

HARDINESS Fully hardy, but best against a warm wall in cold areas to protect the spring flowers from frost.

HEIGHT AND SPREAD 20ft x 12ft (6m x 4m), but can be kept smaller with pruning.

PRUNING NOTES
■ Growth can become congested if stems are allowed to twine around each other. Thin stems regularly to avoid this.

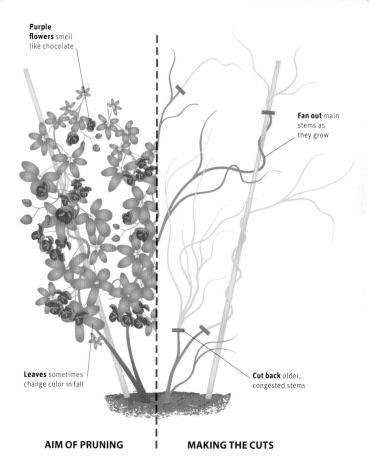

Purple flowers smell like chocolate

Fan out main stems as they grow

Leaves sometimes change color in fall

Cut back older, congested stems

AIM OF PRUNING

MAKING THE CUTS

Alnus *Alder*
DECIDUOUS TREES
■ **Prune in late fall to midwinter**

Alnus glutinosa 'Imperialis'

Alders are commonly used as "utility trees" to strengthen wet ground. Their late-winter catkins—which appear on bare stems—are ornamental; some varieties are also grown for their leaves, which can be lacy or bright golden-yellow when young.

Some naturally grow as trees with a main central trunk while others (such as the gray alder, *A. incana*) branch freely from the base. Encourage plants to branch by cutting them to near ground level at the end of the first winter after planting. Alternatively, plants can be grown with a single trunk—select the strongest stem, and remove all the others. Otherwise prune only as required between late fall and midwinter when the branches are bare. Damaged branches can be removed in summer, but only if strictly necessary.

PLANT PROFILE

NATURAL HABIT Fast-growing trees, some of which shoot freely from the base.

HARDINESS Fully hardy.

HEIGHT AND SPREAD 20ft x 10ft (6m x 3m), although some named varieties are less vigorous.

PRUNING NOTES
■ Pruning can be kept to a minimum.

■ Established trees respond well to renovative pruning.

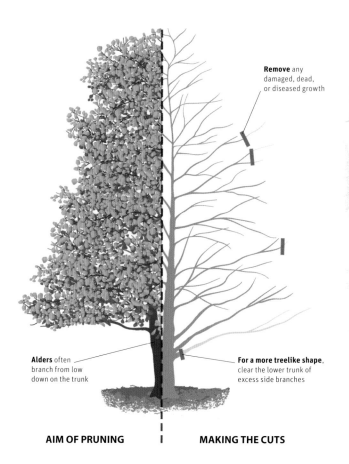

Remove any damaged, dead, or diseased growth

Alders often branch from low down on the trunk

For a more treelike shape, clear the lower trunk of excess side branches

AIM OF PRUNING

MAKING THE CUTS

Aloysia *Verbena*
DECIDUOUS OR EVERGREEN SHRUBS
■ **Prune after the last hard frost**

Aloysia triphylla

Verbena is an upright shrub that often loses its leaves over winter in cold areas. The leaves, which give off a delicious lemon aroma when crushed, are its main attraction, though white to pinkish lilac flowers often appear in small upright spikes in late summer.

Regular pruning encourages fresh leaf production, but this is generally at the expense of the flowers. In spring once all danger of frost has passed, shorten the previous year's growth to strong buds lower down the stems. Thereafter—till midsummer, or later in warm areas—pinch off the shoot tips regularly. This encourages the plant to become bushy but will prevent flowering. During summer, reduce the number of stems to relieve congestion, if necessary. Plants are not long-lived, so older, woody specimens will need replacing.

PLANT PROFILE

NATURAL HABIT Dainty, upright shrubs.

HARDINESS Plants are vulnerable to frost, so should be grown in a sheltered spot in cold areas.

HEIGHT AND SPREAD Usually within 3ft x 3ft (1m x 1m) in cold regions; plants can grow bigger in warmer climates.

PRUNING NOTES
■ Regular pruning is required to maintain production of new stems and leaves.

■ Regularly pinch off the shoot tips in summer to promote bushiness.

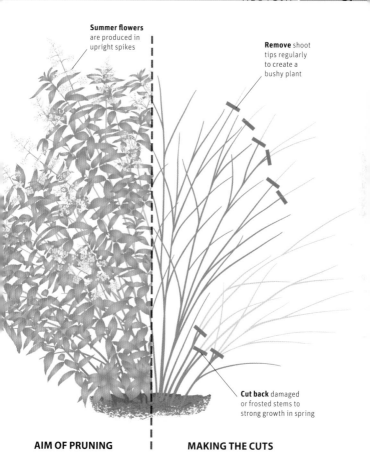

Summer flowers are produced in upright spikes

Remove shoot tips regularly to create a bushy plant

Cut back damaged or frosted stems to strong growth in spring

AIM OF PRUNING

MAKING THE CUTS

Amelanchier *Serviceberry*
DECIDUOUS TREES AND SHRUBS
■ **Prune in late spring/summer after plants have flowered**

Amelanchier lamarckii

These dainty, spring-flowering shrubs or small trees are an excellent substitute for flowering cherries (*Prunus*), which can be too large for many gardens. They also have vivid fall leaf color. Most are naturally multi-stemmed, although these stems become bare at the base with age.

For a treelike shape, remove all but the strongest stem and allow this to grow upright. Clear the trunk of its lower shoots as it grows—this job is most easily done in winter when the plant has shed its leaves.

For multi-stemmed plants, thin the shoots in winter, removing old, thickened branches and any thin, weak ones. Some serviceberries tend to produce suckers; to restrict their spread, cut them back as soon as you see them.

PLANT PROFILE

NATURAL HABIT Graceful trees or multi-stemmed shrubs.

HARDINESS Fully hardy, although flowers may be susceptible to late frost damage in very cold regions.

HEIGHT AND SPREAD 6–10ft (2–3m) in both directions.

PRUNING NOTES
■ Remove older branches and any thin, unproductive growth.

■ Cut back suckers as seen.

■ Hard pruning to invigorate old, multi-stemmed plants is usually successful.

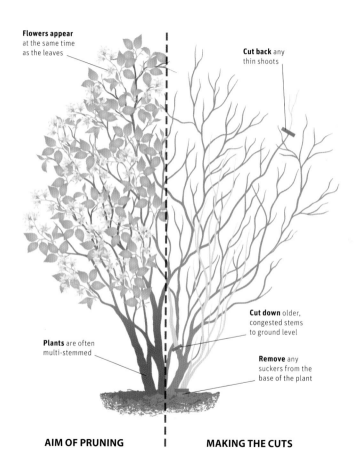

Flowers appear at the same time as the leaves

Cut back any thin shoots

Cut down older, congested stems to ground level

Plants are often multi-stemmed

Remove any suckers from the base of the plant

AIM OF PRUNING

MAKING THE CUTS

Aralia
DECIDUOUS AND EVERGREEN TREES AND SHRUBS
■ Prune in early spring, before new leaves unfurl

Aralia elata
'Variegata'

These hardy shrubs are valued for their frothy, white, late-summer flowers and elegant foliage, which is sometimes attractively variegated. The plants can be either treelike or multi-stemmed and do not take kindly to extensive pruning. Young plants should be allowed to develop with minimum intervention—they will decide for themselves whether to form a single trunk or a cluster of several.

Prune them, if necessary, in early spring. Since the plants are late to leaf, it can be difficult to distinguish dead from merely dormant growth, so prune with caution. Shorten any obviously frost-damaged stems back to a suitably placed strong bud. Cut out plain green shoots on variegated varieties as you spot them. All plants have a tendency to produce suckers around the base, and these should also be removed on sight.

PLANT PROFILE

NATURAL HABIT Spreading shrubs or trees, usually with multiple stems at the base.

HARDINESS Mostly fully hardy.

HEIGHT AND SPREAD 12ft x 12ft (4m x 4m); sometimes more.

PRUNING NOTES
■ Plants do not respond well to heavy pruning, so this is best kept to a minimum.

■ Routinely remove suckers and—on variegated varieties—plain green growth.

Flowers are carried at the ends of branches

Cut out any shoots with plain green leaves on variegated forms

Remove suckers from the base of the plant

AIM OF PRUNING

MAKING THE CUTS

Arbutus *Manzanita*

EVERGREEN TREES AND SHRUBS

■ **Prune in spring, when risk of hard frost has passed**

Arbutus x andrachnoides

Evergreen manzanitas have a naturally good shape and are well balanced, often branching freely from near ground level like a large shrub, even if they have a strong central trunk. The fruits—orange-red and edible, although not very tasty—last on the tree over the winter, only ripening during the following fall. Their presence as the new white or pink flowers appear in spring gives trees a delightful appearance. The reddish bark is also appealing, particularly if trees are placed where it will be lit up by the winter sun.

Grow them with minimal pruning. Any necessary work, such as removing damaged or awkwardly placed shoots, should be done in spring, well after all danger of hard frost has passed. This may be best left to a professional tree trimmer.

PLANT PROFILE

NATURAL HABIT Usually shapely, often rounded evergreen trees that sometimes branch from near the base.

HARDINESS Mainly hardy, although young specimens need protection from hard frosts.

HEIGHT AND SPREAD 25ft x 25ft (8m x 8m), more or less, depending on the species.

PRUNING NOTES
■ Trees are naturally well balanced and are best grown without extensive pruning.

Leaves can be toothed at the margins

New flowers appear at the same time as the previous year's fruits ripen

Remove any damaged branches

AIM OF PRUNING

MAKING THE CUTS

Aronia *Chokeberry*
DECIDUOUS SHRUBS
■ Prune in late winter to early spring

Aronia x prunifolia 'Brilliant'

These deciduous shrubs are grown for their hawthornlike white spring flowers, fall leaf color, and blue-black or red berries that last well into winter. They become naturally rounded shrubs.

For maximum flowering and fruiting, pruning is best kept to a minimum. From late winter to early spring, cut out any crossing or congested shoots, retaining vigorous, healthy growth. On established plants, also cut out older, unproductive stems at the base. Growth can also be thinned in summer after flowering—although this may be at the loss of some berrying wood and other material that may flower the following year. To restrict the spread, remove suckers from around the base of the plant, digging down to their point of origin to sever them. Aronias can also be used for an informal hedge.

PLANT PROFILE

NATURAL HABIT Rounded shrubs.

HARDINESS Fully hardy.

HEIGHT AND SPREAD 6ft x 10ft (2m x 3m), although some forms are more upright than spreading.

PRUNING NOTES
■ Pruning should be minimal, although suckers can be removed to ease congestion within the plant and restrict its spread.

Leaves change color in fall

White flowers are followed by attractive berries

Cut out any older stems in spring

Remove suckers from around the base of the plant

AIM OF PRUNING

MAKING THE CUTS

Artemisia *Wormwood*
DECIDUOUS AND EVERGREEN SHRUBS
■ **Prune in spring, then as necessary in summer**

Artemisia abrotanum

Grown for their mainly silvery gray, aromatic foliage rather than their flowers—which some gardeners consider unattractive—artemisias are often included in herb gardens or used in mixed borders as a foil to flowers planted for summer color. They can be short-lived, especially in damp soils.

Both evergreen and deciduous varieties freely produce copious shoots from near ground level but may become straggly if neglected. Pruning maintains the production of fresh young stems and leaves and can also inhibit flowering, which may be desirable.

For the best foliage, cut all the growth back to a low framework—even into bare wood—in early spring. Trim the plants later in the growing season to neaten them, as necessary.

PLANT PROFILE

NATURAL HABIT Low-growing, sometimes spreading shrubs.

HARDINESS Mainly fully hardy. They are more likely to suffer the effects of cold in poorly drained soils.

HEIGHT AND SPREAD 3ft x 3ft (1m x 1m), although some are taller or more spreading.

PRUNING NOTES
■ Trim plants annually to slow down the build up of old, unproductive stems.

■ Trim the plants throughout the growing season, as necessary.

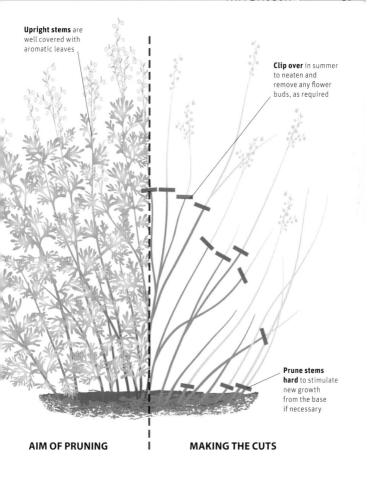

Upright stems are well covered with aromatic leaves

Clip over in summer to neaten and remove any flower buds, as required

Prune stems hard to stimulate new growth from the base if necessary

AIM OF PRUNING

MAKING THE CUTS

Aucuba *Spotted laurel*
EVERGREEN SHRUBS
■ **Prune in spring, and at other times as required**

Aucuba japonica 'Crotonifolia'

Good evergreens for shade and also excellent in containers or as a thick hedge, aucubas are easily taken for granted. They usually become dome-shaped shrubs, although they can be more asymmetrical in the shade as the stems reach toward the light. *A. japonica* 'Crotonifolia', with large leathery leaves splashed and mottled with yellow, is one of the most popular.

Prune young plants to encourage a bushy look. In cold areas shoot tips are sometimes blackened by frost; cut back affected growth to healthy buds in spring. If an over-vigorous shoot spoils the outline, cut it back to its point of origin within the bush. Leaves are prone to blacken when cut, so trim hedges with pruners to avoid shredding individual leaves. If necessary, renovate overgrown shrubs by cutting a portion of stems back hard over two or three years.

PLANT PROFILE

NATURAL HABIT Usually rounded, dome-shaped evergreen shrubs.

HARDINESS Fully hardy, although shoots can be blackened by hard frost.

HEIGHT AND SPREAD Plants can grow to 10ft x 10ft (3m x 3m); less with pruning.

PRUNING NOTES
■ Shorten stems that spoil the outline.

■ Remove any frosted growth.

■ Renovate in stages, cutting back some stems each year over two or three years.

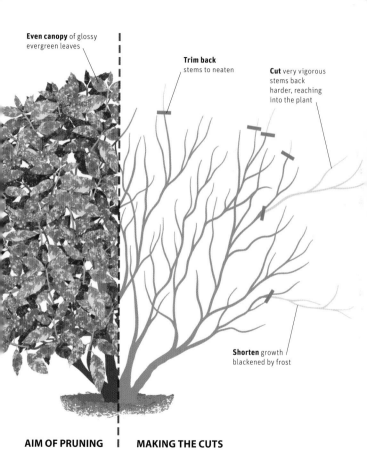

Even canopy of glossy evergreen leaves

Trim back stems to neaten

Cut very vigorous stems back harder, reaching into the plant

Shorten growth blackened by frost

AIM OF PRUNING | **MAKING THE CUTS**

Azara

EVERGREEN SHRUBS

■ Prune in mid-spring, and after flowering if necessary

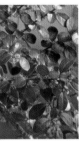

Azara microphylla

Azaras produce their fragrant yellow flowers at various times of the year, depending on the type grown. Not hardy enough to grow as freestanding shrubs in all gardens, most will grow against a wall, and some have arching stems that are suitable for training. In a warm area mauve or white berries succeed the flowers.

In cold areas, remove frosted growth in mid-spring, and shorten wayward stems to neaten. Any other necessary pruning can be done immediately after flowering, although this may reduce the number of berries. On wall-trained plants, cut out old stems, and remove badly placed growth. In warm areas, where some azaras can be used for hedging, freestanding plants need minimal pruning. One of the hardiest, *A. microphylla*, is shade-tolerant and dense-growing, with small leaves. It can be clipped to shape—at the expense of the flowers.

PLANT PROFILE

NATURAL HABIT Elegant, neat, upright to arching shrubs that can become small trees.

HARDINESS Most will tolerate freezing temperatures but are best given the shelter of a wall in very cold areas.

HEIGHT AND SPREAD Plants usually grow to around 10ft x 10ft (3m x 3m).

PRUNING NOTES
■ Prune immediately after flowering.

■ Clip hedges back in spring, or during fall in warm areas.

■ Hard pruning to renovate in late spring is usually successful.

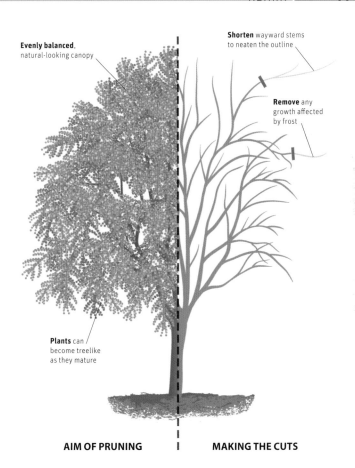

Evenly balanced, natural-looking canopy

Shorten wayward stems to neaten the outline

Remove any growth affected by frost

Plants can become treelike as they mature

AIM OF PRUNING

MAKING THE CUTS

Berberis *Barberry*

DECIDUOUS SHRUBS

■ **Prune in summer or in late winter to early spring**

Berberis thunbergii 'Helmond Pillar'

Deciduous berberis are generally grown for their foliage, which often turns shades of rich orange-red in fall. Forms vary; some are arching shrubs, while others have a much more upright look. Judicious pruning can enhance the fall display, since the best color is produced by older stems. In summer, thin the plant to reduce congestion, cutting back to the ground any older stems that have become bare at the base.

For the most vivid spring foliage, cut all the stems back hard to near ground level annually in late winter to early spring. This will encourage the plant to produce larger leaves, although it will be at the expense of any of the late-spring flowers, and the fall display will not be as good. Deciduous barberries are sometimes used as hedging plants. Clip them over in spring and summer to achieve a neat outline.

PLANT PROFILE

NATURAL HABIT Twiggy shrubs. Some have an upright look; others are arching.

HARDINESS Fully hardy.

HEIGHT AND SPREAD Around 6ft x 6ft (2m x 2m); less if regularly cut back.

PRUNING NOTES
■ Thin stems during summer for good fall foliage effect, or cut back all stems in spring for the best new foliage.

■ The stems carry sharp thorns, so wear protective gloves when pruning.

■ For evergreen berberis see pp.74–75.

Many forms have colorful leaves

Shorten stems after flowering to keep plants within bounds

Thin stems to reduce congestion within the body of the plant

Cut stems hard back in spring for the best young foliage

AIM OF PRUNING

MAKING THE CUTS

Berberis *Barberry*
EVERGREEN SHRUBS
■ Prune in early summer, immediately after flowering

Berberis darwinii

Evergreen berberis make good hedging plants, especially if a thorny barrier is needed for security. They are also excellent additions to a shrub border or on a bank, with arching stems that are wreathed in small yellow or orange flowers in spring followed by attractive red or black berries.

For the best ornamental effect, keep pruning to a minimum. The flowers are borne on the previous year's growth, so cut out older stems after flowering if necessary. Shoots that have flowered can be shortened at the same time, but this will be at the loss of fall fruits and may spoil the overall outline. Shear over hedges in early summer after flowering—this will encourage the densest growth for a security hedge, but results in the loss of most of the berries. Wear gloves when pruning to protect against the thorns.

PLANT PROFILE

NATURAL HABIT Mainly upright to arching shrubs that can have a rounded outline.

HARDINESS Fully hardy.

HEIGHT AND SPREAD 6ft x 6ft (2m x 2m); less with regular pruning.

PRUNING NOTES
■ For the most natural shape, keep pruning to a minimum: prune after flowering if necessary.

■ Trim hedges in summer.

■ Renovate in late winter to early spring.

■ For deciduous berberis, see pp.72–73.

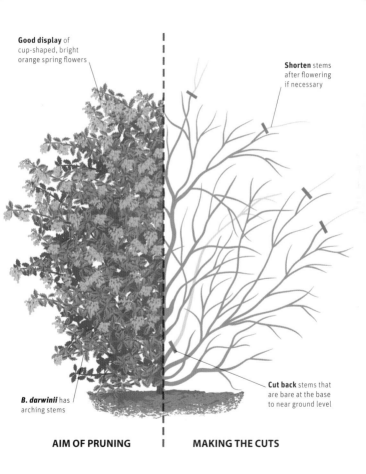

Good display of cup-shaped, bright orange spring flowers

Shorten stems after flowering if necessary

B. darwinii has arching stems

Cut back stems that are bare at the base to near ground level

AIM OF PRUNING

MAKING THE CUTS

Betula *Birch*

DECIDUOUS TREES

■ Prune in late winter

Betula pendula

Birches are airy trees with several seasons of interest. Some have charming spring catkins, and nearly all have excellent fall leaf color. Several are grown for their appealing bark—of particular interest in winter—and many have a very pleasing overall shape that is evident even at an early age. Birches are often grown on a single trunk, though the popular silver birch (*B. pendula*) may develop as a multi-stemmed tree.

Pruning is best kept to a minimum. Around three to five years after planting, twiggy shoots growing low down on the main stem can be removed, as long as the main crown is of good shape. To accentuate the shape of the weeping type of silver birch (*B. pendula* 'Tristis'), clear the trunk to a height of 6ft (2m) or more over a period of two to three years.

PLANT PROFILE

NATURAL HABIT Open, airy trees that sometimes develop several trunks.

HARDINESS Fully hardy.

HEIGHT AND SPREAD Plants grow to around 25ft x 12ft (8m x 4m).

PRUNING NOTES
■ Little routine pruning is needed, but lower stems can be cleared away over a period of years on varieties grown for their bark.

■ You may need to employ a tree surgeon to prune large specimens.

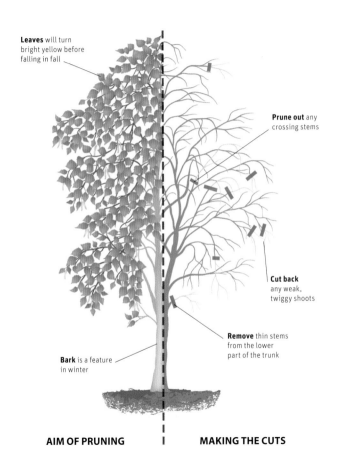

Leaves will turn bright yellow before falling in fall

Prune out any crossing stems

Cut back any weak, twiggy shoots

Remove thin stems from the lower part of the trunk

Bark is a feature in winter

AIM OF PRUNING

MAKING THE CUTS

Bougainvillea
EVERGREEN CLIMBERS
■ **Prune in late winter to early spring**

Bougainvillea glabra 'Variegata'

These rampant, thorny climbers are capable of covering a large area. The plants are not hardy, so in colder areas they should be grown in containers in large sunrooms or greenhouses since they will still need a lot of room. The showy colored bracts that surround the flowers can be white, pink, red, purple, or orange.

For the best display, develop a framework of strong stems during the first two years after planting, creating a broad fan shape. Tie the main stems in as they grow, and shorten the sideshoots. In later years these will produce the flowering shoots. Cut back all unwanted growth. When the framework is established, reduce all the sideshoots produced the previous year to two or three leaves in late winter to early spring. Shorten vigorous new stems, or tie them in as replacement for older framework stems, which can be cut back.

PLANT PROFILE

NATURAL HABIT Very vigorous climbers with long, flexible, very thorny stems.

HARDINESS These plants will not tolerate frost—grow under cover in cold areas.

HEIGHT AND SPREAD Plants grow to around 30ft x 30ft (10m x 10m).

PRUNING NOTES
■ Pruning is essential if the natural vigor of these plants is to be managed.

■ Prune before new growth begins in late winter to early spring.

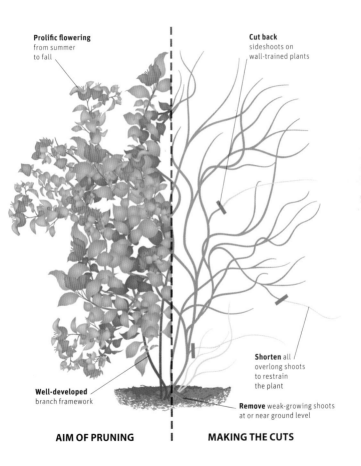

Prolific flowering from summer to fall

Cut back sideshoots on wall-trained plants

Shorten all overlong shoots to restrain the plant

Well-developed branch framework

Remove weak-growing shoots at or near ground level

AIM OF PRUNING

MAKING THE CUTS

Brachyglottis
EVERGREEN SHRUBS
■ **Prune in mid-spring and in summer as necessary**

Brachyglottis 'Sunshine'

These shrubs are grown mainly for their evergreen gray foliage, which makes them an excellent foil to other plants—the yellow flowers are largely unappealing. Stems tend to become woody at the base, leading to bare patches in the coverage since they naturally grow sideways. The most commonly grown is *B.* 'Sunshine', which makes a low, spreading mound, ideal for softening the edge of a mixed planting or even as groundcover in a sunny spot.

Prune in mid-spring—after the worst frost has passed in cold areas—shortening stems by as much as is necessary to achieve a pleasing shape. Cut bare stems back to live buds. Clip over the plants as necessary in summer. Very old and woody specimens are simply best replaced.

PLANT PROFILE

NATURAL HABIT Mound-forming, gray-leaf shrubs with a tendency to accumulate bare, woody stems.

HARDINESS Most are fully hardy.

HEIGHT AND SPREAD Plants grow to around 3ft x 5ft (1m x 1.5m).

PRUNING NOTES
■ To maintain a shapely plant that is well covered with foliage, shorten stems in spring, then clip over again in summer.

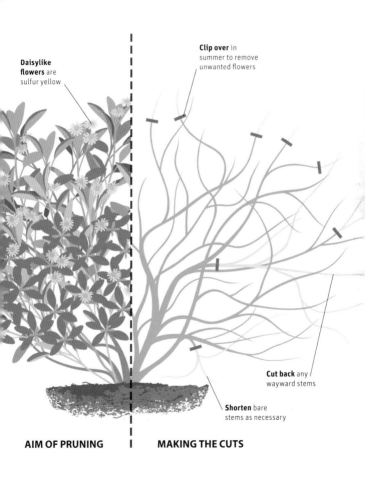

Daisylike flowers are sulfur yellow

Clip over in summer to remove unwanted flowers

Cut back any wayward stems

Shorten bare stems as necessary

AIM OF PRUNING

MAKING THE CUTS

Brugmansia *Angels' trumpets*
EVERGREEN SHRUBS
■ **Prune in late winter to reshape, and during summer**

Brugmansia x candida 'Grand Marnier'

These evergreen shrubs produce large, sweetly scented, trumpetlike flowers. In cold regions they are usually grown in containers and will die back almost completely in winter—cut back all the growth in late winter to a low framework. Overwinter them, dormant, indoors. During the growing season, shorten new shoots that have flowered. This will encourage them to flower again and keep the plant contained.

In frost-free climates brugmansias are large evergreen shrubs or even trees when grown outdoors. In these climates, where the top-growth persists from year to year, the plants can be pruned at any time to shape and encourage new flowering stems. All parts of the plant are toxic, so wear gloves at all times when handling them.

PLANT PROFILE

NATURAL HABIT Shapely shrubs with a domelike crown, often on a thickened stem.

HARDINESS Frost tender. In cold climates plants must be overwintered under cover.

HEIGHT AND SPREAD Plants generally grow to within 4ft x 4ft (1.2m x 1.2m); less when grown as a pot plant.

PRUNING NOTES

■ To give the plant an almost complete renovation, prune each year in late winter.

■ Shorten the new growth throughout summer to keep up the flower production.

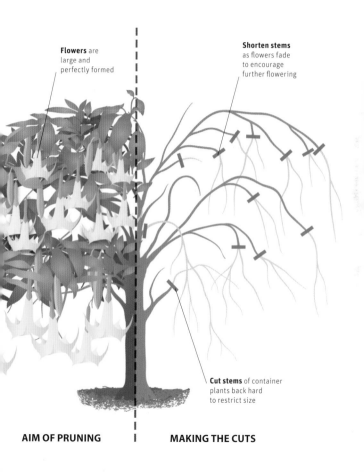

Flowers are large and perfectly formed

Shorten stems as flowers fade to encourage further flowering

Cut stems of container plants back hard to restrict size

AIM OF PRUNING

MAKING THE CUTS

Buddleja *Butterfly bush*
EARLY-FLOWERING DECIDUOUS SHRUBS
■ Prune in early spring, before new growth

Buddleja alternifolia

Buddlejas include a wide range of shrubs that flower throughout the year. While the late-flowering butterfly bush, *B. davidii* (see pp.86–87), is a common garden plant, late-spring or early-summer flowering plants such as *B. alternifolia* are less common, although no less attractive—their arching stems are weighed down by sweetly scented lilac flowers. *B.* 'Argentea' is worth growing for its silver willowlike leaves alone.

A hard pruning should take place early in the spring—before growth increases. Prune the plant down to 12in (30cm). The shrubs also make fine wall plants. Tie in stems in a rough fan formation to enjoy cascades of flowering shoots. Shorten them after flowering, cut back older stems, and tie in vigorous new ones as replacements.

PLANT PROFILE

NATURAL HABIT Deciduous shrub with elegant, arching stems.

HARDINESS Fully hardy.

HEIGHT AND SPREAD 6ft x 10ft (2m x 3m). Wall-trained plants will reach higher.

PRUNING NOTES
■ Prune annually to refresh the plant and reduce the potential buildup of bare stems within the body of the plant.

■ For late-flowering buddlejas see pp.86–87.

Flowers appear on stems produced the previous year

Shorten shoots as the flowers fade, cutting above healthy buds

Cut back older stems to the base, especially if they are bare

AIM OF PRUNING

MAKING THE CUTS

Buddleja *Butterfly bush*
LATE-FLOWERING DECIDUOUS OR EVERGREEN SHRUBS
■ **Prune in late winter to early spring**

Buddleja davidii 'Fascinating'

The butterfly bush annually produces masses of thin, arching stems, which present deliciously scented white, lilac, or rich dark red-purple flowers at the tips in midsummer that are highly attractive to butterflies. The plants are able to seed—and flourish—in small cracks between paving stones and in brickwork, so deadhead the flowers promptly to prevent the plants from spreading like weeds.

Pruning, which should be done annually, is largely a matter of renovation. Cut all the stems back to a low framework up to 12in (30cm) above the ground; you may need loppers or a pruning saw to tackle thicker stems. *B. davidii* is a parent of the hybrid *B* x *weyeriana* (the other being *B. globosa*), and all of these should be treated in the same way.

PLANT PROFILE

NATURAL HABIT These shrubs regularly produce quantities of flexible stems from the base that arch over at flowering time.

HARDINESS Fully hardy.

HEIGHT AND SPREAD 7ft x 5ft (2.1m x 1.5m), if pruned annually. Variegated forms will be smaller.

PRUNING NOTES
■ Refresh the plant on an annual basis, cutting back all the previous year's stems. Plants will regenerate if cut back harder, even to woody trunks near ground level.

■ Variegated forms are less vigorous.

■ For early-flowering buddlejas see pp.84–85.

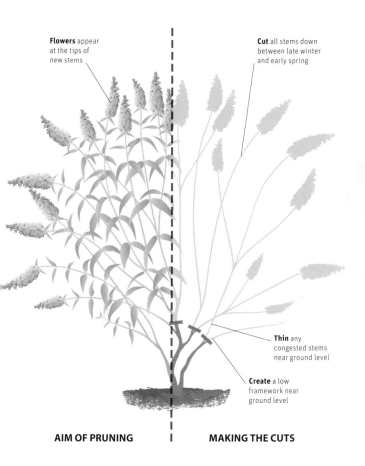

Flowers appear at the tips of new stems

Cut all stems down between late winter and early spring

Thin any congested stems near ground level

Create a low framework near ground level

AIM OF PRUNING

MAKING THE CUTS

Buxus *Boxwood*
EVERGREEN SHRUBS
■ **Prune in spring to midsummer**

Buxus microphylla 'Compacta'

If left unpruned, boxwood eventually becomes treelike but is so slow growing that it is mostly grown as a shrub or hedge. When buying plants, check the rate of growth—unusually, some small- and green-leaf forms can be slower-growing than variegated ones. Larger plants are used for topiary, often in combination with yew. For the densest growth, trim over when planting. Cut twice a year during the growing season.

Plants used in hedges often become bare at the base, particularly if they have been shaded from the sun by other plants. Cutting back hard generally results in speedy regrowth. Box blight is a common problem, resulting in brown leaves and dieback. Cut back any affected parts to healthy wood, and treat with fungicide. In severe cases it may be necessary to replace plants.

PLANT PROFILE

NATURAL HABIT Dense, slow-growing shrubs that become treelike if left to grow.

HARDINESS Mainly hardy, although some types show vulnerability to extreme cold.

HEIGHT AND SPREAD Plants can grow to 5ft x 4ft (1.5m x 1.2m) with age. They can also be kept much smaller with pruning.

PRUNING NOTES
■ Clip to shape in spring to midsummer to give the growth a chance to harden up before winter.

■ Cut old plants back hard to renovate.

Dense, even growth

Clip over plants to neaten

Cut bare stems back hard to a short stub above the ground if necessary

AIM OF PRUNING

MAKING THE CUTS

Callicarpa *Beautyberry*

DECIDUOUS SHRUBS

■ **Prune in early spring, then fall, if necessary**

Callicarpa bodinieri var. giraldii

Unusually, these shrubs are grown more for the appeal of their striking violet-purple fall berries than for their summer flowers. The fruits do not seem to appeal to birds, so stay on the plant well into winter. Regular pruning is essential if plants are to produce the maximum number of berries.

The plants flower in midsummer on a combination of new and older wood, so it is necessary to retain some of the older stems at the same time as allowing space for new ones to develop. In early spring before new growth begins, cut to the base any older stems and any that cross or cause congestion within the plant. Check over the plant again in fall, and cut back any stems broken by the weight of its berries. Pruning involves regular renewal of the plant but should be spread over three or four years.

PLANT PROFILE

NATURAL HABIT Usually dense-growing, twiggy, deciduous shrubs.

HARDINESS Mainly fully hardy.

HEIGHT AND SPREAD Plants grow to around 4ft x 4ft (1.2m x 1.2m).

PRUNING NOTES
■ Remove some of the older growth each year, to make way for the new.

■ Shorten any broken stems.

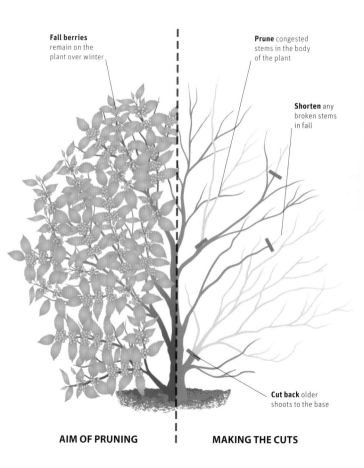

Fall berries remain on the plant over winter

Prune congested stems in the body of the plant

Shorten any broken stems in fall

Cut back older shoots to the base

AIM OF PRUNING

MAKING THE CUTS

Callistemon *Bottlebrush*

EVERGREEN SHRUBS

■ **Prune in mid- to late summer, after flowering**

Callistemon citrinus 'Splendens'

The bottlebrushes—perfectly named for their attractive spikes of red, yellow, or cream flowers—need the shelter of a warm wall in cold areas. They flower in summer, at the tips of shoots on the new growth and usually develop into large shrubs or trees.

They can be grown with minimal pruning. Against a wall, gently attach suitably placed stems at the back of the plant in a rough fan shape. Tip-prune young plants in spring to summer to encourage bushiness. To maintain a compact shape, shorten growth immediately after flowering, cutting just behind the flowers. This also prevents seed formation. At the same time, remove any badly placed or congested stems. Cut older, straggly stems back to outward-facing buds near the base.

PLANT PROFILE

NATURAL HABIT Dense, upright bushes that can be trained up a wall or fence, especially if they have a tall central stem.

HARDINESS Plants need the shelter of a warm, sunny wall in cold areas.

HEIGHT AND SPREAD Plants can grow to around 6ft x 25ft (2m x 8m).

PRUNING NOTES
■ Tip-prune plants when young.

■ Prune mature plants that have outgrown their space to 24in (60cm). Young stems will grow within a year, and the plant will bloom again after two years.

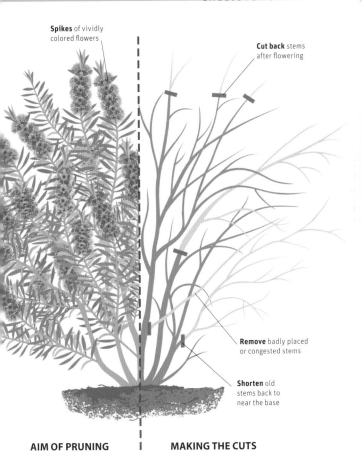

Spikes of vividly colored flowers

Cut back stems after flowering

Remove badly placed or congested stems

Shorten old stems back to near the base

AIM OF PRUNING

MAKING THE CUTS

Calluna *Heather*
EVERGREEN SHRUBS
■ **Clip over the plants in early spring**

Calluna vulgaris 'Multicolor'

There are literally hundreds of varieties of calluna, all flowering between midsummer and late fall. The flowers are produced in a range of colors, from vivid pinks to white and gold. As an additional attraction some have bright yellow, red, or orange foliage, making them especially valued as winter plants; the leaves of others can develop bronze tints when the temperature drops. Calluna heathers are excellent for a massed planting but must have acidic soil.

Pruning is a simple matter of removing the flowered stems in early spring—simply cut them back with shears to neaten the plant. For denser growth, cut them hard but not into bare wood. Old, straggly plants that are leafless toward the base are best dug up and replaced.

PLANT PROFILE

NATURAL HABIT Scrubby, low-growing evergreen shrubs that knit together to form an effective groundcover.

HARDINESS Fully hardy.

HEIGHT AND SPREAD Plants usually grow to within 18in x 18in (45cm x 45cm); some have a wider spread.

PRUNING NOTES
■ Prune regularly to keep the plants neat and well-covered with leaves near the base.

■ Clip over after flowering.

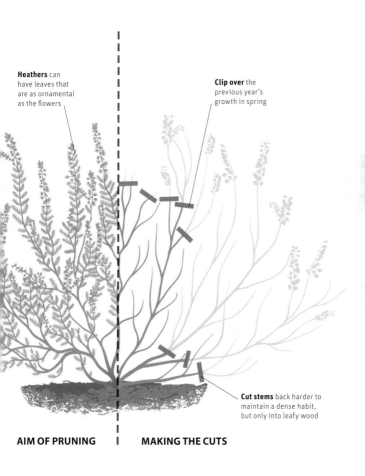

Heathers can have leaves that are as ornamental as the flowers

Clip over the previous year's growth in spring

Cut stems back harder to maintain a dense habit, but only into leafy wood

AIM OF PRUNING

MAKING THE CUTS

Camellia
EVERGREEN SHRUBS
■ Prune immediately after flowering

Camellia japonica 'Janet Waterhouse'

These attractive evergreen shrubs are mainly spring-flowering. There is a vast number of varieties, which produce white, pink, or red blooms in a variety of flower forms, from double and semidouble to rose-form and peony-form. The size of plants can vary, since some have a very compact habit, while others may become more rangy, even treelike with age.

All camellias are very tolerant of pruning, and this should be performed immediately after the plants have flowered. This gives the plants plenty of time to build up an abundance of new flowering growth for the following year. Most plants prefer a sheltered site, and some winter-flowering varieties are suitable for wall training, which offers the flowers valuable protection from the worst of the weather.

PLANT PROFILE

NATURAL HABIT Vigorous shrubs that are usually covered with glossy green foliage.

HARDINESS Mainly fully hardy. Early-flowering varieties benefit from some shelter in cold areas to protect the opening flowers.

HEIGHT AND SPREAD 6ft x 3ft (2m x 1m), or more, depending on the variety.

PRUNING NOTES
■ Plants can be grown without pruning, but an annual prune will keep growth in check.

■ Overgrown specimens respond well to regenerative pruning in spring.

■ Plants can be kept more compact with regular pruning.

Cut back flowered stems once the flowers have faded

Cut stems back to reduce the size of the plant

Stems can be cut hard to the base to renovate, if necessary

Flowers are carried on the previous year's growth

AIM OF PRUNING

MAKING THE CUTS

Campsis *Trumpet vine*
DECIDUOUS CLIMBERS
■ Prune in late winter to early spring

Campsis x tagliabuana 'Madame Galen'

These mainly hardy, deciduous climbers are grown for their coral pink or red trumpetlike flowers, which are borne from late summer to fall. In cold climates a warm, sheltered spot will encourage better flowering. They are very vigorous climbers and produce masses of leafy growth annually.

Performance can be disappointing unless a strong framework is established during the first few years after planting. Tie in strong shoots, and cut out weaker ones, sacrificing the flowers if necessary. Once the framework is established, prune in late winter to early spring before the plant is in leaf, shortening all the sideshoots to two or three buds of the framework. As the plant matures, cut out older branches—especially ones that are bare at the base—and tie in vigorous new ones as replacements.

PLANT PROFILE

NATURAL HABIT Rampant climbers that can amass a large quantity of leafy growth.

HARDINESS Mainly hardy, but flowering is more profuse in a warm, sheltered spot.

HEIGHT AND SPREAD Plants grow to 10ft (3m) in both directions, or more.

PRUNING NOTES
■ Prune annually to keep the plant within limits and to encourage it to produce flowering stems.

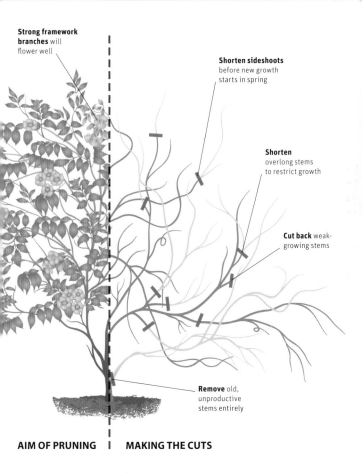

Strong framework branches will flower well

Shorten sideshoots before new growth starts in spring

Shorten overlong stems to restrict growth

Cut back weak-growing stems

Remove old, unproductive stems entirely

AIM OF PRUNING | **MAKING THE CUTS**

Carpinus *Hornbeam*
DECIDUOUS TREES
■ **Prune from late summer to midwinter**

Carpinus betulus 'Pendula'

Hornbeams are deciduous trees that are widely used for hedging because they are faster growing than another very common hedging plant, beech (*Fagus*). Upright types can be planted in a row for screening. With minimal pruning they also make fine specimens—most develop a rounded crown when mature, but some varieties are more narrowly upright or grow in a teardroplike shape. These can be striking even in winter when the branches are bare. All hornbeams have good fall leaf color, and the foliage is sometimes retained over winter.

Prune freestanding specimens any time from late summer to midwinter, otherwise you will cause the plants to bleed sap. Plants need only minimal pruning, but cut back any wayward, broken, and crossing stems. Clip over hedges in late summer.

PLANT PROFILE

NATURAL HABIT Deciduous trees with upright to rounded crowns. Some shoot freely from near the base.

HARDINESS Fully hardy.

HEIGHT AND SPREAD Plants grow to around 20ft x 15ft (6m x 5m).

PRUNING NOTES
■ Keep pruning to a minimum on freestanding specimens.

■ Shear hedges in late summer.

Green leaves will change color in fall

Remove crossing or broken branches

Hornbeams have a naturally elegant shape

Cut out any wayward stems that spoil the outline

AIM OF PRUNING

MAKING THE CUTS

Caryopteris *Bluebeard*
DECIDUOUS SHRUBS
■ **Prune in mid- to late spring, as new growth emerges**

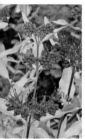

Caryopteris x clandonensis 'Worcester Gold'

These deciduous shrubs most commonly produce blue flowers at the end of summer and into fall. The foliage is aromatic and generally gray-green, although some varieties have yellow leaves. A sunny location is needed for the best performance, and the shelter of a warm wall is desirable in cold areas.

Pruning is a matter of annual renewal. The first spring after planting, cut back all the stems to a low framework. In later years, prune in mid- to late spring, when new shoots are appearing. Shorten the previous year's stems to live buds near the base—not into the framework, which will probably be bare. Against a wall, pruning can be less drastic to achieve greater height.

PLANT PROFILE

NATURAL HABIT Deciduous shrubs that freely produce arching shoots from near ground level.

HARDINESS Mainly fully hardy.

HEIGHT AND SPREAD 4ft x 4ft (1.2m x 1.2m), although the spread may slightly exceed the height.

PRUNING NOTES
■ Pruning is a matter of annual renewal, cutting all the previous year's stems back to near the base of the plant.

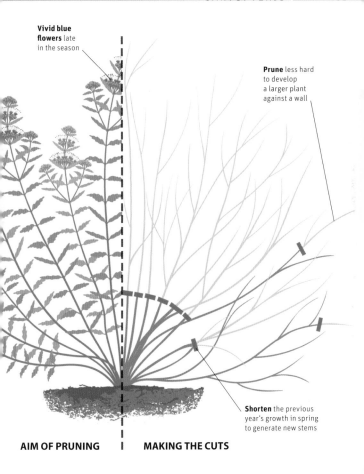

Vivid blue flowers late in the season

Prune less hard to develop a larger plant against a wall

Shorten the previous year's growth in spring to generate new stems

AIM OF PRUNING   **MAKING THE CUTS**

Catalpa *Indian bean tree*
DECIDUOUS TREES
■ Prune in late winter to early spring

Catalpa bignonioides

The white late-spring flowers of the Indian bean tree are carried in upright panicles—reliably on established specimens, and always in greatest profusion in years that follow a hot summer. The trees are excellent for shade due to their large, handsome, heart-shaped foliage; yellow- and purple-leaf forms are also available. The trees are sometimes recommended as suitable for small gardens—in the short term they make shapely well-balanced trees, but older specimens are large. Consider hard pruning if they outgrow their space.

Prune before the foliage appears; hard pruning encourages larger, more impressive leaves. Pollarded or coppiced annually, catalpas can even be used in mixed borders for the effect of their leaves, although this will be at the expense of any flowers. For a flowering tree, keep pruning to a minimum.

PLANT PROFILE

NATURAL HABIT Potentially large trees that can be kept within bounds through regular pruning.

HARDINESS Fully hardy, but flowering is most prolific in areas with warm summers.

HEIGHT AND SPREAD To 30ft x 20ft (10m x 6m); less with restrictive pruning.

PRUNING NOTES
■ For the largest leaves, cut back hard annually—this will be at the expense of any flowers.

■ The trees are very responsive to pruning.

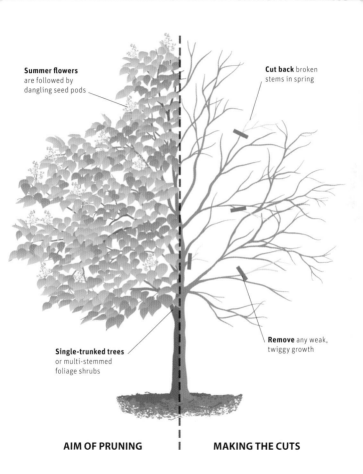

Summer flowers are followed by dangling seed pods

Cut back broken stems in spring

Single-trunked trees or multi-stemmed foliage shrubs

Remove any weak, twiggy growth

AIM OF PRUNING

MAKING THE CUTS

Ceanothus *Mountain snowbell*

DECIDUOUS SHRUBS

■ **Prune in spring, as new growth begins**

Ceanothus x delileanus 'Topaze'

Deciduous ceanothus are hardier than the more commonly grown evergreen types (see pp.108–109) but still do best when planted against a warm wall in cold areas. They usually bear blue flowers, carried from midsummer to early fall on the current year's growth.

To encourage flowers to cover the entire plant, build up a framework of main stems that fan out from near the base. Each spring, shorten strong stems produced the previous year by one-half to two-thirds, then trim back sideshoots to strong buds. After two to three years, leave the framework branches unpruned, or lightly trim back any that are too long. Then simply prune out any congested and crossing stems, and shorten the sideshoots to strong buds. These will then produce flower-bearing stems. In later years, cut out older, unproductive framework branches and train in replacements.

PLANT PROFILE

NATURAL HABIT Usually spreading shrubs that are suitable for informal wall training.

HARDINESS Fully hardy but best in a warm, sheltered site for the best flowering.

HEIGHT AND SPREAD Plants usually grow to around 5ft x 5ft (1.5m x 1.5m), depending on the variety.

PRUNING NOTES
■ Prune back any older and awkwardly placed stems in spring.

■ Shorten sideshoots in spring.

■ Cut stems back hard to renovate.

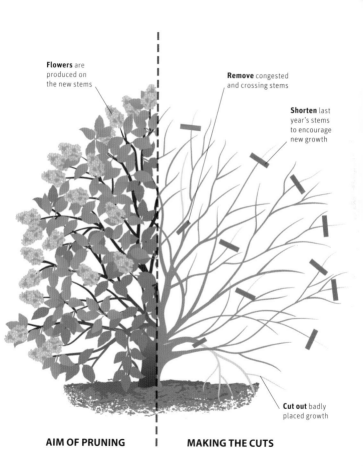

Flowers are produced on the new stems

Remove congested and crossing stems

Shorten last year's stems to encourage new growth

Cut out badly placed growth

AIM OF PRUNING

MAKING THE CUTS

Ceanothus *Mountain snowbell*
EVERGREEN SHRUBS
■ Prune in spring or in early to midsummer

Ceanothus
'Blue Mound'

Depending on the variety, evergreen ceanothus flower either in spring or in late summer into fall—some flower during both periods. In cold areas they are best grown against a warm wall and are suitable for informal training. To achieve this, tie in the main stem vertically and fan out strong sideshoots, attaching them to the support as they grow.

While repeat-flowering types are best left unpruned, early-flowering varieties can be pruned in summer, after flowering. Shorten stems that have flowered by one-third to one-half. To keep plants compact, trim them in late summer. Prune late-flowering types in spring. Trim the previous year's stems by between one-third to one-half. All do best with minimal pruning. Ceanothus are not long-lived, and though renovation is possible, very old plants may be better replaced.

PLANT PROFILE

NATURAL HABIT Rounded to upright or spreading evergreen shrubs that are usually well-covered with foliage.

HARDINESS Most need protection from hard frosts, which can kill them outright.

HEIGHT AND SPREAD 5ft x 5ft (1.5m x 1.5m), although dimensions can vary.

PRUNING NOTES
■ Keep pruning to a minimum: prune early-flowering types after flowering; prune late-flowering types in spring.

■ Renovative pruning is unlikely to be successful; replace older specimens.

■ For deciduous ceanothus see pp.106–107.

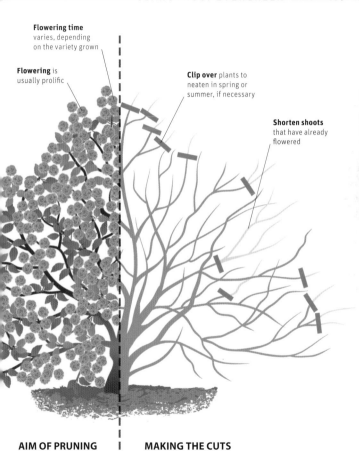

Flowering time varies, depending on the variety grown

Flowering is usually prolific

Clip over plants to neaten in spring or summer, if necessary

Shorten shoots that have already flowered

AIM OF PRUNING

MAKING THE CUTS

Cedrus *Cedar*
EVERGREEN CONIFERS
■ Prune in late winter to early spring or in summer

Cedrus atlantica Glauca Group

Stately and magnificent, cedars are often grown in large gardens and public parks. Most are best left unpruned with any necessary work on mature trees done by an arborist—in late winter to early spring, or in summer.

Some cedars, such as *C. atlantica* 'Glauca Pendula', can be trained on a support or against a wall. When the main stem reaches the desired height, pull its tip down to the horizontal, and tie it in. Any strong shoot that forms at the bend in the leader can be used to extend the framework in the opposite direction. Sideshoots will hang down from strong framework branches like a curtain. Remove awkwardly placed growth in summer. Other types, such as the deodar (*C. deodara*) and the blue atlas cedar (*C. atlantica* f. *glauca*), have weeping shapes that respond well to pruning. They can be grafted onto tall stems of other conifers to create weeping standards.

PLANT PROFILE

NATURAL HABIT Usually very tall trees that become more spreading with age.

HARDINESS Fully hardy, although young plants should be protected from hard frost and cold drying winds.

HEIGHT AND SPREAD 100ft x 30ft (30m x 10m). Weeping forms can be kept smaller.

PRUNING NOTES
■ Extensive pruning is not usually necessary, but weeping types can be pruned regularly to maintain a good shape.

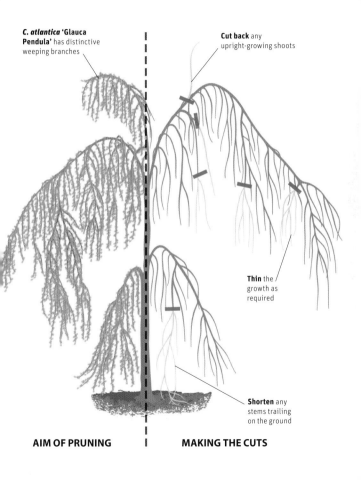

C. atlantica 'Glauca Pendula' has distinctive weeping branches

Cut back any upright-growing shoots

Thin the growth as required

Shorten any stems trailing on the ground

AIM OF PRUNING

MAKING THE CUTS

Celastrus *Bittersweet*
DECIDUOUS CLIMBERS
■ Prune in late winter to early spring, while dormant

Celastrus orbiculatus

These vigorous, twining climbers are grown for the fall interest of their orange or yellow fruit, which split to reveal pink or red seeds, and the butter yellow color of their leaves. The plants can be wall trained but grow best when allowed to scramble through an informal planting of trees and shrubs. Since male and female flowers are produced by different plants, two must be grown to ensure fruit production. If you only have room for one, look for a hermaphrodite variety.

Regular pruning is not essential, but if necessary, remove badly placed stems, and thin congested growth in late winter to early spring. Shorten any wayward sideshoots to improve the shape, and cut older, thickened stems to the base if they are unproductive. Prune to keep the plants to size if necessary.

PLANT PROFILE

NATURAL HABIT Vigorous, twining climbers that shoot freely from the base.

HARDINESS Mainly fully hardy.

HEIGHT AND SPREAD 30ft x 30ft (10m x 10m), although plants can be kept within reasonable bounds with regular pruning.

PRUNING NOTES
■ Thin congested stems, and shorten growth as necessary.

■ Cut any old, unproductive stems down to near the base of the plant.

■ Renovate in late winter to early spring.

Small, decorative fruits in fall

Shorten wayward shoots back to a main branch

Cut back old, thick growth that is less productive

AIM OF PRUNING | **MAKING THE CUTS**

Celtis *Hackberry*
DECIDUOUS TREES
■ **Prune in winter, when trees are dormant**

Celtis australis

Although capable of surviving hard frosts, celtis do best in areas with long, hot summers. They are shapely trees, and the leaves often color well before dropping in fall. In cold climates they can be multi-stemmed.

Any necessary pruning should be done while the trees are still young since wounds made to mature branches do not always heal successfully. Rub out any shoots that appear next to the pruning wounds to avoid having to make further cuts later on. Thereafter, pruning should be minimal. Remove any strongly upright stems on the main branches on sight. To develop a single trunk, remove sideshoots from the lowest quarter of the main stem during the first two years. Celtis often develop several strong branches low down the trunk. Those that are well-spaced and form a wide angle with the main trunk can be retained. Prune out any competing leaders.

PLANT PROFILE

NATURAL HABIT Upright, sometimes multi-stemmed deciduous trees that form a spreading canopy.

HARDINESS Fully hardy, but growth is best in areas with long, hot summers.

HEIGHT AND SPREAD Plants grow to 43ft x 43ft (13m x 13m), sometimes more.

PRUNING NOTES
■ Prune young trees to establish a good shape.

■ Rub out any shoots that form around pruning wounds.

■ Remove any strongly vertical stems that develop within the canopy.

Cut out any strongly vertical shoots on established trees

Single or multi-stemmed trunk

Leafy canopy that often turns vivid colors in fall

Clear any unwanted sideshoots from the lower part of the trunk

AIM OF PRUNING   **MAKING THE CUTS**

Cercis *Redbud*
DECIDUOUS TREES
■ Prune mainly in early summer

Cercis canadensis var. *alba*

These dainty trees are grown mainly for their profusion of spring flowers, which open just before or as the leaves are opening. Some also have attractive foliage that colors well in fall. They sometimes shoot freely from the base and are either multi-stemmed from ground level or from low down on a single main trunk.

To encourage bushiness, cut back the central stem to just above the uppermost of three to five well-spaced and vigorous strong shoots during the first winter after planting. Otherwise, allow a trunk to develop and produce a crown. Once established, prune in early summer only to remove damaged shoots. Types of *C. canadensis* such as 'Forest Pansy', which is grown for its heart-shaped leaves, can be coppiced or pollarded, although annual cutting back of the stems in spring will be at the expense of the flowers.

PLANT PROFILE

NATURAL HABIT Neat-growing trees.

HARDINESS Fully hardy. In frost-prone areas they are best grown in a sheltered location to avoid frost damage to the flowers.

HEIGHT AND SPREAD 15ft x 10ft (5m x 3m), sometimes more. Coppiced and pollarded trees will be smaller.

PRUNING NOTES
■ Prune the plants in early summer after they have flowered, if necessary.

■ Coppice or pollard in spring.

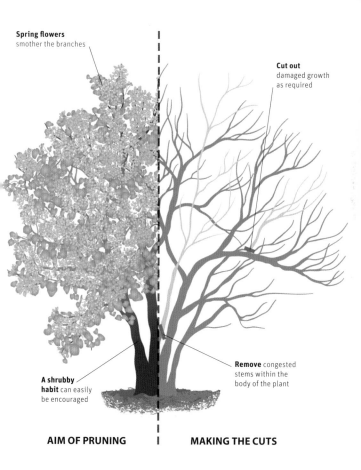

Spring flowers smother the branches

Cut out damaged growth as required

A shrubby habit can easily be encouraged

Remove congested stems within the body of the plant

AIM OF PRUNING

MAKING THE CUTS

Cestrum
DECIDUOUS AND EVERGREEN SHRUBS
■ Prune in early spring, when new growth begins

Cestrum parqui

With their scented tubular flowers, cestrums are desirable shrubs, although most are evergreen and are not hardy enough for growing outdoors in cold regions. Deciduous types are the hardiest, but even so the young top-growth is likely to be killed during a hard winter. In spring, cut back all the old stems to the ground—replacements will soon appear.

The deciduous *C. parqui* is perhaps the hardiest example. With its night-scented flowers it would no doubt be better appreciated were it not that all parts of the plant are toxic. Deadheading will remove the risk of seeding—though the plants flower so late that in cool climates seed is unlikely to ripen. Evergreen species are sometimes grown as houseplants. Prune them lightly when young for extra bushiness.

PLANT PROFILE

NATURAL HABIT These upright shrubs are usually shapely and rounded and well-clothed with foliage.

HARDINESS Borderline hardy, they generally die back in cold areas.

HEIGHT AND SPREAD Plants grow to around 5ft x 4ft (1.5m x 1.2m).

PRUNING NOTES
■ In frost-prone areas a complete renewal of the plant is necessary each year. Cut back all the growth to near ground level in early spring.

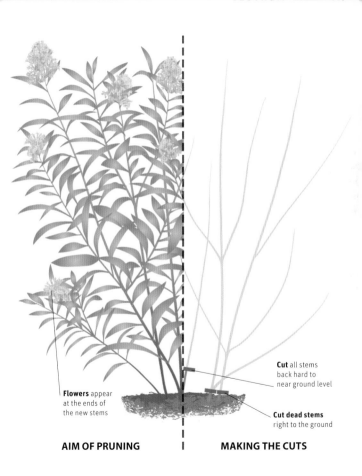

Flowers appear
at the ends of
the new stems

Cut all stems
back hard to
near ground level

Cut dead stems
right to the ground

AIM OF PRUNING

MAKING THE CUTS

Chaenomeles *Flowering quince*
DECIDUOUS SHRUBS
■ **Prune in winter, late spring, and summer**

Chaenomeles x superba 'Nicoline'

These deciduous, sometimes thorny shrubs have two seasons of interest: the vivid spring flowers—white, pink, or most commonly red—are followed by rounded, applelike fall fruits. While they can be grown as freestanding shrubs, they can also be very effective when wall trained. For border plants, prune to reduce congestion in the body of the plant in winter. Trimming new growth in summer, after flowering, improves the performance the following spring. For wall shrubs, tie in vigorous stems to form a framework, cutting out shoots unsuitable for training. Once established, shorten sideshoots to two or three leaves in late spring. New shoots will emerge—cut these back to two or three buds the following winter. Developing short, stubby shoots (spurs) in this way greatly improves flowering. Thin plants in winter if they become congested.

PLANT PROFILE

NATURAL HABIT Twiggy shrubs that are suitable for wall training.

HARDINESS Fully hardy.

HEIGHT AND SPREAD Plants grow to 4ft x 4ft (1.2m x 1.2m). Wall-trained plants can extend much further in both directions.

PRUNING NOTES
■ Prune to maintain a framework of established, older stems.

■ Shorten flowered stems to develop spurs.

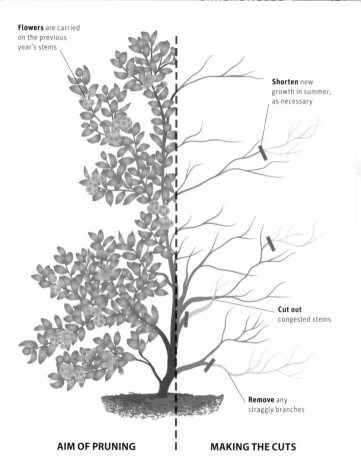

Flowers are carried on the previous year's stems

Shorten new growth in summer, as necessary

Cut out congested stems

Remove any straggly branches

AIM OF PRUNING

MAKING THE CUTS

Chimonanthus *Wintersweet*
DECIDUOUS SHRUBS
■ Prune in late winter to early spring, after flowering

Chimonanthus praecox 'Grandiflorus'

Sweetly scented flowers produced in the depths of winter make this shrub fully deserving of a choice location against a warm wall. The plant itself is hardy, but the flowers need protection from frost.

Plants flower reliably only when mature, so grow them with minimal pruning initially. Against a wall main stems can be tied in to form a framework. Once established, shorten flowered shoots after flowering, and remove any that are awkwardly placed in late winter to early spring. Shorten older shoots if necessary. Wintersweet can also be grown without training. Keep pruning to a minimum on freestanding specimens. Old plants can be renovated, but stems should be reduced to no less than 24in (60cm). Hard-pruned plants will not flower well for several years.

PLANT PROFILE

NATURAL HABIT Vigorous, twiggy shrubs.

HARDINESS Fully hardy but best against a wall in cold areas to protect the winter flowers from frost.

HEIGHT AND SPREAD 10ft x 8ft (3m x 2.5m); sometimes more with wall training.

PRUNING NOTES

■ On freestanding plants, pruning should be kept to a minimum.

■ On wall-trained plants, shorten sideshoots after flowering. Thin congested growth, and cut older stems back to near ground level.

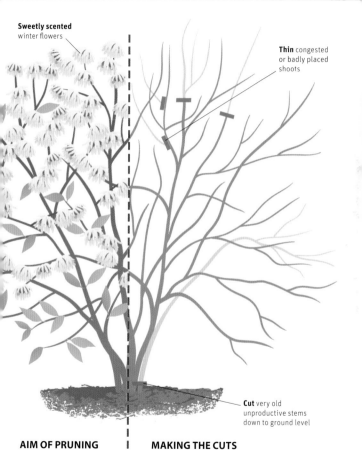

Sweetly scented winter flowers

Thin congested or badly placed shoots

Cut very old unproductive stems down to ground level

AIM OF PRUNING

MAKING THE CUTS

Choisya *Mock orange tree*
EVERGREEN SHRUBS
■ **Prune in early spring and in summer, after flowering**

Choisya ternata

Mock orange trees are mainly compact evergreen shrubs that bear clusters of scented white flowers in late spring. Generally plants grow as neat domes and little pruning is required, although they may become asymmetrical over time, particularly if they have suffered frost damage. Popular types include *C. ternata* 'Sundance', which is grown for its bright yellow foliage, and *C.* 'Aztec Pearl', which is a dainty hybrid with much narrower leaves.

In spring, cut out any frost-damaged stems. Shorten the stems immediately after flowering to encourage more flowers later in the season. Even up the plants, cutting out stems that spoil the outline and any that are bare at the base. Hard pruning of the whole plant is tolerated, but is best done in early spring to allow maximum recovery time.

PLANT PROFILE

NATURAL HABIT Usually neat-growing, domelike evergreen shrubs.

HARDINESS Mainly fully hardy, although soft growth can be vulnerable to frosts.

HEIGHT AND SPREAD Plants grow to 4ft (1.2m) in both directions, or more. Plants can spread wider than they grow tall.

PRUNING NOTES
■ Prune the plant to maintain a balanced and compact shape.

■ Routinely remove frost damaged stems and any that are bare or spoil the outline.

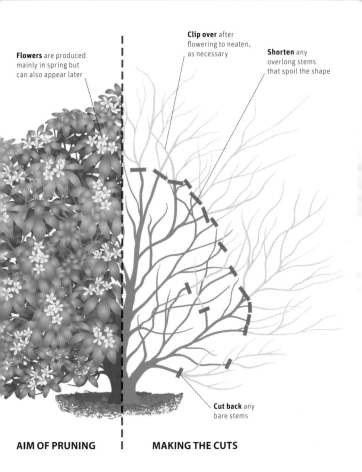

Flowers are produced mainly in spring but can also appear later

Clip over after flowering to neaten, as necessary

Shorten any overlong stems that spoil the shape

Cut back any bare stems

AIM OF PRUNING

MAKING THE CUTS

Cistus *Rock rose*

EVERGREEN SHRUBS

■ **Prune in spring, as the plants are coming into growth**

Cistus x aguilarii 'Maculatus'

These attractive evergreen shrubs are ideal for a Mediterranean garden, producing aromatic foliage and large white or pink flowers with papery petals from late spring and into summer. They must be grown in well-drained soil and benefit from a sunny site since they have a tendency to develop bare patches in cold areas.

The plants do not do well with pruning except when they are very young. To encourage bushiness, cut back stems by as much as two-thirds after planting. In spring, lightly trim the previous year's growth. On established plants, restrict pruning to the removal of any dead and damaged growth; this is always best done in spring. Old, straggly specimens should be replaced. Prune the related *Halimiocistus* (hybrids of cistus and halimium) in the same way.

PLANT PROFILE

NATURAL HABIT Usually rounded, sometimes sprawling shrubs.

HARDINESS Plants are vulnerable to frost, so grow in well-drained soil in a sunny spot.

HEIGHT AND SPREAD 4ft x 4ft (1.2m x 1.2m), although some varieties are more spreading than they are tall.

PRUNING NOTES
■ Prune new plants to encourage bushiness.

■ Restrict the pruning of established plants to a light trim and the removal of any dead or damaged growth in spring.

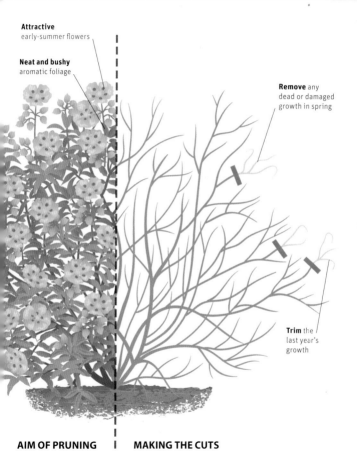

Attractive
early-summer flowers

Neat and bushy
aromatic foliage

Remove any
dead or damaged
growth in spring

Trim the
last year's
growth

AIM OF PRUNING | **MAKING THE CUTS**

Clematis

GROUP 1: EARLY-FLOWERING CLEMATIS

■ Prune immediately after flowering, if necessary

Clematis montana

Clematis that flower from late winter to midsummer form a variable set known as Group 1. Spring-flowering *C. alpina* and *C. macropetala* are weak-growing, while the last to flower, *C. montana*, is rampant. Winter-flowering *C. cirrhosa*, and late spring *C. armandii*, are evergreen. None need regular pruning.

If necessary, after flowering, remove dead or damaged stems. If growth is congested, cut older stems to the base, then thin the rest, cutting to healthy buds. On *C. armandii* and *C. cirrhosa*, shorten any overlong stems. Most have sufficient time to build new growth for good flowering the following year, apart from *C. montana*. Any extensive pruning, while necessary, may affect flowering the following year.

PLANT PROFILE

NATURAL HABIT Vigorous climbers that in time can become very woody toward the base with masses of tangled, soft stems.

HARDINESS Fully hardy.

HEIGHT AND SPREAD Plants can grow to around 30ft x 30ft (10m x 10m).

PRUNING NOTES

■ If necessary, prune after flowering to remove dead or damaged growth.

■ New growth on stems that are pruned hard may not flower the following year.

■ Renovation is usually successful, but normal flowering will not resume for 2–3 years.

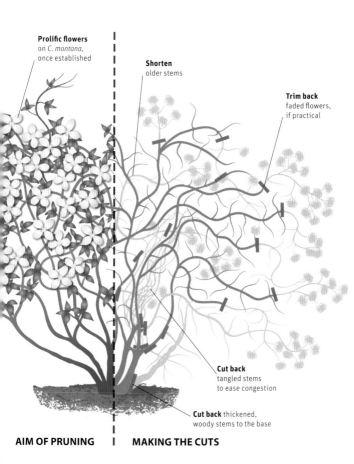

Prolific flowers
on *C. montana*,
once established

Shorten
older stems

Trim back
faded flowers,
if practical

Cut back
tangled stems
to ease congestion

Cut back thickened,
woody stems to the base

AIM OF PRUNING   **MAKING THE CUTS**

Clematis
GROUP 2: MID-SEASON CLEMATIS
■ **Prune in late winter to early spring, as buds are swelling**

Clematis 'Fireworks'

Group 2 clematis are high-value plants, bearing two flushes of flowers, in late spring and summer; some will produce double flowers in their first flush, and then single flowers thereafter. Plants can be grown with minimal pruning, although stems are likely to become congested over time. While pruning can reduce the first crop of flowers, it will allow extra room for the new growth, producing a better second crop.

In late winter to early spring as the buds are swelling, prune all dead, weak, and older tangled stems. Cut back the remainder to the highest pair of strong buds. These, and buds below them, will carry the first flowers. Tie in new growth as it appears in mid-spring. Group 2 clematis can also be pruned hard annually as for Group 3 (see pp.132–133); you will lose the first crop of flowers, but more blooms will be borne later and over a longer period.

PLANT PROFILE

NATURAL HABIT Often vigorous climbers that can accumulate a mass of dead, tangled stems over time.

HARDINESS Fully hardy.

HEIGHT AND SPREAD Plants grow to around 10ft x 6ft (3m x 2m).

PRUNING NOTES
■ Cut back old, dead stems to the ground.

■ Fan out stems to reduce congestion.

■ Renovative pruning is usually successful, but it will be at the loss of any early flowers.

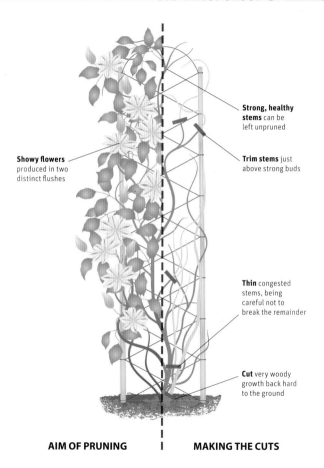

Strong, healthy stems can be left unpruned

Trim stems just above strong buds

Showy flowers produced in two distinct flushes

Thin congested stems, being careful not to break the remainder

Cut very woody growth back hard to the ground

AIM OF PRUNING

MAKING THE CUTS

Clematis
GROUP 3: LATE-FLOWERING CLEMATIS
■ Prune in late winter to early spring

Clematis 'Madame Julia Correvon'

Group 3 contains the greatest number of clematis, including many large-flowered varieties with white, red, pink, blue, or purple flowers, and a few very vigorous species such as yellow *C. orientalis*, white *C. flammula*, and greenish-yellow *C. rehderiana*. They flower from midsummer, often into fall. The group also includes the so-called texensis hybrids, which have flowers like inverted tulips, and viticellas, which have starlike flowers but are smaller than the large-flowered types.

Pruning is straightforward. In late winter to early spring when the buds are swelling, cut down all the stems to pairs of strong buds about 12in (30cm) above ground level. The species mentioned above can also be grown without pruning and allowed to ascend unchecked into the crown of an established tree to add interest late in the season.

PLANT PROFILE

NATURAL HABIT Often very vigorous climbers that can develop masses of tangled, congested stems.

HARDINESS Fully hardy.

HEIGHT AND SPREAD 20ft x 20ft (6m x 6m), depending on the type grown. Some are weaker-growing and more compact.

PRUNING NOTES
■ Cut all stems back hard annually to strong buds 12in (30cm) from the ground.

■ For a larger plant, prune lightly or not at all.

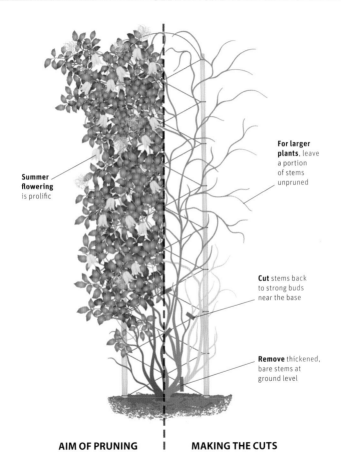

Summer flowering is prolific

For larger plants, leave a portion of stems unpruned

Cut stems back to strong buds near the base

Remove thickened, bare stems at ground level

AIM OF PRUNING

MAKING THE CUTS

Clerodendrum *Glorybower*
DECIADUOUS AND EVERGREEN TREES OR SHRUBS
■ **Prune in early to mid-spring, as new growth begins**

Clerodendrum trichotomum var. fargesii

Clerodendrums can be deciduous or evergreen, although the latter are slightly less hardy. Most are shrubby, but they can become treelike with age. They are valued for their red, pink, or white late-summer flowers, which are often fragrant. These are sometimes followed by shiny blue berries. Most plants need minimal pruning, but if necessary, thin the stems of deciduous plants in spring. On evergreens, shorten any shoots that spoil the shape. Remove suckers as seen.

The commonly grown *C. bungei* is best if cut back hard annually to a low framework of stems about 2ft (60cm) above ground level in spring. If the top-growth is often frosted in the winter, cut back all stems to ground level. The tender *C. speciosissimum* is sometimes grown in containers under glass. Shorten stems to 6in (15cm) immediately after flowering.

PLANT PROFILE

NATURAL HABIT Upright to arching shrubs or small trees, often suckering.

HARDINESS Many withstand frost or recover well after freezing weather. Some will not tolerate low temperatures.

HEIGHT AND SPREAD 15ft x 15ft (5m x 5m), or more in favorable areas.

PRUNING NOTES
■ Prune in early to mid-spring.

■ Remove any suckers from around the base of the plant as seen.

■ Most respond well to renovative pruning.

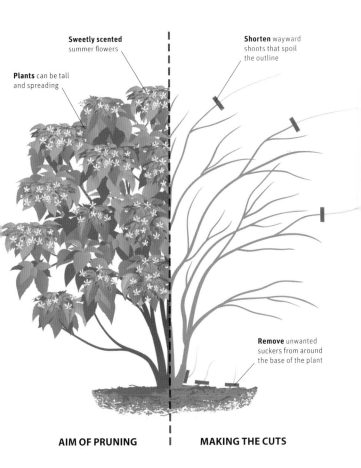

Sweetly scented summer flowers

Plants can be tall and spreading

Shorten wayward shoots that spoil the outline

Remove unwanted suckers from around the base of the plant

AIM OF PRUNING

MAKING THE CUTS

Clethra *Pepperbush*
DECIDUOUS AND EVERGREEN SHRUBS
■ **Prune in spring, as growth begins**

Clethra alnifolia

Suitable only for acidic soils, clethras are grown for their fragrant white or, less commonly, pink summer flowers. A few will not tolerate frost but are suitable for growing in containers under glass. Deciduous types often have good fall leaf color, including *C. barbinervis*, which also has attractive peeling bark. Some have a suckering habit.

Most deciduous types can be grown with minimal pruning. In late winter to early spring, remove any wayward or crossing shoots. On *C. alnifolia*, cut back some of the older stems to ground level, allowing vigorous suckers to replace them. Remove any unwanted suckers in spring or summer. The evergreen *C. arborea* is large and treelike but suitable only for frost-free gardens. Shorten wayward growth as necessary in spring. Under glass, prune harder to restrict its size.

PLANT PROFILE

NATURAL HABIT Often suckering, sometimes treelike shrubs.

HARDINESS Hardiness varies: deciduous types are generally tolerant of frost, but some will not withstand freezing temperatures.

HEIGHT AND SPREAD 10ft x 10ft (3m x 3m); some forms are much smaller.

PRUNING NOTES
■ Most require only minimal pruning.

■ On *C. alnifolia*, cut back some of the older stems annually in spring.

■ Renovative pruning can be staggered over two to three years.

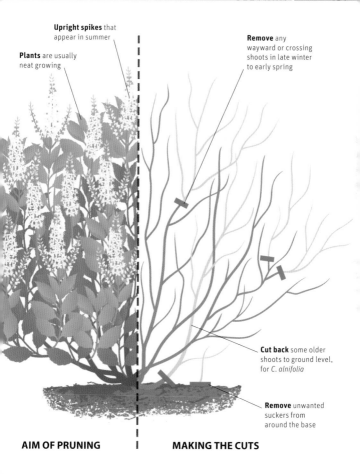

Upright spikes that appear in summer

Plants are usually neat growing

Remove any wayward or crossing shoots in late winter to early spring

Cut back some older shoots to ground level, for *C. alnifolia*

Remove unwanted suckers from around the base

AIM OF PRUNING

MAKING THE CUTS

Clianthus *Parrot's bill*
EVERGREEN SHRUBS
■ **Prune in summer after flowering**

Clianthus puniceus

This small group of plants contains only one that is commonly grown: *C. puniceus*, an evergreen shrub with long, trailing, lax stems. Not reliably hardy, it is excellent for training against a warm wall in cold areas and is ideal for covering a horizontal stretch under a window. The white, pink, or red flowers, which look like claws, appear from spring to early summer on growth produced the previous year.

Prune plants cautiously after flowering. Do no more than cut out dead or damaged shoots, and shorten other stems by no more than a third of their length. The stems are brittle, so wall training must be done while the stems are growing and still reasonably flexible. Create a framework of mainly horizontal stems, and tie in healthy young shoots as they develop.

PLANT PROFILE

NATURAL HABIT Evergreen shrubs that have lax, trailing stems.

HARDINESS Susceptible to frost but can withstand low temperatures if given the protection of a warm wall.

HEIGHT AND SPREAD 12ft x 12ft (4m x 4m); growth is less vigorous in cold areas.

PRUNING NOTES
■ Stems are brittle, and pruning should be kept to a minimum.

■ Hard pruning is not tolerated.

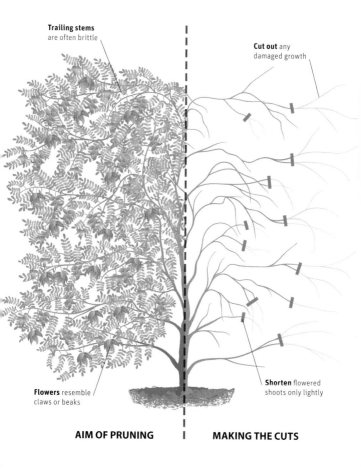

Trailing stems are often brittle

Cut out any damaged growth

Flowers resemble claws or beaks

Shorten flowered shoots only lightly

AIM OF PRUNING

MAKING THE CUTS

Colutea
DECIDUOUS SHRUBS
■ Prune in spring, as new growth is beginning

Colutea x media

These branching shrubs have feathery foliage and bear yellow or orange pealike flowers over a long period in summer, followed by inflated papery seed cases. They naturally produce multiple shoots at or near ground level but can otherwise be grown with a single central trunk, which will rise above lower growing plants.

Prune the plants in spring. For a large, single-stemmed plant, simply remove any thin and weak shoots, then shorten the previous year's stems by up to half. On multi-stemmed plants, cut back any older, thickened shoots to the base of the plant. Alternatively, coppice the plant by cutting all the stems back to a low framework 2in (5cm) above the ground. Do this annually, shortening the previous year's stems to two buds. This will delay flowering slightly.

PLANT PROFILE

NATURAL HABIT Multi-stemmed, generally upright to spreading shrubs.

HARDINESS Mainly fully hardy.

HEIGHT AND SPREAD Plants grow to around 7ft x 7ft (2.2m x 2.2m).

PRUNING NOTES
■ On single-stemmed plants, shorten the previous year's stems if necessary, and remove any thin, weak shoots.

■ On multi-stemmed plants, cut back old stems to the base of the plant.

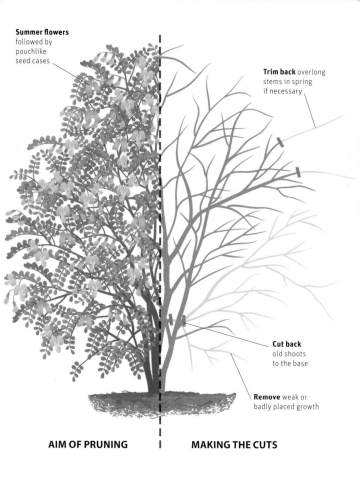

Summer flowers followed by pouchlike seed cases

Trim back overlong stems in spring if necessary

Cut back old shoots to the base

Remove weak or badly placed growth

AIM OF PRUNING

MAKING THE CUTS

Cornus *Dogwood*
DECIDUOUS TREES
■ Prune between late winter and early spring

Cornus controversa 'Variegata'

Dogwoods grown as trees are valued for their flowers and elegant look, although their attractive fall leaf color is also a strong incentive. Pruning is best kept to a minimum—any necessary work can be done in the dormant period between fall and late winter.

The most commonly grown types have very distinct pruning needs. *C. kousa* has large, white, early-summer flowers. When pruning, take care not to damage twiggy stems since these may flower later. *C. alternifolia* and *C. controversa* have a distinctive tiered shape. After planting, select the strongest stem as the leader, and attach it to a pole. Remove any other upright stems from near the base. Prune carefully to maintain the shape. Evergreen *C. capitata* is not reliably hardy and is best grown as a multi-stemmed shrub in cold areas.

PLANT PROFILE

NATURAL HABIT Elegant trees; some produce upright shoots from near the base.

HARDINESS Mainly hardy. Most are best with shelter from hard frost and cold winds.

HEIGHT AND SPREAD Plants grow to around 20ft x 10ft (6m x 3m). Variegated varieties are less vigorous.

PRUNING NOTES
■ Prune when trees are dormant—employ an arborist if necessary.

■ Cut back very vigorous upright shoots on *C. alternifolia* and *C. controversa*.

■ For cornus grown as shrubs, see pp.144–145.

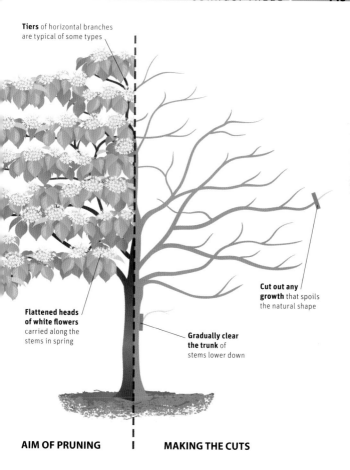

Tiers of horizontal branches are typical of some types

Flattened heads of white flowers carried along the stems in spring

Cut out any growth that spoils the natural shape

Gradually clear the trunk of stems lower down

AIM OF PRUNING

MAKING THE CUTS

Cornus *Dogwood*
DECIDUOUS SHRUBS
■ Prune in late winter or early spring

Cornus alba

Those dogwoods that grow as shrubs have several attractive features and can be pruned in a number of ways, depending on the type. The cornelian cherry (*C. mas*) is grown for its clusters of yellow-green spring flowers and fall leaf color. After flowering, thin the stems to maintain an open, airy look, if necessary.

Varieties of *C. alba* and *C. stolonifera* are grown mainly for the winter interest of their bare stems, which are usually bright yellow or red. Cut back all the stems in the first spring after planting to 2in (5cm) high. Thereafter, annually or every other year in early spring, shorten the previous year's stems to buds at the base. This drastic technique gives the best winter display, but it is at the expense of flowers and fruit. It may also cause variegated varieties to produce plain green leaves; in these instances, limit pruning to the removal of older stems only.

PLANT PROFILE

NATURAL HABIT Elegant shrubs that shoot freely from the base.

HARDINESS Fully hardy.

HEIGHT AND SPREAD 5ft x 4ft (1.5m x 1.2m); larger without extensive pruning.

PRUNING NOTES
■ On *C. mas*, keep pruning to a minimum.

■ Cut forms that are grown for their colorful stems back hard annually.

■ Prune variegated forms less rigorously.

■ For cornus grown as trees see pp.142–143.

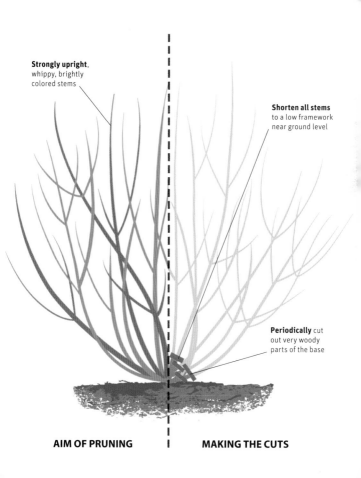

Strongly upright, whippy, brightly colored stems

Shorten all stems to a low framework near ground level

Periodically cut out very woody parts of the base

AIM OF PRUNING

MAKING THE CUTS

Corylopsis *Winterhazel*
DECIDUOUS SHRUBS
■ **Prune in mid-spring, immediately after flowering**

Corylopsis pauciflora

These undemanding shrubs have two seasons of interest: catkinlike, scented yellow flowers in early spring and excellent fall leaf color. Do not plant them too close to other shrubs in a border since this may prevent them from achieving their graceful shape.

Prune to remove older, unproductive wood. Corylopsis flower on stems that grew in the previous year so tackle them as soon after flowering as possible. Cut back thicker stems to the base, then if necessary, thin others to reduce congestion. The plants are suitable for informal wall training, which protects the flowers from frost in very cold areas. Tie in a basic framework of strong stems. After flowering, shorten flowered sideshoots, and remove any others that are awkwardly placed.

PLANT PROFILE

NATURAL HABIT Mainly upright but open, twiggy shrubs of naturally good shape.

HARDINESS Fully hardy, although flowers can be vulnerable to frost damage.

HEIGHT AND SPREAD Plants grow to 10ft x 10ft (3m x 3m), depending on the type. Some have a spread that exceeds the height.

PRUNING NOTES
■ Prune as soon after flowering as possible.

■ Cut older stems back to the base.

■ Renovation should be spread over two to three years to prevent damage to the plant.

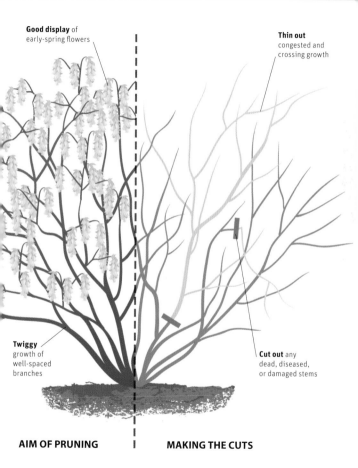

Good display of early-spring flowers

Thin out congested and crossing growth

Twiggy growth of well-spaced branches

Cut out any dead, diseased, or damaged stems

AIM OF PRUNING

MAKING THE CUTS

Corylus *Hazel*
DECIDUOUS TREES AND SHRUBS
■ Prune in winter, or at other times as required

Corylus avellana 'Contorta'

Hazels are grown for their catkins and nuts, and they are commonly planted in wildlife hedges. Naturally producing a number of stems from ground level, they are often cut to the ground annually to produce quantities of whiplike stems that are ideal for traditional basket- and fence-making, although this is at the expense of the flowers and nuts. Otherwise, pruning can be restricted to the removal of older stems in spring.

One distinctive, commonly grown form with different pruning needs is the corkscrew hazel (*C. avellana* 'Contorta'). Its twisted stems are highly ornamental, and its attractive catkins dangle from the branches in spring. Thin any congested stems in winter, and shorten any stems showing cracked bark. Cut back any straight or strongly vertical shoots that arise from the plant to their point of origin as soon as they are seen.

PLANT PROFILE

NATURAL HABIT Deciduous shrubs that naturally shoot from the base.

HARDINESS Fully hardy.

HEIGHT AND SPREAD Plants can grow to 10ft x 6ft (3m x 2m) but are often smaller.

PRUNING NOTES
■ Prune to maintain a good, even shape.

■ Remove suckers and other unruly stems that spoil the overall shape.

Catkins hang from the bare stems in late winter

Shorten congested growth

Cut out any straight shoots

AIM OF PRUNING | **MAKING THE CUTS**

Cotinus *Smoke bush*
DECIDUOUS SHRUBS
■ Prune in late winter to early spring

Cotinus coggygria f. purpureus

Smoke bushes have large, coinlike leaves. Most have purple or golden-yellow foliage that assumes brilliant orange or scarlet tints in the fall before being shed. In warm areas plants produce a froth of flowers in summer, which earns them their common name.

To encourage the largest leaves, which are particularly striking during the first months of the growing season, cut all stems back hard to strong shoots near the base in late winter to early spring. This regime also keeps plants within bounds. However, it is at the expense of any flowers, and the fall color will not be so good. Otherwise, keep pruning to a minimum. Simply remove crossing or wayward shoots in late winter to early spring, and allow the plant to achieve its natural dome-shaped habit. It will become more treelike in shape with age.

PLANT PROFILE

NATURAL HABIT Spreading to upright deciduous shrubs that shoot freely from or near the base.

HARDINESS Fully hardy, although plants flower best in areas with warm summers.

HEIGHT AND SPREAD 10ft x 10ft (3m x 3m); coppiced plants will be smaller.

PRUNING NOTES
■ Prune hard annually for the best leaves.

■ For flowers and better fall color, keep pruning to a minimum.

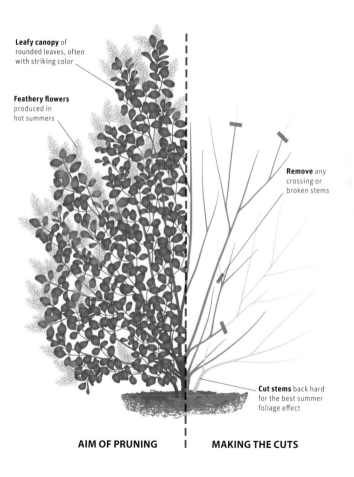

Leafy canopy of rounded leaves, often with striking color

Feathery flowers produced in hot summers

Remove any crossing or broken stems

Cut stems back hard for the best summer foliage effect

AIM OF PRUNING   **MAKING THE CUTS**

Cotoneaster
DECIDUOUS SHRUBS
■ **Prune in early spring**

Cotoneaster horizontalis

Besides the creamy white flowers that are produced in late spring and early summer, deciduous cotoneasters often have good fall leaf color to coincide with their bright red berries. Habits vary from low and spreading to more upright, even treelike. No regular pruning is necessary, but growth can be reduced in late winter if a plant has outgrown its allotted space.

C. horizontalis has an unusual and attractive look. The sideshoots on the stiffly arching stems are arranged in a herringbone pattern. It can be grown on banks or encouraged to ascend a wall, since it will tolerate some shade. To wall train, attach suitably placed branches to the wall after planting. As the plant grows, simply attach stems to the wall as required—most will grow flat against it. Cut back any awkwardly placed growth in late winter.

PLANT PROFILE

NATURAL HABIT Usually stiff-branched, upright to spreading deciduous shrubs.

HARDINESS Fully hardy.

HEIGHT AND SPREAD Plants grow to around 10ft x 10ft (3m x 3m), depending on the type. Against a wall, *C. horizontalis* can reach 15ft (5m) or more.

PRUNING NOTES

■ Prune in early spring, if necessary.

■ Hard pruning to renovate is best spread over two or three years.

■ For evergreen cotoneasters, see pp.154–155.

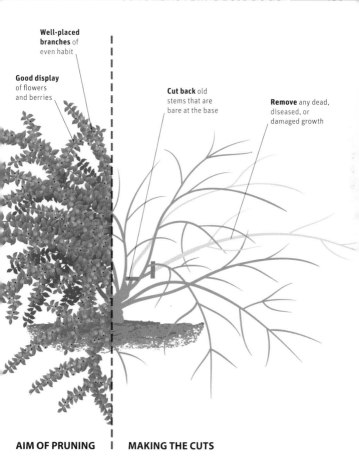

Well-placed branches of even habit

Good display of flowers and berries

Cut back old stems that are bare at the base

Remove any dead, diseased, or damaged growth

AIM OF PRUNING | **MAKING THE CUTS**

Cotoneaster
EVERGREEN SHRUBS
■ **Prune in early spring, or in summer after flowering**

Cotoneaster lacteus

Evergreen cotoneasters produce creamy white flowers in late spring or summer followed by red or yellow fruits. Some are prostrate and make excellent groundcover in lightly shaded situations, while others are more upright, taking the place of a tree in a small garden. Some will lose their leaves in a very cold winter.

Prune either in early spring or immediately after flowering in summer. To encourage open growth on upright or mound-forming varieties, thin stems, and remove any crossing branches in the center of the bush during the first few years after planting. Thereafter, pruning can be kept to a minimum. Shorten any overlong upright shoots on prostrate and mound-forming varieties, and clip hedges after flowering to neaten, retaining as many of the berrying shoots as possible.

PLANT PROFILE

NATURAL HABIT Upright to arching, mound-forming or prostrate shrubs.

HARDINESS Fully hardy, although some will lose their leaves during a very cold winter.

HEIGHT AND SPREAD 12ft x 12ft (4m x 4m) or less. Mound-forming and prostrate forms have a greater spread than height.

PRUNING NOTES
■ Prune carefully when the plants are young to encourage an open shape.

■ Trim wayward shoots on established plants.

■ Renovation is generally successful.

■ For deciduous cotoneasters, see pp.152–153.

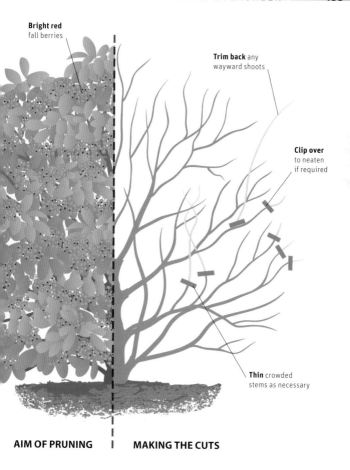

Bright red fall berries

Trim back any wayward shoots

Clip over to neaten if required

Thin crowded stems as necessary

AIM OF PRUNING   **MAKING THE CUTS**

Crataegus *Hawthorn*
DECIDUOUS TREES AND SHRUBS
■ **Prune in winter or after flowering**

Crataegus monogyna

Hawthorns are hardy, deciduous trees that can be kept relatively small with regular pruning. Usually dense growing, they are suitable for hedging and are good for attracting wildlife to the garden. The late-spring flowers are creamy white or pink, with single or double petals.

To keep plants within bounds, prune them after flowering by thinning the dense growth within the body of the plant. Hedges can be clipped to neaten their shape after flowering, but if you want to retain some of the fruits for feeding wildlife over the winter, leave some of the flowered wood. For those with a weeping habit, such as *C. monogyna* 'Pendula', thin congested stems in the canopy in late winter. The remaining branches can be shortened back to an outward-facing bud, if required.

PLANT PROFILE

NATURAL HABIT Dense-growing, deciduous shrubs or small trees.

HARDINESS Fully hardy and tolerant of wind and exposed sites.

HEIGHT AND SPREAD 10ft x 10ft (3m x 3m), or more. Growth can be restricted by regular pruning.

PRUNING NOTES
■ Thin any congested or damaged stems within the body of the plant in winter.

■ Neaten growth after flowering.

Dark red berries follow the flowers

Cut back untidy stems to neaten

Remove awkwardly placed branches

Trim excess growth after flowering

AIM OF PRUNING

MAKING THE CUTS

Cryptomeria
EVERGREEN CONIFERS
■ **Prune in spring as plants are coming into growth**

Cryptomeria japonica 'Cristata'

Unlike nearly all other conifers, cryptomerias respond well to pruning—even a renovative prune in spring can be tolerated. Some form tall, strongly upright trees, while others are much more compact. Many assume rich bronze tints in fall as a response to a drop in temperature. The normally cream leaves of the slow-growing *C.* 'Sekka-sugi' turn white.

There are hundreds of named varieties, some with variegated foliage, others with flattened stems that are fused together. Remove any atypical growth or any shoots that spoil the outline in spring. Cut out badly placed shoots, and stake or wire them into the desired position. Main stems often bend under the weight of the dense foliage. If necessary, large, out-of-shape specimens can be cut back to a 2ft (60cm) stump in spring.

PLANT PROFILE

NATURAL HABIT Plants are extremely variable. Some become very tall trees, while others are more compact or spreading.

HARDINESS Fully hardy.

HEIGHT AND SPREAD Plants can grow to 52ft x 15ft (16m x 5m). Some are much more compact, growing to within 6ft (2m).

PRUNING NOTES
■ Prune in spring if necessary.
■ Plants respond well to renovative pruning.

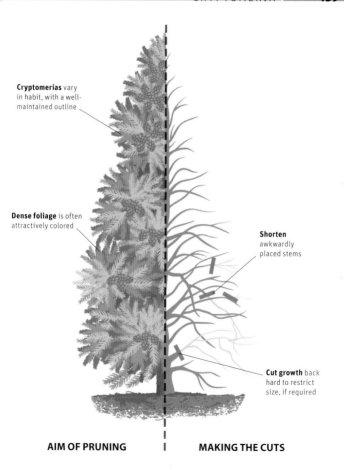

Cryptomerias vary in habit, with a well-maintained outline

Dense foliage is often attractively colored

Shorten awkwardly placed stems

Cut growth back hard to restrict size, if required

AIM OF PRUNING

MAKING THE CUTS

Cupressus *Cypress*
EVERGREEN CONIFERS
■ **Prune in late spring, if necessary**

Cupressus macrocarpa 'Goldcrest'

Cypresses are mainly strongly upright-growing conifers, although some, such as the Monterey cypress (*C. macrocarpa*), can become more spreading as they mature, while other types are compact. Some varieties have very attractive silvery blue or bright golden-yellow foliage—the neat-growing *C. macrocarpa* 'Goldcrest' produces particularly vivid yellow new foliage in spring. Some have attractive hanging sprays of foliage, such as *C. cashmeriana*. Cypresses are especially effective when grown as specimens, hedging, or screening.

If necessary, clip over plants in late spring to encourage a new flush of foliage, being careful not to cut into older growth. Extensive pruning is not successful, so cut out any dead patches, and tie in surrounding branches to conceal the area.

PLANT PROFILE

NATURAL HABIT Upright-growing and often pencil-like conifers.

HARDINESS Mainly hardy, although some will not withstand temperatures below freezing and should be grown under cover.

HEIGHT AND SPREAD Plants grow to around 30ft x 12ft (10m x 4m), depending on the type. Some named forms are compact.

PRUNING NOTES
■ Pruning should be very minimal—simply trim plants in late spring, if necessary.

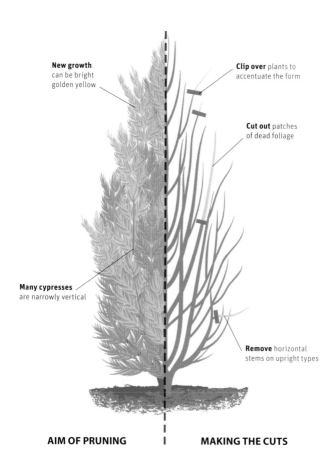

New growth can be bright golden yellow

Clip over plants to accentuate the form

Cut out patches of dead foliage

Many cypresses are narrowly vertical

Remove horizontal stems on upright types

AIM OF PRUNING

MAKING THE CUTS

Cytisus *Broom*

DECIDUOUS SHRUBS AND TREES

■ **Prune in summer, after the plants have flowered**

Cytisus battandieri

Ideal for a tropical garden, brooms are mainly short-lived deciduous shrubs that revel in full sun. Many have twiggy stems that are covered in flowers—white, cream, yellow, or red—in late spring and early summer. Annual pruning limits the buildup of bare wood but does not prolong their lives; old specimens are always better replaced. After flowering, clip over the plants, reducing stems by up to two-thirds in length. Cut back dead stems to the base. New stems will flower the following year.

A popular example, which has summer flowers that both look and smell like pineapple and silky gray-green leaves, is the Moroccan broom (*C. battandieri*). It is best trained loosely against a warm wall in cold areas and should be pruned accordingly. Shorten sideshoots after flowering, and tie in vigorous new shoots to replace any bare framework stems.

PLANT PROFILE

NATURAL HABIT Airy, twiggy plants with stems that tend to become bare at the base.

HARDINESS Mainly hardy—some need the protection of a warm wall in frost-prone areas.

HEIGHT AND SPREAD 4ft x 4ft (1.2m x 1.2m), although some can become larger.

PRUNING NOTES
■ While hard pruning is not successful, stems should be cut back annually—the younger growth is always more productive.

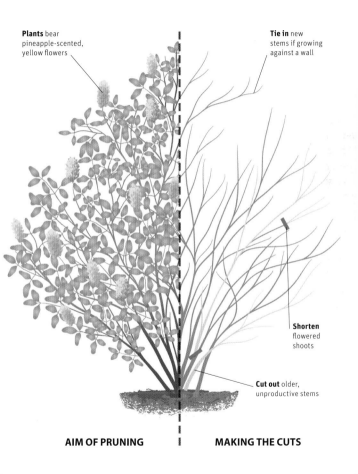

Plants bear pineapple-scented, yellow flowers

Tie in new stems if growing against a wall

Shorten flowered shoots

Cut out older, unproductive stems

AIM OF PRUNING

MAKING THE CUTS

Deutzia
DECIDUOUS SHRUBS
■ Prune in spring and summer

Deutzia scabra

Attractive clusters of dainty, pink or white, spring or summer flowers belie this plant's general hardiness and vigorous growth. In spring, cut out any frost-damaged growth, and after flowering has finished, shorten stems that have flowered, cutting down to just above strong buds. This encourages an attractive bushiness, even though it can lead to congestion within the plant after a few years.

Since deutzias produce new shoots freely from the base, some of the older, less productive wood can be thinned out in early spring every year by cutting them to the ground or to strong buds near the base. Be aware that the plants flower on stems produced the previous year, so do not remove too much established growth at one time.

PLANT PROFILE

NATURAL HABIT Deciduous shrubs that regularly produce shoots from ground level.

HARDINESS Mainly fully hardy.

HEIGHT AND SPREAD 4ft x 4ft (1.2m x 1.2m). Some varieties are taller, others have a more spreading habit.

PRUNING NOTES
■ Prune to refresh the plant, occasionally removing older growth to allow young shoots to develop.

Flowers open in spring or summer

Lightly shorten shoots that have flowered

Thin growth after flowering to reduce congestion

New stems appear from the base every year

Prune out older stems, cutting them right to the base

AIM OF PRUNING

MAKING THE CUTS

Elaeagnus
DECIDUOUS SHRUBS
■ **Prune in early to midsummer, after flowering**

Elaeagnus angustifolia 'Quicksilver'

Deciduous elaeagnus are large, open, elegant shrubs that can be treelike with a spreading crown. They make excellent specimens or back-of-the-border plants, with small but sweetly scented early summer flowers and silvery foliage. The trunks naturally become bare at the base over time.

They can be allowed to develop as multi-stemmed bushes or trained with a single main trunk—either way, they make vase-shaped plants, but the crown will be more spreading if there are several main stems. Prune after flowering to maintain good shape in the canopy. Remove crossing and damaged branches, and shorten any overlong shoots. The job may be easier in late winter when the stems are bare, but this may result in the loss of some of the flowers.

PLANT PROFILE

NATURAL HABIT Spreading, arching shrubs that can become treelike.

HARDINESS Fully hardy.

HEIGHT AND SPREAD Plants grow to around 12ft x 12ft (4m x 4m).

PRUNING NOTES
■ Prune after flowering, if necessary, removing any wayward branches.

■ Plants tolerate hard pruning to renovate.

■ For evergreen elaeagnus see pp.168–169.

Silvery leaves are attractive over a long period

Shorten stems after flowering to neaten

Flowers are small but very sweetly scented

Prune old stems hard to generate replacement growth

AIM OF PRUNING

MAKING THE CUTS

Elaeagnus
EVERGREEN SHRUBS
■ **Prune in mid-spring and late summer**

Elaeagnus x ebbingei 'Gilt Edge'

Evergreen elaeagnus are grown for their leaves rather than their flowers, which are inconspicuous but often highly fragrant. Some foliage is boldly margined or splashed with yellow, while some is pewter-silver. These elaeagnus make excellent hedging material, especially in coastal areas, because they are tolerant of wind and salt spray. They are often used for year-round interest in mixed borders.

Individual plants can be grown with minimal pruning or clipped to a loose "egg" shape. Cut to shape twice a year, as necessary, in mid-spring and late summer. Ideally, use pruners to avoid damaging individual leaves. If it's more practical to use shears—for instance on hedges—do the job during a period of mild, dry weather so that the cuts will heal rapidly. Remove plain green shoots on variegated varieties.

PLANT PROFILE

NATURAL HABIT Dense-growing shrubs.

HARDINESS Fully hardy.

HEIGHT AND SPREAD 10ft x 10ft (3m x 3m), although plants can be kept smaller with regular pruning.

PRUNING NOTES
■ Prune to shape as necessary twice a year, although this will reduce flowering.

■ For deciduous elaeagnus see pp.166–167.

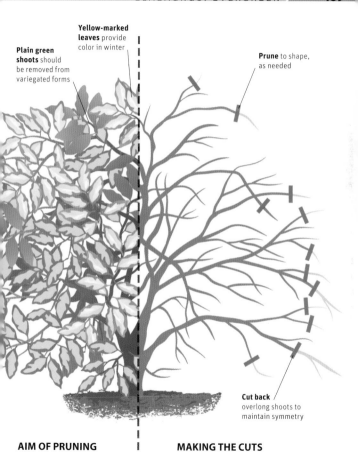

Plain green shoots should be removed from variegated forms

Yellow-marked leaves provide color in winter

Prune to shape, as needed

Cut back overlong shoots to maintain symmetry

AIM OF PRUNING

MAKING THE CUTS

Enkianthus
DECIDUOUS SHRUBS
■ Prune in late winter to early spring

Enkianthus deflexus

Related to the rhododendrons, enkianthus have somewhat similar needs, the principal one being an acidic or neutral soil. Spreading or sometimes treelike shrubs, their bell-like white, pink, cream, or red flowers are carried on the previous year's stems in late spring to early summer. The leaves color well in fall before falling, sometimes making a more impressive display than the flowers.

Extensive pruning is not necessary. Anything needed to improve the balance of branches can be done between winter and early spring. Renovate overgrown or misshapen plants by cutting back old stems. Vigorous younger stems can be left unpruned or shortened less drastically. Damaged wood should be removed in summer.

PLANT PROFILE

NATURAL HABIT Open, spreading, often treelike shrubs.

HARDINESS Fully hardy, but a spot sheltered from strong winds is desirable so that plants hold on to their colorful leaves for as long as possible in fall.

HEIGHT AND SPREAD 6ft x 4ft (2m x 1.2m); bigger in favorable situations.

PRUNING NOTES
■ Though pruning is tolerated, plants are best grown with minimal intervention.

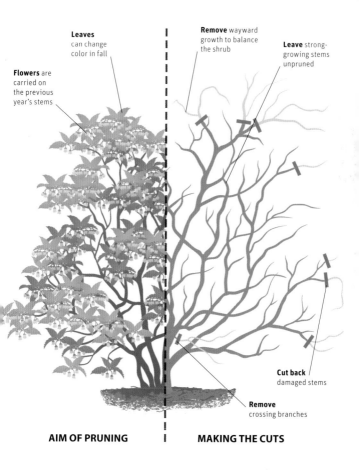

Leaves can change color in fall

Flowers are carried on the previous year's stems

Remove wayward growth to balance the shrub

Leave strong-growing stems unpruned

Cut back damaged stems

Remove crossing branches

AIM OF PRUNING

MAKING THE CUTS

Erica *Heath*
EVERGREEN SHRUBS
■ Prune in spring or early summer, after flowering

Erica carnea 'Springwood White'

Heaths can be used to provide color throughout the year. Depending on the type, white, pink, red, or purple flowers are borne in winter, spring, or summer, with some types producing yellow or orange foliage. Many make excellent groundcover on peaty, sandy soils.

To prevent leggy growth, clip the plants over to remove most of the previous year's growth—without cutting into bare wood at the base. Prune summer- and winter-flowering varieties in early spring, and spring-flowering types after flowering. Replace old, straggly plants.

Prune the tree heath (*E. arborea*) and similar species when young to promote sturdy, bushy growth. In the first two springs, reduce the top-growth by one-half to two-thirds. Thereafter, shorten stems after flowering in early summer. Old stems can be cut back hard into bare wood.

PLANT PROFILE

NATURAL HABIT Scrubby, mound-forming or more upright evergreen shrubs.

HARDINESS Mainly hardy, although some types will not tolerate freezing temperatures.

HEIGHT AND SPREAD Plants grow to around 12in x 30in (30cm x 75cm). Tree heaths are taller and narrower, to 10ft (3m).

PRUNING NOTES
■ Clip or shear over plants to remove most of the previous year's growth.

■ On tree heaths, shorten the previous year's growth by up to half its length.

■ Tree heaths respond well to renovation, producing new growth from bare stems.

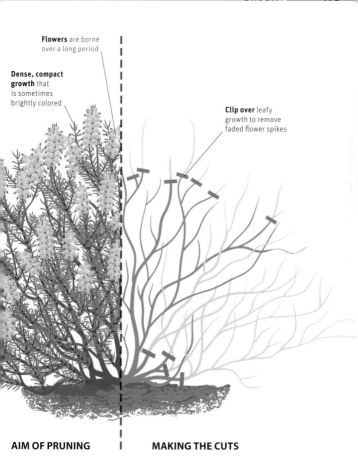

Flowers are borne over a long period

Dense, compact growth that is sometimes brightly colored

Clip over leafy growth to remove faded flower spikes

AIM OF PRUNING

MAKING THE CUTS

Escallonia

EVERGREEN SHRUBS

■ **Prune in spring, then in summer after flowering**

Escallonia 'Langleyensis'

These mainly evergreen shrubs are often used as hedging. They generally produce a mass of arching stems that are covered with small, attractive, white, pink, or red flowers throughout summer and fall. They are mainly hardy but can suffer from frost damage in a very hard winter if they are not given a sheltered location.

Unusual for shrubs that flower late in the season, the flowers are produced not on the new stems but on one-year-old wood. Spring pruning should therefore be restricted to simply removing any frost-damaged growth. After flowering, thin the growth by removing all the stems that have flowered, pruning to maintain a good shape and to keep the plant within bounds. The current year's growth should be retained for flowering in the following year. Clip over hedges twice a year between spring and summer. Flowering will be sparse.

PLANT PROFILE

NATURAL HABIT Generally neat-growing and compact evergreen shrubs.

HARDINESS Mainly hardy, although some benefit from shelter in a cold climate.

HEIGHT AND SPREAD Plants grow to around 6ft x 6ft (2m x 2m).

PRUNING NOTES
■ Pruning is largely a matter of cutting back flowered stems to maintain a neat shape.

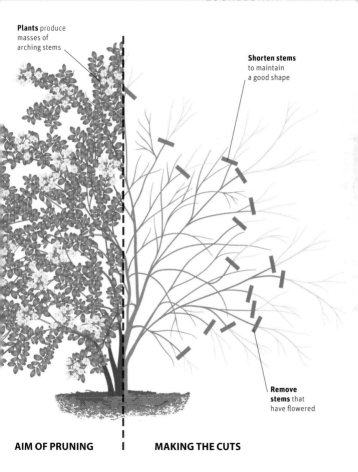

Plants produce masses of arching stems

Shorten stems to maintain a good shape

Remove stems that have flowered

AIM OF PRUNING | **MAKING THE CUTS**

Eucalyptus *Gum*
EVERGREEN TREES AND SHRUBS
■ **Prune in midsummer**

Eucalyptus gunnii

Eucalyptus are potentially large evergreen trees that sometimes develop multiple trunks. They are grown mainly for their foliage, although mature specimens also have attractive bark. Flowers are produced only in reliably warm areas. Given adequate space, multi-trunked trees develop an impressive, spreading shape.

Some eucalyptus, such as *E. gunnii*, can be treated as a coppice or pollard: cut all the stems back hard each summer either to ground level or a tall stump. This will help to keep the tree within bounds and also maintain the production of its gleaming, silver, coinlike young leaves, which become duller and sickle-shaped as they age. On other eucalyptus, cut out any frost-damaged growth in the spring. Most respond well to pruning even after significant dieback. Eucalyptus often develop crooked trunks, so should be well staked on planting.

PLANT PROFILE

NATURAL HABIT Upright, often multi-stemmed trees and shrubs.

HARDINESS Most show some sensitivity to hard frost. Established plants often survive periods of freezing weather.

HEIGHT AND SPREAD 30ft x 20ft (10m x 6m) or more in both directions.

PRUNING NOTES
■ Cut out damaged growth in summer.

■ For the best leaves, cut all stems back hard annually to a low framework.

■ Mature specimens may not respond well to renovative pruning.

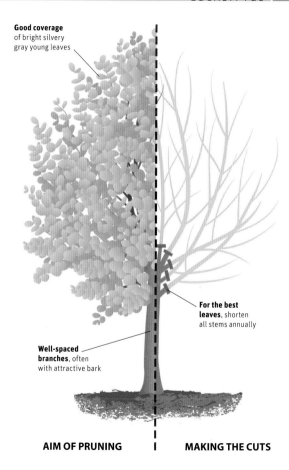

Good coverage of bright silvery gray young leaves

For the best leaves, shorten all stems annually

Well-spaced branches, often with attractive bark

AIM OF PRUNING | **MAKING THE CUTS**

Eucryphia
EVERGREEN TREES
■ **Prune mainly in spring, after the last hard frost**

Many of these evergreen trees are strongly upright. They become pillars of white when studded with their flowers, which appear mainly in late summer. They need a sheltered spot since they are vulnerable not only to hard frosts but to cold, drying winds, especially when they are young. Most are best grown in acidic soil, although *E.* x *nymansensis* 'Nymansay'—one of the most commonly grown—tolerates lime.

Eucryphia x *nymansensis* 'Nymansay'

Plants need minimal pruning—it is usually only necessary to repair any frost or wind damage. Cut back any affected growth in spring, cutting to just above a healthy shoot. New stems will be upright growing.

E. lucida is something of an exception because it flowers from early summer on older shoots. Prune it to shape after flowering, if necessary.

PLANT PROFILE

NATURAL HABIT Imposing, usually strongly upright, evergreen trees. Some are fast-growing.

HARDINESS Mainly hardy but susceptible to freezing weather and cold winds.

HEIGHT AND SPREAD Plants grow to around 30ft x 10ft (10m x 3m).

PRUNING NOTES
■ Keep pruning to a minimum.

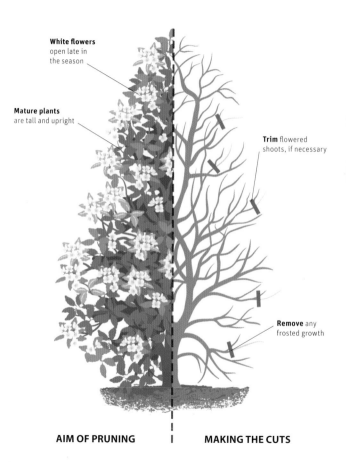

White flowers open late in the season

Mature plants are tall and upright

Trim flowered shoots, if necessary

Remove any frosted growth

AIM OF PRUNING

MAKING THE CUTS

Euonymus *Spindle tree*
DECIDUOUS SHRUBS
■ **Prune in late winter to early spring**

Euonymus europaeus

Deciduous euonymus are shrubs for fall, with fine leaf color in shades of deep red or purple and ornamental fruits that split to reveal their seeds. In winter corky wings borne on the stems prolong the interest. The greenish yellow late-spring flowers are inconspicuous. The plants can be used for informal hedging, either on their own or in combination with other plants to create a wildlife hedge.

Deciduous euonymus can be slow growing, so extensive pruning is not necessary. In late winter to early spring, before new growth begins, thin any congested growth. Older stems can be cut hard to the base to open up the center of the plant. Clip over hedges to neaten them in late spring to early summer, after flowering. This is best done selectively, with pruners, to retain as much fruiting material as possible.

PLANT PROFILE

NATURAL HABIT Slow-growing, spreading, sometimes dense shrubs that can be treelike when mature.

HARDINESS Fully hardy.

HEIGHT AND SPREAD 8ft x 10ft (2.5m x 3m) where grown as a specimen.

PRUNING NOTES
■ For the best shape, restrict pruning to cutting out older and congested stems.

■ Neglected plants respond well to renovation. Cut all stems down to a low framework in late winter to early spring.

■ For evergreen euonymus see pp.182–183.

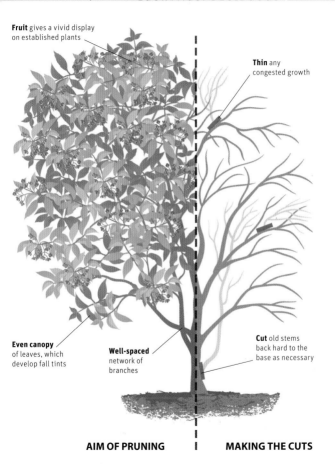

Fruit gives a vivid display on established plants

Thin any congested growth

Even canopy of leaves, which develop fall tints

Well-spaced network of branches

Cut old stems back hard to the base as necessary

AIM OF PRUNING

MAKING THE CUTS

Euonymus

EVERGREEN SHRUBS

■ **Prune in spring and mid- to late summer, as required**

Evergreen types of euonymus are valuable foliage shrubs, and of these the variegated varieties are most commonly grown. Some varieties are spreading and mound-forming, which makes them useful for billowing groundcover or low hedging, although they cannot be clipped to a formal shape. Others, such as *E. japonicus*, are more upright and are suitable for a boundary hedge.

Clip over plants in spring and again in mid- to late summer to neaten them. As a matter of routine, cut back any plain green shoots on variegated types. Some forms are suitable for informal wall training, such as the popular *E. fortunei* 'Silver Queen'. This slow-growing shrub is one of the best, with at least as much cream in the leaf as green. Once established, shorten overlong sideshoots, and remove any plain green shoots as necessary. Hard pruning variegated forms to renovate may not be successful.

Euonymus fortunei 'Emerald 'n' Gold'

Cut out any stems with plain green leaves on variegated types

Sprawling or spreading growth

AIM OF PRUNING

PLANT PROFILE

NATURAL HABIT Mound-forming to spreading, generally dense, compact shrubs.

HARDINESS Mainly fully hardy, although foliage can collapse following a hard frost, recovering as the temperature rises.

HEIGHT AND SPREAD 3ft x 4ft (1m x 1.2m), or more. Hedging types are taller.

PRUNING NOTES

■ Cut back plain shoots on variegated forms.

■ Trim over as necessary during the growing season.

■ Shorten overlong sideshoots on wall-trained plants.

■ For deciduous euonymus, see pp.180–181.

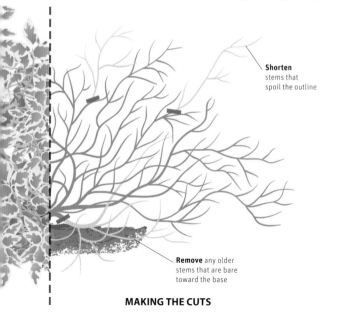

Shorten stems that spoil the outline

Remove any older stems that are bare toward the base

MAKING THE CUTS

Euphorbia *Spurge*
EVERGREEN SHRUBS
■ Prune in midsummer as the flowers start to fade

Euphorbia characias subsp. *wulfenii* 'John Tomlinson'

There are hundreds of different euphorbias, some of them perennials and used in mixed borders, and others that are tropical plants suitable as houseplants in cold areas. While the majority have soft or fleshy stems and only need very minimal pruning, *E. characias*—a popular, variable species—has stems that tend to become woody arising from ground level. The large heads of greenish gold flowers last for many weeks in spring and early summer. In cold areas it does best with the shelter of a wall. Plants flower at the tips of the previous year's stems. In midsummer, cut the flowered stems right back or near to the base, reaching inside the plant to do so—next year's flower stems will have already formed. Leave the new stems unpruned unless they need thinning. Cut stems bleed a milky sap that can cause a rash, so wear gloves when pruning.

PLANT PROFILE

NATURAL HABIT This group varies from hardy, upright shrubs and clump-forming perennials to low-growing succulents.

HARDINESS Plants are sensitive to frost but normally thrive if grown against a warm wall.

HEIGHT AND SPREAD 4ft x 4ft (1.2m x 1.2m); often more when grown against a wall.

PRUNING NOTES
■ For hardy shrubs such as *E. characias*, remove older stems annually, cutting back to the base to allow room for newer growth.

■ Other euphorbias require far less pruning —simply trim them back after flowering.

■ Protect eyes, and cover skin when pruning.

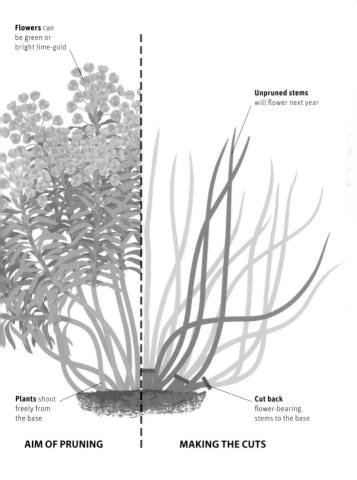

Flowers can be green or bright lime-gold

Unpruned stems will flower next year

Plants shoot freely from the base

Cut back flower-bearing stems to the base

AIM OF PRUNING

MAKING THE CUTS

Fagus *Beech*
DECIDUOUS TREES
■ **Prune in winter, when dormant, or in midsummer**

Fagus sylvatica 'Tortuosa'

Beech trees have a remarkable variety of shapes. While many are grand and spreading in maturity, there are also weeping and upright types. Some have yellow or purple leaves, and all have excellent fall color. Thriving after trimming, beech is often used as a slow-growing hedge and can be cut to a sheer, wall-like finish. As freestanding trees, most develop and maintain a good shape without intervention.

Any pruning necessary can be carried out during the dormant period in winter or in midsummer. On weeping types, shorten overlong stems that trail on the ground, cutting to an outward-facing bud further up the stem. Unpruned, these trailing stems will root and send up another main stem, gradually increasing the spread of the plant. Shear over hedges in winter and midsummer, and at other times to neaten.

PLANT PROFILE

NATURAL HABIT Slow-growing, spreading, weeping, or upright trees.

HARDINESS Fully hardy.

HEIGHT AND SPREAD Plants can grow to around 43ft x 43ft (13m x 13m). Named varieties are often much smaller.

PRUNING NOTES
■ Prune upright, weeping, or arching varieties to maintain the shape. Otherwise, keep pruning to the minimum.

■ Clip hedges throughout the year as necessary to maintain a firm outline.

Even, sweeping canopy that colors well in fall

Cut back strongly upright-growing shoots

Shorten overlong shoots to suitably placed buds

Remove any unwanted stems from the trunk

AIM OF PRUNING

MAKING THE CUTS

Fatsia

EVERGREEN SHRUBS

■ **Prune in mid- to late spring, when frost has passed**

Fatsia japonica

With their big, glossy, hand-shaped leaves and large clusters of white fall flowers, fatsias bring a tropical touch to a garden. Not reliably hardy, they benefit from a sheltered location in cold gardens and can be trained against a shady wall; they are sometimes grown indoors as houseplants. Top-growth sometimes collapses after a frost but then recovers once the temperature rises.

Pruning is seldom strictly necessary, but when it is, it is best to remove entire stems rather than just shortening them. In mid- to late spring, cut back stems blackened by frost. Any stems that spoil the outline can be taken back to the base. On wall-trained plants, cut out badly placed stems. The cross between fatsia and ivy, x *Fatshedera*, is best wall-trained or used as groundcover. Prune as necessary in mid- to late spring.

PLANT PROFILE

NATURAL HABIT Usually elegant, architectural evergreen shrubs.

HARDINESS Plants need shelter from extreme cold in frost-prone areas.

HEIGHT AND SPREAD Plants can grow to 6–10ft (2–3m) in both directions.

PRUNING NOTES
■ Cut back frost-damaged growth.

■ Remove any badly placed stems.

■ To renovate, cut back older stems only, retaining younger, more vigorous ones.

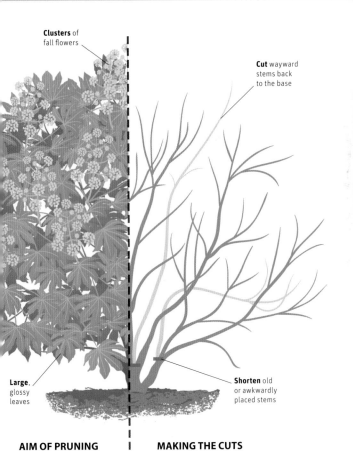

Clusters of fall flowers

Cut wayward stems back to the base

Large, glossy leaves

Shorten old or awkwardly placed stems

AIM OF PRUNING

MAKING THE CUTS

Ficus *Fig*

EVERGREEN TREES

■ **Prune any time when plants are in active growth**

Ficus elastica 'Doescheri'

Besides the hardy outdoor fruiting fig (*F. carica*, see pp.452–453), there are a number of tropical evergreen ficus that are most commonly grown as houseplants in cold areas—principally the weeping fig (*F. benjamina*) and the rubber plant (*F. elastica*). In their country of origin both are large trees; in containers they are slower growing and much more compact. Both have variegated forms that are less vigorous than those with plain green leaves.

To prevent them from getting out of hand, prune in spring and summer, shortening stems as required. Cut back stems of the weeping fig that show signs of dieback; *F. lyrata* can be treated in the same way. Plants usually recover well if fed and kept well watered in the weeks following. Shorten fast-growing stems on the climbing *F. repens* as required.

PLANT PROFILE

NATURAL HABIT Often vigorous, potentially large evergreen trees and shrubs.

HARDINESS The figs given above do not tolerate frost—grow indoors in cold areas.

HEIGHT AND SPREAD 6ft x 4ft (2m x 1.2m). Plants are capable of growing bigger, but can also be kept smaller with regular pruning.

PRUNING NOTES
■ Prune to keep plants in bounds and to remove dead or damaged material.

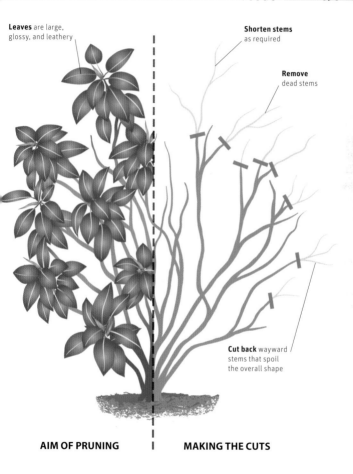

Leaves are large, glossy, and leathery

Shorten stems as required

Remove dead stems

Cut back wayward stems that spoil the overall shape

AIM OF PRUNING

MAKING THE CUTS

Forsythia
DECIDUOUS SHRUBS
■ Prune in mid- to late spring, after flowering

Forsythia x
intermedia
'Lynwood'

While the cheery yellow flowers of forsythias cover their bare branches and light up the garden in early spring, for the rest of the year they can be shapeless shrubs with an untidy shape.

Forsythias respond well to regular pruning, and this is best tackled immediately after flowering, before their leaf growth is fully advanced. Shorten stems that have flowered by one-third to one-half, or more if you need to restrict the size. To balance growth and encourage a vase-shaped habit, prune very vigorous stems only lightly; weaker-growing stems should be pruned back much harder. You may be able to leave some stems unpruned. Cut back older, thicker branches to the base, especially if the lower portion is bare. If necessary, thin the remaining stems to ease congestion.

PLANT PROFILE

NATURAL HABIT Upright to arching, sometimes ungainly shrubs.

HARDINESS Fully hardy.

HEIGHT AND SPREAD Plants can grow to around 7ft x 6ft (2.2m x 2m), although some forms are more compact.

PRUNING NOTES
■ Prune annually to keep within bounds and to improve the overall shape.

■ Shorten stems that have flowered.

■ Renovative pruning is generally successful.

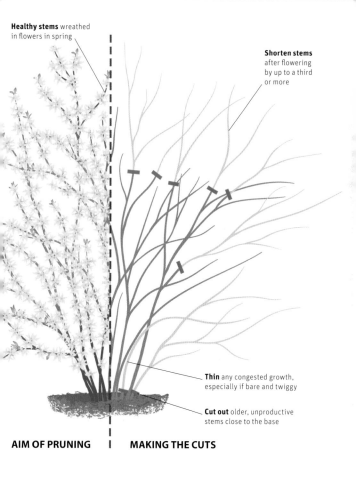

Healthy stems wreathed in flowers in spring

Shorten stems after flowering by up to a third or more

Thin any congested growth, especially if bare and twiggy

Cut out older, unproductive stems close to the base

AIM OF PRUNING　　**MAKING THE CUTS**

Fothergilla
DECIDUOUS SHRUBS
■ **Prune in spring, immediately after flowering**

Fothergilla major

These slow-growing deciduous shrubs require an acidic soil. They are grown for their bottlebrushlike spikes of white and occasionally pinkish spring flowers and spectacular fall leaf color; the flowers usually appear before or at the same time as the new foliage emerges. Both of these features develop best if the plants are given a location in full sun.

Pruning should be kept to a minimum. If necessary, remove any damaged stems in spring, immediately after the plants have flowered, cutting back to strong, outward-facing buds. Also remove any crossing or rubbing stems in the body of the plant and any weak and unhealthy growth. Otherwise, fothergillas should be allowed to develop their natural shapely form without intervention.

PLANT PROFILE

NATURAL HABIT Slow-growing, usually rounded, twiggy, deciduous shrubs.

HARDINESS Fully hardy.

HEIGHT AND SPREAD Plants grow to around 4ft x 4ft (1.2m x 1.2m), or more.

PRUNING NOTES
■ Keep pruning to a minimum.

■ Remove any damaged stems in spring.

■ Renovate only if strictly necessary, staggering the process over a two- or three-year period.

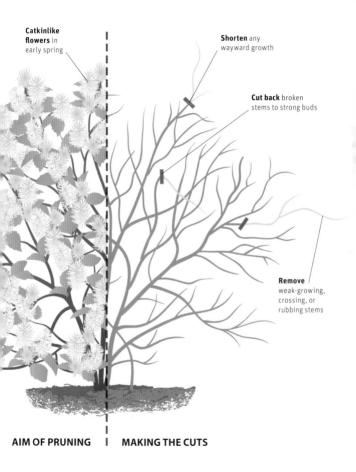

Catkinlike flowers in early spring

Shorten any wayward growth

Cut back broken stems to strong buds

Remove weak-growing, crossing, or rubbing stems

AIM OF PRUNING | MAKING THE CUTS

Fremontodendron *Flannel bush*

EVERGREEN SHRUBS

■ **Prune in summer, immediately after flowering**

Fremontodendron 'California Glory'

These stiffly upright plants are smothered in bright yellow flowers for a couple of weeks in summer and may produce a scattering of additional flowers later in the season. Since they are not reliably hardy, they need the shelter of a warm wall in cold regions. Attach the main stems to the wall as they grow, but remember that strict training is not possible, because the stems do not bend easily.

Prune with some caution: plants do not tolerate hard cutting back, and the stems are also covered in irritant hairs, so wear protective gloves and a mask, if necessary, when handling the plant. After the plant has flowered, shorten stems that are growing outward from the wall. Prune out crowded stems, leaving the younger, vigorous shoots to grow on.

PLANT PROFILE

NATURAL HABIT Stiffly branching shrubs that often have a main central stem.

HARDINESS Hardy, if given the protection of a warm wall in frost-prone areas.

HEIGHT AND SPREAD 15ft x 10ft (5m x 3m). In warm climates, plants may become larger.

PRUNING NOTES

■ Prune to achieve good coverage of the chosen support.

■ Cut back flowered stems in summer.

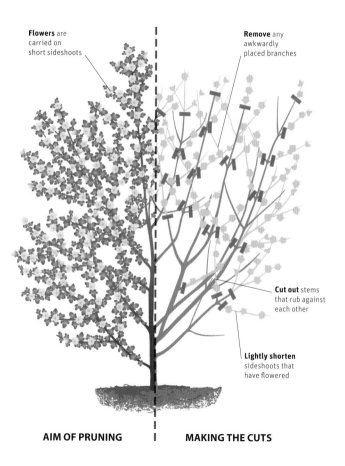

Flowers are carried on short sideshoots

Remove any awkwardly placed branches

Cut out stems that rub against each other

Lightly shorten sideshoots that have flowered

AIM OF PRUNING

MAKING THE CUTS

Fuchsia

HARDY VARIETIES

■ **Spring and, optionally, in fall**

All fuchsias are useful for summer containers, but hardy varieties also make excellent permanent border plants, wall shrubs, and hedging material. They are not evergreen however, and top-growth can be damaged or even killed outright by a hard frost. Leave this on the plant over winter to protect the lower part of the plant.

In spring, cut back all dead stems to near the base. New growth may appear from below ground. If there are signs of new growth, stems can be shortened by up to two-thirds if you want to promote a more compact shape, or just lightly tipped back. Shear over hedges in spring to shorten the sideshoots, then cut older stems back to near the base. In exposed gardens, shortening all the current year's growth after flowering in fall will make the plant less vulnerable to wind damage.

Fuchsia magellanica var. molinae

PLANT PROFILE

NATURAL HABIT Twiggy shrubs that shoot from the base. They sometimes produce tall, arching stems.

HARDINESS Mainly hardy, although top-growth is often killed outright over winter in cold areas.

HEIGHT AND SPREAD 6ft x 6ft (2m x 2m).

PRUNING NOTES

■ Prune annually in spring either to the ground or to a low framework of stems.

■ For hedges, shorten sideshoots only, and remove old stems at the base.

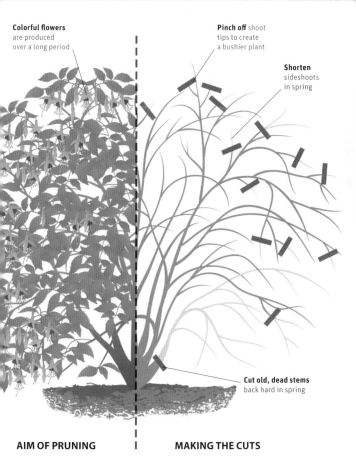

Colorful flowers are produced over a long period

Pinch off shoot tips to create a bushier plant

Shorten sideshoots in spring

Cut old, dead stems back hard in spring

AIM OF PRUNING

MAKING THE CUTS

Garrya
EVERGREEN SHRUBS
■ **Prune in spring, after flowering**

Garrya elliptica

These evergreen shrubs have gray-green flowers that appear from midwinter to spring in long, dangling catkins at the tips of branches. Young stems have a tendency to shoot upward, but the weight of the flowers bends the tips down. Although plants can be grown as freestanding specimens or in shrub borders, they can be very effective trained loosely against a wall, which also protects the catkins from frost. Any exposure is suitable.

Freestanding specimens need little regular pruning beyond the removal of frost-damaged growth. Against a wall, establish an informal framework of branches, and allow new stems to cascade forward—they naturally achieve a pleasing shape. In early spring, thin congested or badly placed shoots, and shorten any overlong or wayward branches.

PLANT PROFILE

NATURAL HABIT Evergreen shrubs that look elegant when in full flower in late winter.

HARDINESS Mainly fully hardy, although flowers can be damaged by frost in an exposed location.

HEIGHT AND SPREAD Plants grow to around 10ft x 10ft (3m x 3m).

PRUNING NOTES
■ Prune to accentuate the natural shape and to remove any frost-damaged growth.

■ Trim the plants back in spring as the catkins begin to fade.

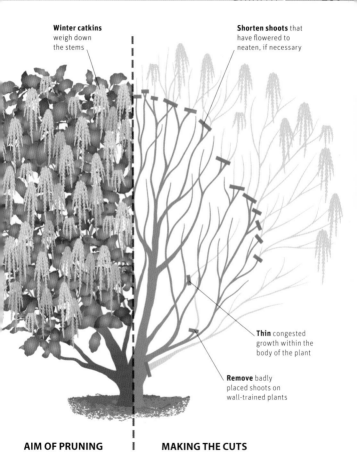

Winter catkins weigh down the stems

Shorten shoots that have flowered to neaten, if necessary

Thin congested growth within the body of the plant

Remove badly placed shoots on wall-trained plants

AIM OF PRUNING

MAKING THE CUTS

Gaultheria *Wintergreen*
EVERGREEN SHRUBS
■ **Prune in mid- to late spring, or after flowering**

Gaultheria. mucronata 'Wintertime'

Related to the heathers and also requiring acidic soil, gaultherias are mainly low-growing evergreens, grown less for their small spring and summer flowers than for their beadlike, white, pink, red, or purple berries; these last into winter and stand out vividly against the dark foliage. Plants look good planted as a group, but small specimens (varieties of *G. mucronata*) can also add color to winter window boxes and containers.

Regular pruning is not required, but plants can be neatened in mid- to late spring, or after flowering. Established plants often produce suckers—remove these to restrict the spread. Older plants can be cut back hard into old wood. *G. shallon* forms a thicket and can be used as hedging; regular clipping maintains dense growth but may be at the expense of flowers and fruit.

PLANT PROFILE

NATURAL HABIT Low-growing, dense, sometimes suckering evergreen shrubs.

HARDINESS Mainly fully hardy, although some will not withstand frost.

HEIGHT AND SPREAD Plants grow to 4–6ft x 4–6ft (1.2–2m x 1.2–2m), depending on the type grown.

PRUNING NOTES
■ Keep pruning to a minimum.

■ Remove suckers as seen.

■ Renovative pruning is usually successful—cut into old wood if necessary.

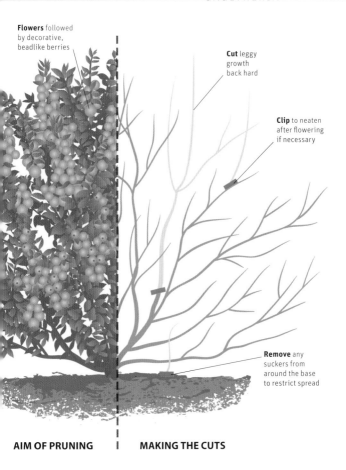

Flowers followed by decorative, beadlike berries

Cut leggy growth back hard

Clip to neaten after flowering if necessary

Remove any suckers from around the base to restrict spread

AIM OF PRUNING

MAKING THE CUTS

Genista *Broom*
DECIDUOUS SHRUBS
■ **Prune in spring or summer, depending on the type**

Genista aetnensis

A profusion of pealike flowers, usually bright yellow, cover the arching stems, often in late spring to early summer. Most genistas form low, rounded mounds, although *G. aetnensis*, commonly known as the Mount Etna broom, can be treelike—its flowering stems cascade down in mid- and late summer. It is excellent for providing height without creating too much shade.

Pruning is not generally necessary. Forms of popular *G. lydia* are best with no pruning at all. Trim lightly after flowering to encourage a bushy look. Thin crowded shoots on older plants, but prune carefully since stems cut back hard into bare wood will not regenerate.

To encourage the Mount Etna broom to achieve its full height, insert a tall cane next to a strong stem when planting, and tie it to the cane as it grows. Prune in spring only if absolutely necessary.

PLANT PROFILE

NATURAL HABIT Mound-forming or more upright shrubs with flexible, arching stems.

HARDINESS Most are hardy if grown in gritty, well-drained soil. Some need a sheltered spot in frost-prone areas.

HEIGHT AND SPREAD 2ft x 3ft (60cm x 1m). *G. aetnensis* can reach 15ft (5m) or more.

PRUNING NOTES
■ Keep pruning to a minimum.

■ Renovative pruning is unlikely to be successful. Plants are not long-lived, and unproductive specimens are best replaced.

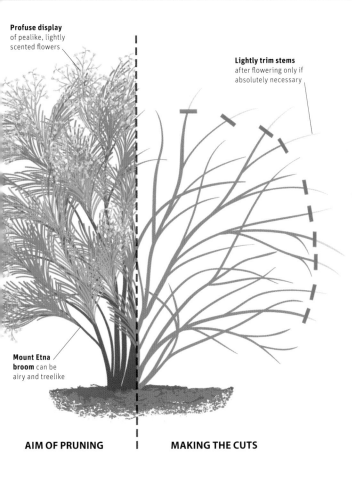

Profuse display of pealike, lightly scented flowers

Lightly trim stems after flowering only if absolutely necessary

Mount Etna broom can be airy and treelike

AIM OF PRUNING

MAKING THE CUTS

Ginkgo *Maidenhair tree*
DECIDUOUS TREES
■ Prune between fall and early spring

Ginkgo biloba

Most ginkgos make potentially large trees, usually upright when young, then spreading. The waxy, fanlike leaves turn butter yellow before falling in fall. The main trunk sometimes curves toward the top but will straighten with age. Female types bear yellowish, plumlike fruits. Some are slow-growing and shrubby.

Pruning should be kept to a minimum. Remove any damaged growth between leaf fall in autumn and early spring. Cut back any horizontal branches that spoil the outline on upright forms. The prostrate variety, *G. biloba* 'Horizontalis', which is normally very flat-growing, occasionally produces strongly upright shoots. Cut these back to their point of origin as seen. Variegated forms may not show good variegation every year. Cut out plain green shoots only if they are very strong growing and affect the balance of the plant.

PLANT PROFILE

NATURAL HABIT Generally strongly upright deciduous trees.

HARDINESS Fully hardy.

HEIGHT AND SPREAD 30ft x 10ft (10m x 3m) or more. Some forms are narrower. Prostrate varieties are lower growing.

PRUNING NOTES
■ Keep pruning to a minimum.

■ After leaf fall, remove dead branches and any that cross or spoil the shape.

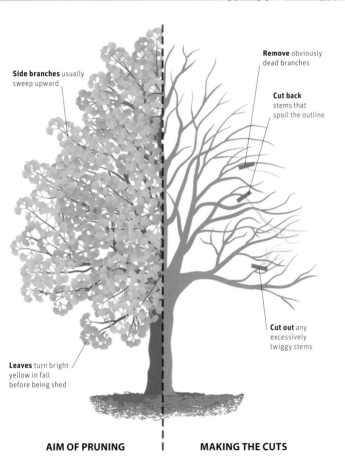

Side branches usually sweep upward

Remove obviously dead branches

Cut back stems that spoil the outline

Leaves turn bright yellow in fall before being shed

Cut out any excessively twiggy stems

AIM OF PRUNING

MAKING THE CUTS

Gleditsia *Honeylocust*
DECIDUOUS TREES
■ **Prune in fall, after the leaves have fallen**

Gleditsia triacanthos 'Sunburst'

These dainty deciduous trees are grown for their feathery foliage, a particular delight in spring. Any pruning is best done immediately after leaves fall—earlier, and sap may bleed from the cuts. Thin congested growth within the crown, and shorten any damaged stems. The trees naturally develop a good shape without much intervention.

The popular *G. triacanthos* 'Sunburst' naturally develops a spreading crown. Its bright golden-yellow spring foliage turns green by summer, briefly turning yellow again before dropping in fall. *G. triacanthos* 'Rubylace' has reddish young leaves that are tinged bronze in summer before yellowing in fall. The stems of all gleditsias are usually spiny. Many are extremely tolerant of urban pollution.

PLANT PROFILE

NATURAL HABIT Graceful trees that are airy when young but develop a fuller canopy as they mature.

HARDINESS Fully hardy.

HEIGHT AND SPREAD 30ft x 25ft (10m x 8m). Varieties with colored leaves are often less vigorous.

PRUNING NOTES
■ Prune only to improve the balance of the canopy and the shape of the tree.

Cut out any damaged growth in fall

Thin congested growth, as necessary

Trees often develop spreading crowns

AIM OF PRUNING

MAKING THE CUTS

Grevillea
EVERGREEN SHRUBS

■ **Prune in spring and during the growing season**

Grevillea 'Poorinda Constance'

With their showy white, red, orange, or yellow flowers grevilleas bring an exotic touch to a garden. Depending on the type, they flower at various times of the year, sometimes in two flushes and sometimes all year round. In cool climates some can be grown outdoors against a warm wall, while others are only suitable for containers under glass. None is reliably hardy.

Most respond well to regular pruning in spring. Tip-prune young plants to encourage a bushy habit. On mature plants, cut back awkwardly placed stems to their point of origin, and remove any crossing stems. Shorten the sideshoots, and reduce the strong stems that grew in the previous year by one-third—or by two-thirds for more vigorous types. Deadhead repeat-flowering types during the growing season to prolong their flowering.

PLANT PROFILE

NATURAL HABIT Fast-growing, usually open and spreading evergreen shrubs.

HARDINESS Many will not tolerate prolonged cold, but others will survive low temperatures in a sheltered location.

HEIGHT AND SPREAD 6ft x 6ft (2m x 2m). Some types are prostrate and spreading.

PRUNING NOTES
■ Tip-prune young plants.
■ Prune plants annually to improve flowering.
■ Deadhead regularly.
■ Some respond well to hard pruning.

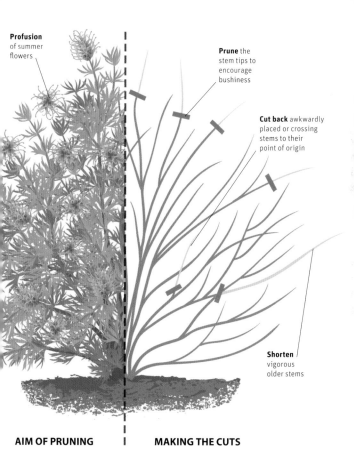

Profusion of summer flowers

Prune the stem tips to encourage bushiness

Cut back awkwardly placed or crossing stems to their point of origin

Shorten vigorous older stems

AIM OF PRUNING

MAKING THE CUTS

Halesia *Silverbell*
DECIDUOUS SHRUBS OR TREES
■ **Prune between fall and early spring**

Halesia carolina

Masses of white, or occasionally pink, snowdroplike flowers adorn the branches of halesias in spring, just before or at the same time as the leaves emerge; their fall leaf color is also an attractive feature. Slow growth makes these graceful trees an ideal choice for small gardens, but they must have neutral to acidic soil.

The trees branch freely and are sometimes multi-stemmed. If you do not want plants to develop this shrubby habit and prefer to encourage a shapely, well-balanced plant, select the strongest stem to form a leader, and remove the remainder. Halesias can be encouraged to develop a short trunk—apart from *H. monticola*, which is one of the largest. Young trees can appear uneven, but keep any pruning to a minimum because of the slow growth rate. Once established, prune out any congested growth during the dormant period.

PLANT PROFILE

NATURAL HABIT Slow-growing, upright to vase-shaped or spreading, sometimes multi-stemmed trees and shrubs.

HARDINESS Fully hardy.

HEIGHT AND SPREAD Up to 25ft x 20ft (8m x 6m), but only after many years.

PRUNING NOTES
■ Grow with a central trunk for the most balanced appearance.

■ Prune during the dormant period.

■ Renovative pruning may not be successful.

Prune out congested stems within the body of the plant

Cut out older branches that are less productive

Bell-like flowers hang from the branches in spring

Single or multi-stemmed trunk

AIM OF PRUNING

MAKING THE CUTS

Hamamelis *Witch hazel*
DECIDUOUS SHRUBS
■ **Prune in spring, immediately after flowering**

Hamamelis mollis

Witch hazels produce attractive spidery yellow or orange-red flowers in the depths of winter, well before their foliage appears. The fall leaf color, usually in shades of bright red, can also be spectacular. There are several named varieties, and plants are often grafted onto rootstocks of *H. virginiana*.

Witch hazels are very slow-growing, so keep pruning to a minimum wherever possible. Immediately after flowering, remove any damaged or straggly branches, cutting back to strong, outward-facing buds. On grafted plants, remove any shoots that appear below the graft union. Witch hazels growing on their own roots sometimes sucker around the base. If necessary, these suckers can be removed to restrict the spread of the plant and ease congestion.

PLANT PROFILE

NATURAL HABIT Open, vase-shaped shrubs that sometimes sucker from the base.

HARDINESS Fully hardy.

HEIGHT AND SPREAD 6ft x 6ft (2m x 2m), but only when well established.

PRUNING NOTES
■ Keep pruning to a minimum.

■ Remove suckers on grafted plants.

■ For plants growing on their own roots, thin any suckers produced as required.

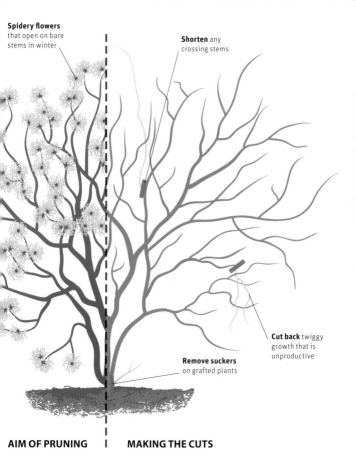

Spidery flowers that open on bare stems in winter

Shorten any crossing stems

Cut back twiggy growth that is unproductive

Remove suckers on grafted plants

AIM OF PRUNING | MAKING THE CUTS

Hebe
EVERGREEN SHRUBS
■ **Prune in spring**

Hebe 'Great Orme'

Hebes come in a variety of forms—some are large and even treelike, while others are compact with a neat shape. Small hebes, which are good rock garden or container plants, also make excellent low hedges, although their rather billowing shape means that they do not lend themselves to formal clipping. Large-leaf types are less hardy and wind-tolerant than the others and benefit from the shelter of a warm wall in cold areas. The white, pink, blue, or purple summer flowers are extremely attractive to bees.

For all hebes, remove any frosted stems in spring, cutting these right back to the base. Any dead material you notice on plants at other times can be dealt with in the same way. Trim over small, domelike hebes (such as *H. pinguifolia*) after flowering to maintain a good shape.

PLANT PROFILE

NATURAL HABIT These evergreen shrubs are naturally shapely.

HARDINESS Mainly hardy, although large-leaf types show sensitivity to cold weather.

HEIGHT AND SPREAD Plants can grow to 5ft x 4ft (1.5m x 1.2m); small-leaf types are naturally much more compact.

PRUNING NOTES
■ Prune to maintain and encourage their natural shape.

■ Clear the plant of all dead and frosted material.

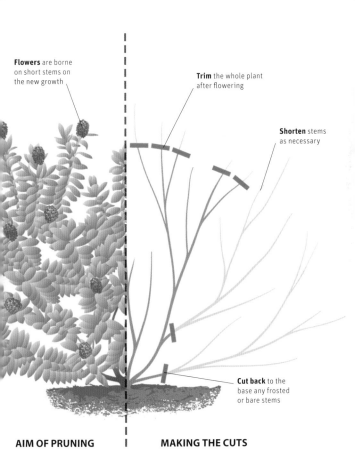

Flowers are borne on short stems on the new growth

Trim the whole plant after flowering

Shorten stems as necessary

Cut back to the base any frosted or bare stems

AIM OF PRUNING

MAKING THE CUTS

Hedera *Ivy*

EVERGREEN CLIMBERS, ALSO USED AS GROUNDCOVER

■ **Prune in early spring, and in summer as necessary**

Hedera helix
'Little Diamond'

Ivies are vigorous evergreen climbers that cling by means of aerial roots. They can also be used as groundcover and will tolerate dry soil in shade, making them useful for planting under evergreen trees and shrubs where little else will thrive. Small-leaf types are excellent trailing plants for a winter window box; train them over wire or up canes to produce a topiary effect. Unpruned ivies flower in fall, providing a late source of nectar for bees.

Pruning is a matter of keeping them within bounds. In early spring, shorten any stems that have outgrown their allotted space, cutting them back to allow for new growth. During the growing season, remove any plain-leaf stems on variegated forms. On wall-trained plants, shear over the growth in late spring or early summer to neaten if necessary.

PLANT PROFILE

NATURAL HABIT Vigorous climbers that will cling to their support.

HARDINESS Large-leaf forms sometimes curl at the edges as a response to frost but generally recover.

HEIGHT AND SPREAD Plants can grow to 20ft x 15ft (6m x 5m), depending on the type.

PRUNING NOTES

■ Established plants are very tolerant of clipping to neaten.

■ Remove any plain green shoots on variegated forms.

■ To renovate, cut all growth back to 12in (30cm) or more from the base.

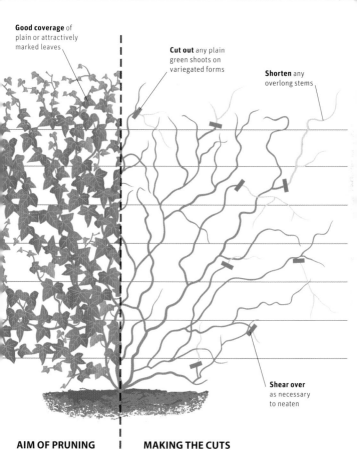

Good coverage of plain or attractively marked leaves

Cut out any plain green shoots on variegated forms

Shorten any overlong stems

Shear over as necessary to neaten

AIM OF PRUNING

MAKING THE CUTS

Helichrysum
EVERGREEN SHRUBS
■ **Prune in spring, then during the summer as required**

Helichrysum italicum

If silver foliage is desired, helichrysums are unrivaled. Often the daisylike yellow flowers are routinely removed, and the plants are used as a foil for brightly colored annuals and other summer-flowering plants in borders, containers, and hanging baskets.

One of the most common types, the curry plant (*H. italicum*), has strongly aromatic foliage. Naturally mound-forming, it can be used as an edging plant or as a low hedge. In early to mid-spring, trim back the previous year's growth. Old stems can be cut back hard, either to near the base or to strong buds low down. Trim over the plants during summer to neaten if required; this may reduce flowering. *H. petiolare* has long, trailing stems; it is not hardy but is often used as a foliage plant in summer containers. Simply nip off the stem tips on young plants to encourage branching.

PLANT PROFILE

NATURAL HABIT Usually mound-forming, very occasionally spreading shrubs.

HARDINESS Mainly hardy, provided they are grown in well-drained soil. *H. petiolare* will not tolerate frost.

HEIGHT AND SPREAD To 24in x 36in (60cm x 90cm). *H. petiolare* is trailing.

PRUNING NOTES
■ Prune in spring to refresh the plant.

■ Trim over in summer as required.

■ Complete renovation is unlikely to be successful; old plants are best replaced.

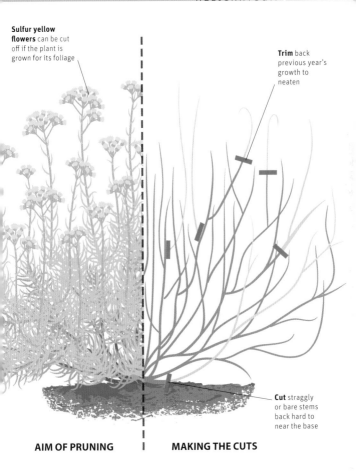

Sulfur yellow flowers can be cut off if the plant is grown for its foliage

Trim back previous year's growth to neaten

Cut straggly or bare stems back hard to near the base

AIM OF PRUNING

MAKING THE CUTS

Hibiscus
EVERGREEN AND DECIDUOUS SHRUBS
■ Prune in late spring, when danger of frost has passed

Hibiscus syriacus 'Blue Bird'

Shrubby hibiscus can be either deciduous or evergreen —the former is considerably hardier. They are grown for their attractive white, pink, red, blue, or yellow flowers and make a valuable addition to late summer plantings. In cold climates evergreen hibiscus make excellent container plants if given appropriate winter protection.

Prune both evergreen and deciduous types in late spring—for plants grown outdoors this reduces the risk of frost damage on new growth. On evergreens, cut out dead wood and shorten the main branches to keep the plants compact. Pruning of deciduous types should be more cautious: shorten shoots that show signs of dieback, and remove any crossing branches. Trim any weak or very thin shoots near the tips of branches.

PLANT PROFILE

NATURAL HABIT Generally neat-growing shrubs with an upright look.

HARDINESS Evergreens will not tolerate frost, but deciduous types will perform reliably in cold areas.

HEIGHT AND SPREAD 6ft x 6ft (2m x 2m). Container-grown plants will be less vigorous.

PRUNING NOTES
■ Prune to repair damage and to reduce congestion within the plant.

■ Evergreen plants can be pruned to restrict size, especially when grown in containers.

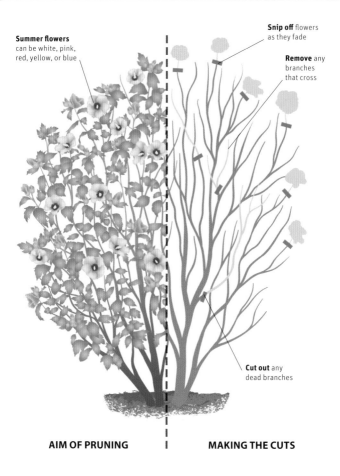

Summer flowers can be white, pink, red, yellow, or blue

Snip off flowers as they fade

Remove any branches that cross

Cut out any dead branches

AIM OF PRUNING

MAKING THE CUTS

Humulus *Hops*

HERBACEOUS CLIMBERS

■ **Prune in early spring, then in summer as required**

Humulus lupulus 'Aureus'

These vigorous climbers are actually herbaceous perennials, dying back completely in winter. While *H. lupulus* is an important economic crop grown for its hops—which are used to make beer—the plant most commonly seen in gardens is its gold-leaf type *H. l.* 'Aureus'. This attractive plant can be used to provide summer cover for walls, fences, arches, and outbuildings and can also be grown over trellis or trained along wires for screening—it produces the best color when grown in a location in full sun.

In early spring, cut all growth down to ground level. The shoots are easily broken, so train in the twining stems with care as they grow. Established plants produce quantities of growth annually: if a plant becomes too large or unruly, shear back any wayward shoots in summer.

PLANT PROFILE

NATURAL HABIT Very vigorous herbaceous climbers with twining stems.

HARDINESS Mainly fully hardy, although some types will not survive freezing temperatures.

HEIGHT AND SPREAD Plants can grow to around 20ft x 15ft (6m x 5m).

PRUNING NOTES

■ Prune back all the old growth to ground level annually in early spring.

■ Trim over to neaten in summer as needed.

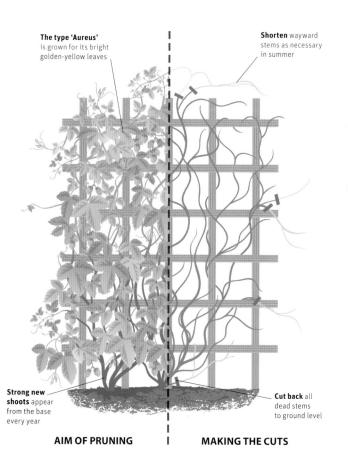

The type 'Aureus' is grown for its bright golden-yellow leaves

Shorten wayward stems as necessary in summer

Strong new shoots appear from the base every year

Cut back all dead stems to ground level

AIM OF PRUNING

MAKING THE CUTS

Hydrangea
SHRUBS WITH MOPHEAD AND LACECAP FLOWERHEADS
■ **Prune in mid-spring**

Hydrangea macrophylla 'Blue Bonnet'

With their late-season flowers hydrangeas are perfect shrubs for a mixed border and also thrive in containers. Mopheads produce domed heads of large flowers while the flowers of the lacecaps are more open, with large blooms surrounding a central cluster of much smaller ones. The flowers are produced in shades of white, pink, or blue, although blue varieties often revert to pink.

Not reliably hardy, hydrangeas need a spot sheltered from hot sun and strong winds in cold areas. As an extra precaution against frost, old flowers can be left on the plant over winter to protect the new growth buds lower down the stem. In mid-spring, once the risk of hard, overnight frosts has passed, shorten the stems by up to 12in (30cm), cutting just above strong buds. Cut older, unproductive stems back to the base, and remove any weak or crossing shoots.

PLANT PROFILE

NATURAL HABIT Domed to spreading deciduous shrubs.

HARDINESS Mainly hardy, but best given some protection in frost-prone areas.

HEIGHT AND SPREAD Plants grow to around 4ft x 5ft (1.2m x 1.5m).

PRUNING NOTES
■ Shorten flowered stems in mid-spring, or earlier in milder areas.

■ Cut back older wood entirely.

■ Renovation is usually successful, but plants will not flower well until the following year.

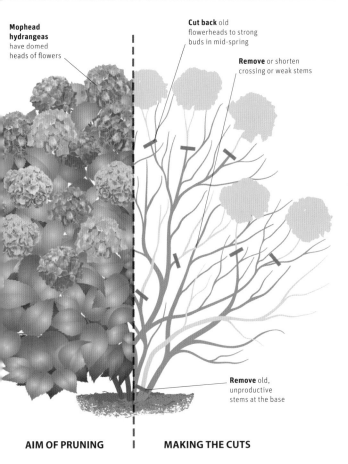

Mophead hydrangeas have domed heads of flowers

Cut back old flowerheads to strong buds in mid-spring

Remove or shorten crossing or weak stems

Remove old, unproductive stems at the base

AIM OF PRUNING

MAKING THE CUTS

Hydrangea paniculata

DECIDUOUS SHRUBS WITH PANICLES OF LATE-SUMMER FLOWERS
■ **Prune in late winter to early spring**

Hydrangea paniculata

The treatment of these late-flowering shrubs is quite different from that of other hydrangeas—and much simpler. Their large flower panicles, which vary in color from green to greenish white, are carried at the tips of the upright stems, and pruning is merely a matter of maximizing the production of these blooms. The flowers are long-lasting, usually becoming paler as they age and sometimes developing pink tints. They can also be dried for use indoors.

In late winter to early spring, simply cut down the previous year's stems to a low framework. Thicker stems, particularly if they are crowded, can be cut back to ground level. These plants are excellent in large containers but will need frequent watering. There are many named varieties.

PLANT PROFILE

NATURAL HABIT Upright shrub with large flower clusters at the ends of the stems.

HARDINESS Fully hardy.

HEIGHT AND SPREAD 4ft x 3ft (1.2m x 1m); if necessary restrict spread by reducing the number of stems and tying the remainder to short upright stakes.

PRUNING NOTES
■ For even larger—but fewer—flowers, reduce the number of stems in spring.

■ In cold areas, delay pruning until spring; the old stems will protect the new buds from hard frosts.

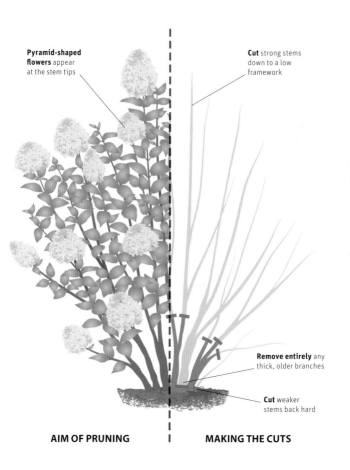

Pyramid-shaped flowers appear at the stem tips

Cut strong stems down to a low framework

Remove entirely any thick, older branches

Cut weaker stems back hard

AIM OF PRUNING

MAKING THE CUTS

Hydrangea
DECIDUOUS CLIMBERS
■ Prune in summer, immediately after flowering

Hydrangea petiolaris

Besides the many shrubby hydrangeas there are also a couple of climbing varieties, which are valued for their ability to cover a shady wall. They bear large heads of white or greenish white flowers in summer. Climbing hydrangeas cling by means of aerial roots, so no particular training is required beyond guiding their stems toward and onto the support in the early years after planting. They are too heavy for growing against fence panels but can be very effective if allowed to ascend into the crown of an established tree.

H. petiolaris is the most commonly grown. It is slow to establish so pruning should be kept to a minimum. Once it has reached the desired size, cut back overlong shoots and any sideshoots that are badly placed immediately after flowering. Deadhead to neaten. The evergreen *H. seemannii* can be treated in the same way.

PLANT PROFILE

NATURAL HABIT Vigorous but slow-growing climbers with aerial roots.

HARDINESS Mainly hardy, but evergreens are slightly more vulnerable to frost.

HEIGHT AND SPREAD 20ft x 10ft (6m x 3m) or potentially more.

PRUNING NOTES

■ Keep pruning to a minimum.

■ Shorten growth as necessary in summer.

■ Plants respond to renovative pruning, but this should be staggered over two to three years since recovery is usually slow.

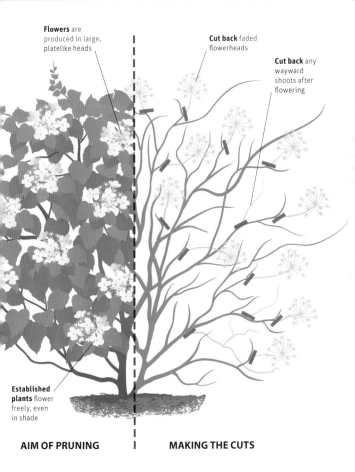

Flowers are produced in large, platelike heads

Cut back faded flowerheads

Cut back any wayward shoots after flowering

Established plants flower freely, even in shade

AIM OF PRUNING

MAKING THE CUTS

Hypericum *St. John's wort*
EVERGREEN AND DECIDUOUS SHRUBS
■ Prune in spring, as plants come into growth

Hypericum 'Hidcote'

Hypericums can be evergreen or deciduous and vary from upright and rounded shrubs to creeping groundcover plants. All have bright yellow flowers that are often borne over a long period from late spring into fall, sometimes followed by attractive berries.

Most respond well to pruning. Deciduous types can be cut back annually to a low framework in early spring. Evergreens have varying needs. Compact rock garden-types, such as *H. balearicum*, need minimal pruning. For larger types, remove some older stems entirely in spring, then shorten the remainder back to strong buds. *H. calycinum* is a rampant evergreen that spreads by runners. To control it, shear over the plant annually in spring. Restrict the spread by digging out new plants that form from runners at the periphery.

PLANT PROFILE

NATURAL HABIT Mainly rounded to spreading, sometimes mat-forming shrubs.

HARDINESS Mainly fully hardy, but some are vulnerable to freezing temperatures.

HEIGHT AND SPREAD 3ft x 4ft (1m x 1.2m), depending on the type. Groundcover plants can have an unlimited spread.

PRUNING NOTES
■ Prune according to the type grown.

■ Shear over groundcover types as needed.

■ Renovative pruning is usually successful.

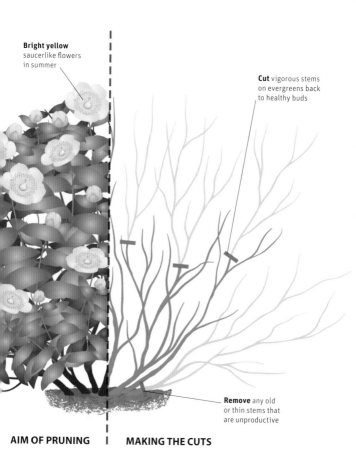

Bright yellow saucerlike flowers in summer

Cut vigorous stems on evergreens back to healthy buds

Remove any old or thin stems that are unproductive

AIM OF PRUNING   MAKING THE CUTS

Ilex *Holly*

EVERGREEN SHRUBS AND TREES

■ **Prune during spring and summer, as necessary**

Ilex aquifolium

Hollies are handsome evergreens. Large-leaf forms of *I.* x *altaclarensis* are relatively fast growing and often have a slightly more open habit than those of *I. aquifolium*, which are slow and dense. Several forms have bright red or, less commonly, yellow berries. These appear on female specimens if a compatible male is nearby; a few varieties are self-pollinating. Hollies make excellent hedges and can be clipped to shape, although this will be at the loss of any berries.

Most can be grown with minimal pruning. To shape, shear over plants in spring and in mid- to late summer as necessary. Cut out plain green shoots on variegated types on sight. *I. crenata* has small leaves and can be used as an alternative to boxwood (*Buxus*) where a low hedge is needed. Clip the plants over twice, or more if necessary, during the growing season.

PLANT PROFILE

NATURAL HABIT Often dense-growing, long-lived trees and shrubs.

HARDINESS Mainly fully hardy, but some types show some vulnerability to hard frost.

HEIGHT AND SPREAD Plants can grow to 25ft x 15ft (8m x 5m). Some are more compact and all can be kept smaller with pruning.

PRUNING NOTES
■ Clip to neaten in spring and summer.

■ For berry production, trim lightly, or selectively remove some of the older stems.

■ Cut a portion of stems back hard in spring to renovate, staggering the process over two or three years.

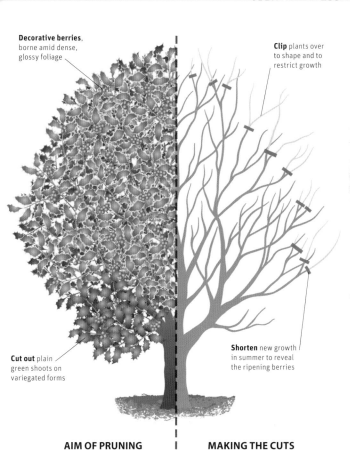

Decorative berries, borne amid dense, glossy foliage

Clip plants over to shape and to restrict growth

Cut out plain green shoots on variegated forms

Shorten new growth in summer to reveal the ripening berries

AIM OF PRUNING

MAKING THE CUTS

Indigofera *Indigo*
DECIDUOUS SHRUBS
■ **Prune in spring, as new growth begins**

Indigofera decora

Shooting freely from the base, these colorful shrubs are wreathed in pink or purple flowers in summer, with some varieties also flowering into early fall. In frost-prone areas pruning is a matter of annual renovation. In early spring, cut back all the previous year's stems to near ground level. In warmer areas pruning can be less drastic and will produce a larger, more arching plant; shorten the previous year's stems by no more than half.

Indigoferas can also be trained against a warm, sunny wall. Create a framework of branches, and tie them in as they grow. In early spring, shorten flowered sideshoots, and remove any that are awkwardly placed. Cut out older shoots near the base to encourage new growth, then tie in the new stems as they grow to form replacements.

PLANT PROFILE

NATURAL HABIT Usually arching shrubs that shoot freely from the base.

HARDINESS Mainly fully hardy. Some are best given wall protection in very cold areas.

HEIGHT AND SPREAD 4ft x 4ft (1.2m x 1.2m). Some varieties are larger; wall-trained plants will be taller.

PRUNING NOTES

■ In cold areas, cut all stems back to near the base annually, unless plants are wall trained.

■ In warmer areas, shorten the previous year's growth as required.

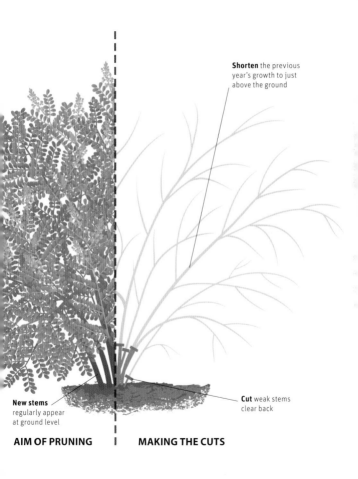

Shorten the previous year's growth to just above the ground

New stems regularly appear at ground level

Cut weak stems clear back

AIM OF PRUNING

MAKING THE CUTS

Jasminum *Jasmine*
EVERGREEN AND DECIDUOUS SHRUBS
■ **Prune in early spring, after flowering**

Jasminum nudiflorum

While most of the jasmines are climbers, a few are shrubby and require different pruning and training techniques. The plants are not natural climbers, and the flexible stems have no means of attaching themselves to a support. Grown against a wall or fence, the stems can be loosely tied in to create a basic framework. Each spring, tie in new shoots to fill in any gaps. Cut out older stems, especially if they are leafless toward the base. Shorten sideshoots, if necessary, and remove awkwardly placed growth.

J. nudiflorum is particularly valued for its bright yellow winter flowers that open when most other plants are fully dormant. It is ideal positioned on a bank so that the flowering stems can cascade down, or it can be wall trained.

PLANT PROFILE

NATURAL HABIT Lax, arching shrubs that can be loosely wall trained.

HARDINESS Fully hardy.

HEIGHT AND SPREAD 7ft x 7ft (2.1m x 2.1m), or more, against a wall. Grown as a shrub, height may not exceed 4ft (1.2m).

PRUNING NOTES
■ Maximize the plant's flowering potential and reduce congestion by cutting back older stems, especially if they are bare and very woody at the base.

■ For climbing jasmines see pp.240–241.

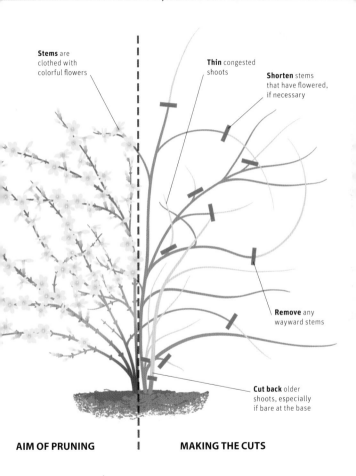

Stems are clothed with colorful flowers

Thin congested shoots

Shorten stems that have flowered, if necessary

Remove any wayward stems

Cut back older shoots, especially if bare at the base

AIM OF PRUNING

MAKING THE CUTS

Jasminum *Jasmine*
EVERGREEN AND DECIDUOUS CLIMBERS
■ **Prune in fall, after flowering**

Jasminum · officinale 'Argenteo-variegatum'

All climbing jasmines are plants of great vigor and are excellent for training against house walls; in cold areas they will flower most freely against a warm wall. Variegated forms are less rampant. Most produce deliciously scented flowers that bloom in summer and into early fall.

Plants flower on a combination of old and new stems. Establish a main framework in the first years after planting by guiding or tying in vigorous twining stems as they grow. After flowering, shorten flowered shoots, and cut back others to relieve congestion. On a large established plant against a wall, it may be simpler to trim all of it, then cut out congested stems. Cut back older, unproductive stems to near the base, if necessary. The following year, train in vigorous new stems as replacements.

PLANT PROFILE

NATURAL HABIT Very vigorous climbers, capable of scaling high walls.

HARDINESS Hardy if given the shelter of a warm wall in cold areas.

HEIGHT AND SPREAD Plants grow to around 20ft x 12ft (6m x 4m).

PRUNING NOTES
■ Prune to prevent the accumulation of excessive leafy growth.

■ Prune to keep the plant within bounds.

■ For shrubby jasmines see pp.238–239.

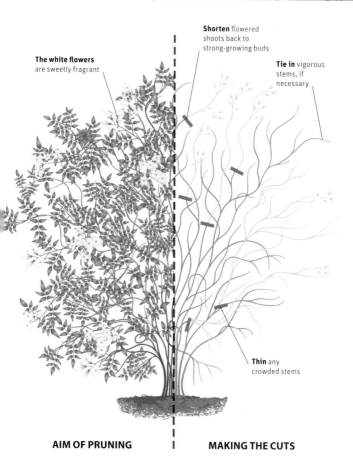

Shorten flowered shoots back to strong-growing buds

Tie in vigorous stems, if necessary

The white flowers are sweetly fragrant

Thin any crowded stems

AIM OF PRUNING

MAKING THE CUTS

Juniperus *Juniper*
EVERGREEN CONIFERS
■ **Prune in spring, and at other times as necessary**

Juniperus communis 'Hibernica'

Junipers vary greatly in size and shape—some are narrowly upright, while others are more bushy and spreading. There are many dwarf varieties that become neat mounds, while prostrate types are suitable for use as groundcover. *J. rigida* and varieties of *J.* x *pfitzeriana* have weeping branches.

Pruning is seldom strictly necessary but may be done to maintain the form. Simply cut out any growth that spoils the outline in spring. Cut back stems that shoot out sideways on upright types, and remove strongly upright stems on prostrate varieties. To accentuate the pencil-like outline of upright types of *J. scopulorum* such as 'Blue Arrow', thin the growth, then wire in the remaining stems close to the central leader. Older branches that bend outward, possibly due to heavy snowfall, should also be wired in.

PLANT PROFILE

NATURAL HABIT Depending on the type, junipers are mound-forming to spreading, weeping, strongly upright, or prostrate.

HARDINESS Mainly fully hardy, although young plants are vulnerable to hard frost and cold, drying winds.

HEIGHT AND SPREAD Depending on the variety, heights vary from 12in (30cm) to 30ft (10m); spreads from 3ft (1m) to 20ft (6m).

PRUNING NOTES
■ Prune in spring, or at other times as necessary to maintain the shape.

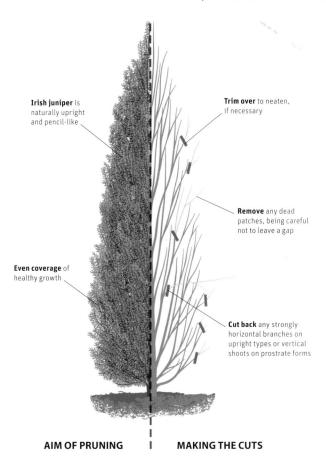

Irish juniper is naturally upright and pencil-like

Trim over to neaten, if necessary

Remove any dead patches, being careful not to leave a gap

Even coverage of healthy growth

Cut back any strongly horizontal branches on upright types or vertical shoots on prostrate forms

AIM OF PRUNING   **MAKING THE CUTS**

Kalmia *Calico bush*
EVERGREEN SHRUBS
■ **Prune in spring, and deadhead after flowering**

Kalmia latifolia

Related to rhododendrons and also requiring an acidic soil, kalmias produce domed heads of pink, white, or purple flowers in late spring or summer. Calico bushes are naturally shapely plants, so pruning can be kept to a minimum. Any wayward shoots that spoil the outline and that are not flower-bearing may be shortened in spring. If it is practical to do so, deadhead after flowering, cutting behind each cluster. This will help the plant to maintain a dense form.

Plants that have outgrown their allotted space can be reduced in size through hard pruning. The process should be spread over three years to prevent damage to the plant. In the spring of the first year, cut back one-third of the stems to near ground level. Tackle the remaining stems over the following two years.

PLANT PROFILE

NATURAL HABIT Mound-forming evergreens, spreading on maturity, that are usually well-covered with foliage.

HARDINESS Mainly hardy but best when given some shelter from cold, drying winds.

HEIGHT AND SPREAD 6ft x 8ft (2m x 2.5m) or sometimes more.

PRUNING NOTES
■ Keep pruning to a minimum.

■ Deadhead after flowering.

■ Plants respond well to renovation, but it is best to spread this process over a number of years.

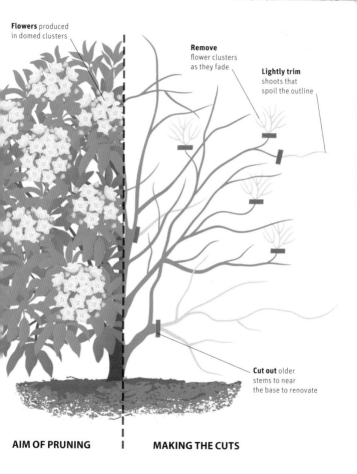

Flowers produced in domed clusters

Remove flower clusters as they fade

Lightly trim shoots that spoil the outline

Cut out older stems to near the base to renovate

AIM OF PRUNING

MAKING THE CUTS

Kerria
DECIDUOUS SHRUBS
■ **Prune in mid- to late spring, after flowering**

Kerria japonica 'Pleniflora'

The suckering or thicket-forming *K. japonica* is the only species in this group and is almost always seen in its double type, 'Pleniflora'; its wandlike stems are topped with attractive fluffy yellow flowers in mid- to late spring. It produces new shoots each year that will flower the year after.

After flowering, shorten all stems that have flowered to strong shoots lower down the stem or near the base. Cutting to different heights will produce a more upright, less thicketlike plant. If necessary, cut back older stems at ground level to reduce congestion. To restrict the unwanted spread of the plant, dig out any new suckers that appear around the base. The variegated type 'Picta' is less vigorous and therefore requires less drastic pruning.

PLANT PROFILE

NATURAL HABIT Suckering deciduous shrubs with whippy stems.

HARDINESS Fully hardy.

HEIGHT AND SPREAD Plants can grow to around 4ft x 5ft (1.2m x 1.5m).

PRUNING NOTES
■ Shorten all stems after flowering.

■ Remove suckers to restrict spread.

■ Hard pruning to renovate plants is generally successful.

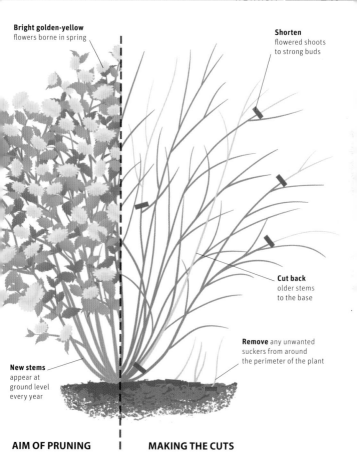

Bright golden-yellow flowers borne in spring

Shorten flowered shoots to strong buds

Cut back older stems to the base

Remove any unwanted suckers from around the perimeter of the plant

New stems appear at ground level every year

AIM OF PRUNING

MAKING THE CUTS

Kolkwitzia *Beautybush*
DECIDUOUS SHRUBS

■ **Prune in summer, immediately after flowering**

Kolkwitzia amabilis

Kolkwitzia amabilis, the only species in this group, is a deciduous, arching shrub that carries its delicate bell-shaped pink flowers between late spring and early summer on growth produced the previous year. Prune immediately after flowering to allow the shrub the maximum amount of time to build new stems for flowering in the following year.

Established plants produce suckers at the base, so pruning is a matter of removing older, unproductive stems to allow new ones to take over. Thin the plant, removing one-quarter to one-third of the old stems, cutting them right to the base or to suitably placed strong shoots low down. Be careful not to remove too many stems that have yet to flower. Pruning to restrict the size of plants is not recommended.

PLANT PROFILE

NATURAL HABIT An arching to rounded shrub that suckers freely from the base.

HARDINESS Fully hardy.

HEIGHT AND SPREAD Plants grow to around 10ft x 8ft (3m x 2.5m) and occasionally more.

PRUNING NOTES
■ Annually thin older stems from established plants.

■ Remove unwanted suckers from around the base of the plant.

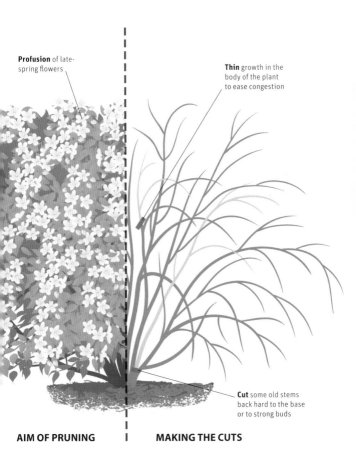

Profusion of late-spring flowers

Thin growth in the body of the plant to ease congestion

Cut some old stems back hard to the base or to strong buds

AIM OF PRUNING

MAKING THE CUTS

Laburnum

DECIDUOUS TREES

■ **Prune in late summer to midwinter**

Laburnum x watereri 'Vossii'

A mature laburnum in full flower is quite a sight, when the long chains of golden-yellow flowers hang from the branches in late spring to early summer. As specimen trees, laburnums can be grown with minimal pruning. Any work necessary to improve the shape of the canopy should be done between late summer and midwinter to avoid causing the tree to bleed sap.

Laburnums are suitable for training over an arch, provided the main stems are tied in when they are young and flexible. Between late summer and midwinter, remove badly placed branches, and tie in new strong stems. Shorten sideshoots growing from the main framework branches to two or three buds to encourage the production of flowering spurs. All parts of the plant are poisonous, so wear gloves when pruning.

PLANT PROFILE

NATURAL HABIT Usually upright deciduous trees with an open, airy crown.

HARDINESS Fully hardy.

HEIGHT AND SPREAD 20ft x 15ft (6m x 5m); less if trained over an arch.

PRUNING NOTES
■ Ideally, keep pruning to a minimum.

■ Any pruning necessary should be done between late summer and midwinter.

Remove any dead and damaged stems

Bright yellow flowers hang in generous clusters

Cut back flowered stems, if necessary

AIM OF PRUNING

MAKING THE CUTS

Lagerstroemia
DECIDUOUS TREES
■ **Prune in early spring, before new growth begins**

Lagerstroemia indica 'Seminale'

Usually multi-stemmed, but sometimes grown on a single trunk, lagerstroemias make handsome specimens in frost-free gardens, producing generous plumes of red, white, pink, or purple flowers in mid- to late summer; mature plants develop attractive peeling bark. Deciduous types are hardier than the evergreens and can be grown in a sheltered spot in colder areas, ideally against a warm wall, although neither are suitable for wall training.

After planting, select three, five, or seven strong shoots, and cut the rest to the ground. In spring, remove lower side branches to clear the lower portion of the trunks. Remove crossing growth and any shoots that are thin or overlong. On established plants, annual pruning can improve flowering. Hard pruning can restrict growth but may be at the expense of the bark.

PLANT PROFILE

NATURAL HABIT Usually vase-shaped to spreading, multi-stemmed trees and shrubs.

HARDINESS None will survive prolonged periods of hard frost, but deciduous types will cope in cold areas if given shelter.

HEIGHT AND SPREAD 25ft x 25ft (8m x 8m), or smaller with pruning.

PRUNING NOTES
■ Thin stems within the canopy to let in light.

■ Clear the trunks to expose the bark.

■ Hard pruning to renovate is usually successful; plants grown under cover can be pruned hard to restrict their size.

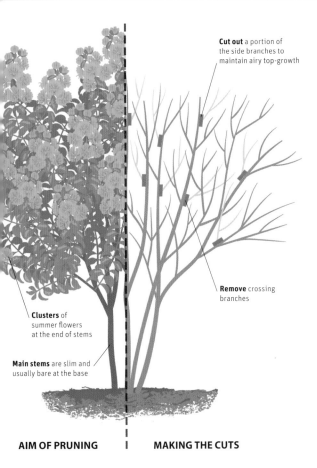

Cut out a portion of the side branches to maintain airy top-growth

Remove crossing branches

Clusters of summer flowers at the end of stems

Main stems are slim and usually bare at the base

AIM OF PRUNING | **MAKING THE CUTS**

Larix *Larch*
DECIDUOUS CONIFERS
■ **Prune in midsummer, and at other times as required**

Larix decidua

Unusual among conifers, larches are deciduous, and the needles turn bright red or yellow before dropping in fall. With minimal pruning most become upright trees with conical crowns, although dwarf, spreading, and weeping types are relatively compact. All will grow successfully in a range of situations.

Prune to maintain the shape of named varieties, such as the weeping *L. decidua* 'Pendula', removing any stems that spoil the outline. Larches can create a very effective windbreak hedge when planted in combination with evergreen conifers such as cypresses. Planted alternately, the bare branches of the larches filter strong fall winds while the cypresses provide shelter. Shear them at least twice between spring and summer.

PLANT PROFILE

NATURAL HABIT Mainly strongly upright-growing conifers with conical crowns. Some are fairly spreading.

HARDINESS Fully hardy and wind tolerant.

HEIGHT AND SPREAD Plants can grow to 70ft x 20ft (20m x 6m). Dwarf forms are often within 3ft (1m).

PRUNING NOTES
■ Prune in midsummer, if necessary, to maintain the form of named varieties.

■ Shear hedges at least twice a year during the growing season.

■ Consider hiring an arborist if necessary.

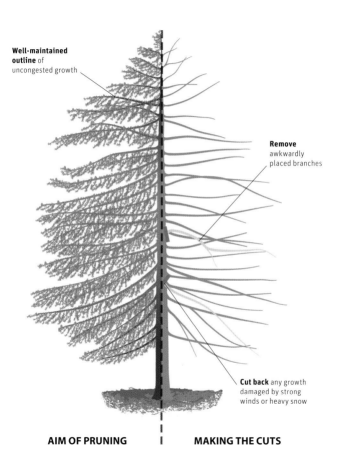

Well-maintained outline of uncongested growth

Remove awkwardly placed branches

Cut back any growth damaged by strong winds or heavy snow

AIM OF PRUNING

MAKING THE CUTS

Laurus *Bay tree*
EVERGREEN SHRUBS AND TREES
■ **Prune in spring and summer, as necessary**

Laurus nobilis

Bay (*L. nobilis*, the only species commonly grown) is a handsome evergreen whose leaves are often used in cooking. It is a much more versatile plant than other herbs, and if given the chance will form a large shrub or tree.

Bay trees can be clipped to shape, although very elaborate topiary is not possible. If you are clipping the plants with shears, choose a day within a settled period of dry, sunny weather so that the cut edges of the leaves will heal rapidly to reduce the risk of rotting. In cold areas, avoid pruning too drastically after midsummer—any new growth will be vulnerable to cold. Mature trees are hardy; young specimens will need some protection to get them through freezing temperatures.

PLANT PROFILE

NATURAL HABIT Bay naturally becomes a tree or large shrub, well-covered with foliage.

HARDINESS Plants are generally hardy, once established, though top-growth can suffer during a hard frost.

HEIGHT AND SPREAD 20ft x 10ft (6m x 3m), if unpruned; much less with regular pruning. Trees in warm climates may well exceed these dimensions.

PRUNING NOTES
■ Prune to shape and keep within bounds.

■ Topiary shapes can be trimmed as necessary during the growing season to keep them in shape.

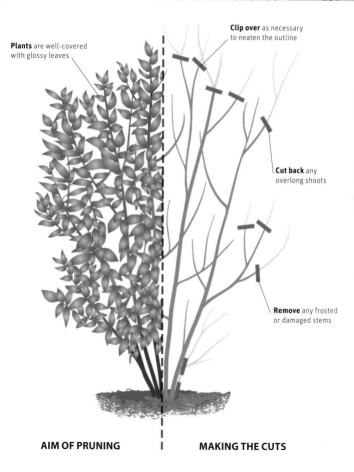

Plants are well-covered with glossy leaves

Clip over as necessary to neaten the outline

Cut back any overlong shoots

Remove any frosted or damaged stems

AIM OF PRUNING

MAKING THE CUTS

Lavandula *Lavender*

EVERGREEN SHRUBS

■ Prune in early spring

Lavandula angustifolia

Lavenders are a common sight in English-style garden designs and are often used as low, evergreen hedging. While they can be regularly clipped to shape during spring and summer for a formal look, this is at the expense of the fragrant flowers—usually lilac or blue, although sometimes white—that appear from late spring to late summer, depending on the type. They are rich in nectar and highly attractive to bees.

Lavender plants can become straggly with age, so to keep them fresh, bushy, and well-covered with their characteristic gray-green foliage, cut back the previous year's growth each spring. Hedging plants can be cut back harder, if necessary, to shoots low down on the stems. Older plants that have become very woody are best replaced, since old wood seldom produces new growth.

PLANT PROFILE

NATURAL HABIT Low-growing shrubs with a tendency to spread.

HARDINESS Mainly hardy, although some species will not withstand frost.

HEIGHT AND SPREAD Plants can grow to 18in x 18in (45cm x 45cm), more or less, depending on the species.

PRUNING NOTES
■ Prune to maintain bushiness and to prevent the accumulation of dead stems.

■ Remove most of the year's growth.

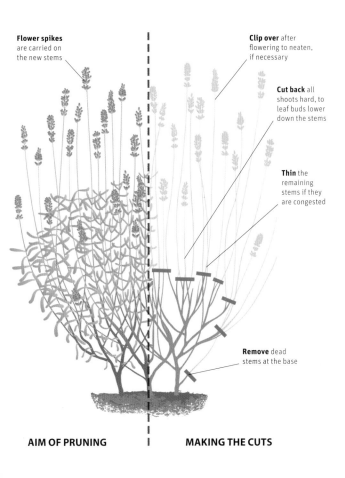

Flower spikes are carried on the new stems

Clip over after flowering to neaten, if necessary

Cut back all shoots hard, to leaf buds lower down the stems

Thin the remaining stems if they are congested

Remove dead stems at the base

AIM OF PRUNING

MAKING THE CUTS

Lavatera *Mallow*
DECIDUOUS SHRUBS
■ **Prune in spring**

Lavatera x clementii 'Barnsley'

Excellent at the back of a border, these shrubs bear clusters of pink or, less commonly, white flowers over a long period during summer—sometimes slightly beyond. The stems are long and flexible and have a tendency to arch over. For this reason lavateras are best planted in a sheltered location, because strong winds are likely to damage the stems if plants are too exposed—particularly older, thicker stems that will have become brittle.

Prune in early spring to maximize the number of new stems that will flower the same year. Cut back strong stems to within 12in (30cm) of the ground, and cut weaker stems back to the base; remove older stems completely. Recovery is brisk. Watch out for any broken stems in summer, and cut these back to a strong bud lower down.

PLANT PROFILE

NATURAL HABIT Vigorous, arching shrubs.

HARDINESS Mainly hardy but best in a sheltered location.

HEIGHT AND SPREAD Plants can reach around 6ft x 4ft (2m x 1.2m).

PRUNING NOTES
■ Prune to keep the plant fresh by allowing young growth to replace older material, which is very susceptible to breaking.

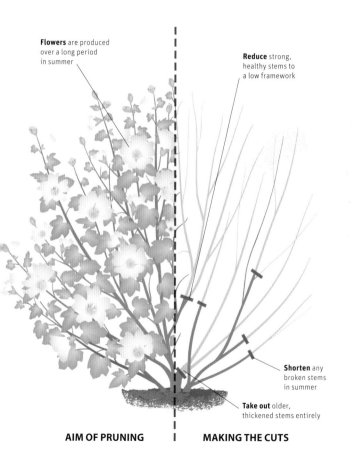

Flowers are produced over a long period in summer

Reduce strong, healthy stems to a low framework

Shorten any broken stems in summer

Take out older, thickened stems entirely

AIM OF PRUNING

MAKING THE CUTS

Leycesteria *Himalayan honeysuckle*
DECIDUOUS SHRUBS
■ Prune in spring, before growth becomes advanced

Leycesteria formosa

The Himalayan honeysuckle is a deciduous shrub with a naturally arching shape. The flowers are of interest over a long period, from summer to fall, because they have colored bracts that persist while the fleshy berries ripen inside. Effective as specimens or in a shrub border, these plants also make fine additions to a woodland planting.

Pruning is a matter of thinning the existing growth to make way for vigorous new stems—congested plants look messy, and their stems will become bare toward the base. Each spring use loppers to cut thickened, older branches back to ground level. Also cut out any weak, thin shoots. Leave healthy, vigorous, young shoots unpruned. Plants should not need any further pruning until the following spring.

PLANT PROFILE

NATURAL HABIT Arching shrubs with a tendency to sucker and spread.

HARDINESS Mainly fully hardy.

HEIGHT AND SPREAD 6ft x 6ft (2m x 2m) or more, with a potentially wider spread.

PRUNING NOTES
■ Thin the stems annually to contain the plant's spread and to maintain vigor.

■ Cut back one-third of the older stems to near ground level each spring.

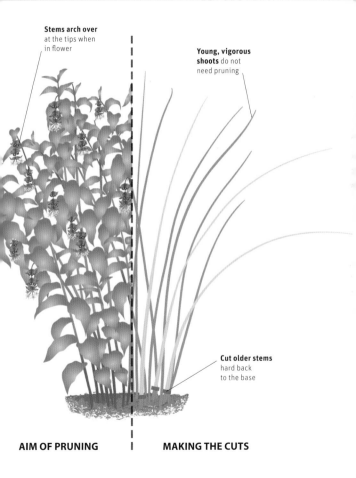

Stems arch over at the tips when in flower

Young, vigorous shoots do not need pruning

Cut older stems hard back to the base

AIM OF PRUNING

MAKING THE CUTS

Ligustrum *Privet*
EVERGREEN SHRUBS AND SMALL TREES
■ Prune in spring and possibly also in summer

Ligustrum lucidum

Widely used as hedging, evergreen privet can also be used in mixed plantings or even as specimens—plants develop a graceful shape with minimal pruning. The vase-shaped plants branch freely at the base, and the creamy white flowers, shaped like miniature lilac blooms, are followed by small, shiny black berries. Some forms have yellow or variegated leaves.

Any pruning should be done in early spring or immediately after flowering. Thin any congested shoots, cutting stems that are bare at the base back hard. Shorten other shoots to neaten the outline. Clip hedges twice a year, in mid-spring and late summer. Hard pruning can renovate them, but may not be successful on variegated forms, which can revert to plain green. Clipping to shape in spring may be at the cost of the flowers.

PLANT PROFILE

NATURAL HABIT Upright to spreading, usually open, vase-shaped shrubs and trees.

HARDINESS Mainly hardy.

HEIGHT AND SPREAD 12ft x 10ft (4m x 3m); often much less with regular pruning.

PRUNING NOTES
■ Privets are very tolerant of pruning, either for shaping or to keep them within bounds.

■ Neglected specimens can become bare at the base over time.

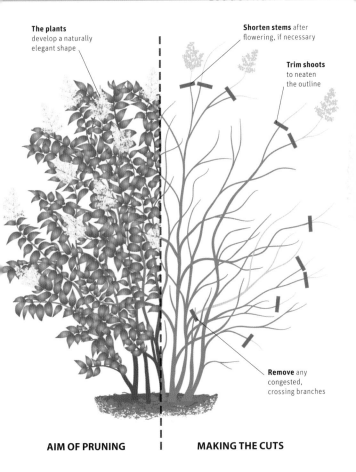

The plants develop a naturally elegant shape

Shorten stems after flowering, if necessary

Trim shoots to neaten the outline

Remove any congested, crossing branches

AIM OF PRUNING

MAKING THE CUTS

Liquidambar *Sweetgum*
DECIDUOUS TREES
■ **Prune in fall to late winter**

Liquidambar styraciflua

Liquidambars are virtually unrivaled for their spectacular fall leaves in shades of bright red, yellow, orange, and occasionally a deeper burgundy red. Though tolerant of lime, they produce their best color on neutral to acidic soils. *L. styraciflua* is the most popular and has a number of named types, some of which are commonly grown as standards. Habits vary: 'Pendula' is a weeping form, but other types are more strongly upright.

Most liquidambars naturally form a strong central leader and can be allowed to develop with minimal help. Remove any competing upright branches that spoil the shape as soon as possible. Otherwise pruning can be kept to a minimum. Prune out any crossing and unwanted branches between fall and winter when plants are dormant. On standards, thin congested stems, and shorten others to suitably placed buds to keep the head balanced.

PLANT PROFILE

NATURAL HABIT Usually upright, open deciduous trees.

HARDINESS Mainly hardy. Young plants can suffer dieback after very severe late-spring frost but usually recover well.

HEIGHT AND SPREAD 25ft x 12ft (8m x 4m) or more. Standards are smaller.

PRUNING NOTES
■ Keep pruning to a minimum.

■ Obviously dead branches can be removed in summer.

■ Prune standards to maintain a well-balanced head.

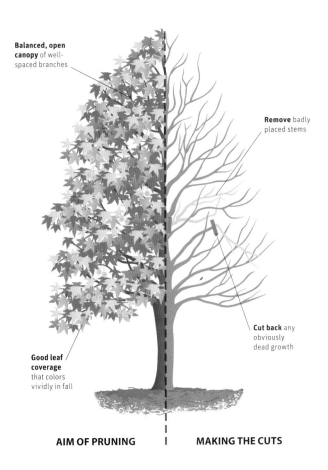

Balanced, open canopy of well-spaced branches

Remove badly placed stems

Cut back any obviously dead growth

Good leaf coverage that colors vividly in fall

AIM OF PRUNING

MAKING THE CUTS

Lonicera *Honeysuckle*
DECIDUOUS OR EVERGREEN SHRUBS
■ Prune in spring and summer, or after flowering

Lonicera fragrantissima

Shrubby honeysuckles include both deciduous shrubs—valued for their scented winter flowers—and evergreens, which are usually used as hedging.

The deciduous types are twiggy shrubs that flower in winter or early summer. Prune them after flowering. Cut back older, unproductive stems to the base, especially if the growth is congested. If necessary, take other stems back to suitably placed strong buds.

Evergreens are naturally dense growing. Clip them over twice a year, in spring and midsummer. Plants such as *L. nitida* 'Baggesen's Gold' are also effective when grown with minimal pruning, producing arching golden-green stems that stand out in the winter garden. Neglected plants respond well to renovation between late winter and early spring.

PLANT PROFILE

NATURAL HABIT Often untidy, sometimes twiggy evergreen and deciduous shrubs.

HARDINESS Mainly fully hardy.

HEIGHT AND SPREAD Plants usually grow to around 6ft x 6ft (2m x 2m), but they can be kept within bounds through pruning.

PRUNING NOTES
■ Prune back deciduous types after flowering as necessary.

■ Prune evergreens in spring and summer.

■ Shrubby types respond well to renovation.

■ For climbing honeysuckles, see pp.270–271.

Shorten flowered stems to keep the plant reasonably compact

Plentiful flowers on deciduous types

Cut out any congested or awkwardly placed stems

Remove old stems at the base

AIM OF PRUNING

MAKING THE CUTS

Lonicera *Honeysuckle*
EVERGREEN AND DECIDUOUS CLIMBERS
■ **Prune in spring (evergreen) or summer (deciduous)**

Lonicera periclymenum 'Serotina'

Climbing honeysuckles are popular English-style garden plants. Beautifully scented and easy to grow, they are natural woodlanders so will tolerate a shady location. All are rampant, and they can easily get out of hand—the twisting stems have a tendency to coil around each other, which can lead to congestion and poor flowering. Train vigorous stems horizontally while they are growing, and cut out weak shoots entirely.

Once established, prune evergreens in spring, cutting out older stems to the base; it can be easiest to cut them in sections. Shorten other growth as necessary, cutting just above strong buds. On deciduous types, shorten stems that have flowered in summer. Thinning of the main shoots is most easily done in late winter, when they are bare. Remove older, thicker stems, retaining healthy younger ones.

PLANT PROFILE

NATURAL HABIT Very vigorous climbers with twining stems.

HARDINESS Mainly hardy.

HEIGHT AND SPREAD 10ft x 10ft (3m x 3m). If they are left unpruned, plants can extend much further.

PRUNING NOTES
■ Aim to reduce the number of stems that wrap around each other—these cause congestion and reduce flowering.

■ For shrubby honeysuckles see pp.268–269.

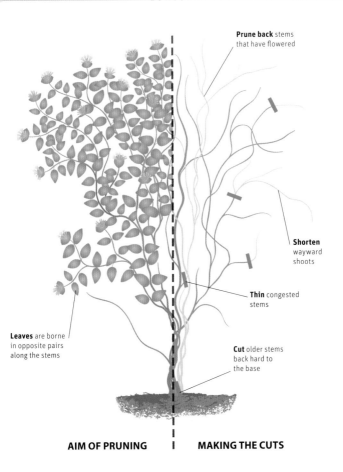

Prune back stems that have flowered

Shorten wayward shoots

Thin congested stems

Leaves are borne in opposite pairs along the stems

Cut older stems back hard to the base

AIM OF PRUNING

MAKING THE CUTS

Magnolia *Magnolia*
DECIDUOUS TREES AND SHRUBS
■ Prune in midsummer during warm, dry weather

Magnolia x soulangeana

As young plants magnolias are definitely shrubs, but many mature as shapely specimens, just as a tree would. Most have creamy white, pink, or occasionally purple chalicelike flowers early in the growing season. These are susceptible to frost damage in very cold areas.

Deciduous magnolias are slow growing, and pruning should be kept to a minimum so as not to interfere with the natural graceful shape. Indiscriminate pruning can result in the production of strongly upright stems that spoil the outline. If absolutely necessary, prune during a dry period in midsummer since wounds will heal more rapidly. Rather than cutting all the growth to shape, shorten only the longest shoots back to within the canopy—but avoid cutting into older wood. The following spring, remove any new shoots that show a tendency to grow strongly upward.

PLANT PROFILE

NATURAL HABIT Rounded to spreading trees and shrubs with an elegant outline.

HARDINESS Mainly fully hardy. Early flowers are susceptible to frost damage, so choose a sheltered spot in very cold areas.

HEIGHT AND SPREAD Around 20ft x 20ft (6m x 6m) although some are much smaller.

PRUNING NOTES
■ If it cannot be avoided, prune in summer when wounds will heal most quickly.

■ Remove any strongly upward-growing shoots that appear after pruning.

■ For evergreen magnolias see pp. 274–275.

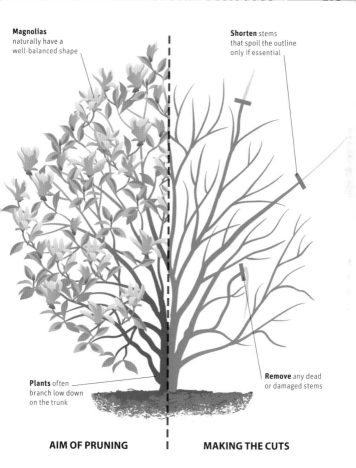

Magnolias naturally have a well-balanced shape

Shorten stems that spoil the outline only if essential

Plants often branch low down on the trunk

Remove any dead or damaged stems

AIM OF PRUNING

MAKING THE CUTS

Magnolia *Magnolia*
EVERGREEN TREES
■ **Prune in summer, as required, and also in winter**

Magnolia grandiflora 'Ferruginea'

Evergreen magnolias are quite distinct from deciduous types because they grow faster and flower later in the year. The flowers never appear in profusion but are carried intermittently over a long period from midsummer into fall. Late-swelling buds often succumb to frost and fail to open; remove them promptly, or they will rot on the plant. Cut back any other frosted growth during winter. Evergreen magnolias are also much more tolerant of pruning than deciduous types and are eminently suitable for wall training. New stems will shoot upward with great vigor, so pull them horizontal before the growth thickens and hardens. In summer, shorten any wayward branches, especially if they are shading flower buds. Pruning is best done with long-handled loppers or—for thicker branches—a saw.

PLANT PROFILE

NATURAL HABIT Vigorous trees whose downy young stems rapidly lose flexibility.

HARDINESS Mainly hardy, but best with shelter in very cold areas.

HEIGHT AND SPREAD 20ft x 10ft (6m x 3m) where grown as a tree (more, in warm climates), less if wall trained.

PRUNING NOTES

■ Trees can be allowed to develop with minimal pruning.

■ As wall shrubs, prune to keep growth close to the wall, cutting out older and badly placed stems.

■ For deciduous magnolias see pp.272–273.

Flowers are scattered over the plant

Shorten frosted or damaged growth

Remove frost-damaged flower buds

Prune out wayward shoots

AIM OF PRUNING

MAKING THE CUTS

Mahonia *Oregon grape*
SPRING-FLOWERING SHRUBS
■ **Prune in late spring to early summer, after flowering**

Mahonia aquifolium 'Smaragd'

These evergreen shrubs produce clusters of bright yellow flowers in spring. Most have a good shape and are well-covered with foliage—the leaves can turn an attractive red color in winter in response to the low temperatures. Creeping forms make good groundcover.

Prune these plants immediately after they flower in spring. Some varieties produce suckers that emerge freely from the base—remove these from around the edge of the plant to restrict its spread. Any older, unproductive stems within the body of the plant can also be removed. Flowered stems may also be shortened, but this will be at the loss of the fall fruits.

Shear over any plants that are grown as groundcover, cutting close to the base either every year or in alternate years.

PLANT PROFILE

NATURAL HABIT Suckering, mound-forming to spreading shrubs, some suitable for use as groundcover.

HARDINESS Mainly fully hardy.

HEIGHT AND SPREAD 3ft x 5ft (1m x 1.5m). Groundcover types are lower growing.

PRUNING NOTES
■ Prune annually to encourage plenty of fresh growth for flowering the following year.

■ For winter-flowering types see pp.278–279.

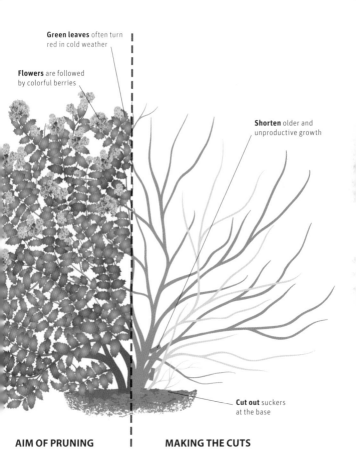

Green leaves often turn red in cold weather

Flowers are followed by colorful berries

Shorten older and unproductive growth

Cut out suckers at the base

AIM OF PRUNING

MAKING THE CUTS

Mahonia *Oregon grape*
WINTER-FLOWERING EVERGREEN SHRUBS
■ Prune in late winter, immediately after flowering

Mahonia x media

Winter-flowering mahonias provide a dazzling display in the depths of winter, when long panicles of soft yellow, sweetly fragrant flowers open at the tops of the stiffly upright branches. Two winter-flowering species, *M. japonica* and *M. lomariifolia*, crossed to produce *M. x media*—a valuable group of the most common cultivars that share the same pruning needs. These architectural evergreen shrubs are often grown for their attractive foliage, but over time older stems may become bare at the base. While this may not be a problem if the plants are at the back of a border and skirted by lower-growing plants, they can easily appear gaunt if they have a more prominent location. This is easily rectified by cutting the stems back hard to near ground level, immediately after flowering in late winter to early spring.

PLANT PROFILE

NATURAL HABIT Stiffly upright shrubs with a tendency to lose their leaves at the base of the stems.

HARDINESS Fully hardy.

HEIGHT AND SPREAD Plants can reach around 10ft x 4ft (3m x 1.2m).

PRUNING NOTES
■ Prune to encourage the production of new stems from the base that will be well-covered with foliage from ground level.

■ For spring-flowering mahonias see pp.276–277.

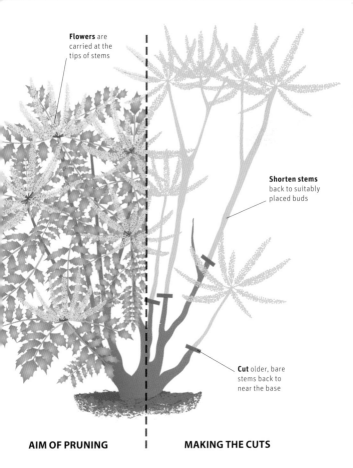

Flowers are carried at the tips of stems

Shorten stems back to suitably placed buds

Cut older, bare stems back to near the base

AIM OF PRUNING

MAKING THE CUTS

Malus *Crabapple*
DECIDUOUS TREES
■ **Prune in late winter to early spring**

Malus 'John Downie'

As well as the hundreds of varieties grown for their edible fruit (see pp.438–439), this group of plants includes several trees of purely ornamental value. They bear a profusion of pink or white spring blossoms followed by small orange, yellow, or red crabapples in fall. The leaves often turn yellow, red, or orange before they are shed. Most form rounded to spreading, open crowns, although *M. tschonoskii* is strongly upright. They make excellent specimen trees in small gardens.

Pruning can be kept to a minimum. If the lower branches are not shed naturally, clear them from the trunks gradually—however they are best retained on *M. floribunda*, which is often shrubby. Remove any dead or damaged growth in late winter or early spring, but be careful not to cut back any branches too hard within the canopy since this can result in strongly upright shoots.

PLANT PROFILE

NATURAL HABIT Deciduous trees with open, rounded or spreading, occasionally upright crowns.

HARDINESS Fully hardy.

HEIGHT AND SPREAD Plants grow to 15ft x 10ft (5m x 3m), or more with age.

PRUNING NOTES
■ Keep pruning to a minimum.

■ Remove any dead or broken branches in late winter to early spring.

Pretty spring flowers followed by ornamental fall fruit

Cut back any badly placed, damaged, or diseased growth

Remove low side branches to create a clear trunk

AIM OF PRUNING

MAKING THE CUTS

Melianthus
TENDER EVERGREEN SHRUBS
■ **Prune in early to mid-spring**

Melianthus major

This small genus of evergreen shrubs is most commonly represented in gardens by *M. major*, also known as the honey bush, which is grown largely for the exotic appearance of its large, soft gray-green leaves. Although they are evergreen, these plants are not fully hardy and need the protection of a warm wall; even with shelter they usually succumb to winter cold, dying back to ground level like herbaceous perennials. Protect the underground parts of the plant with a dry mulch over the winter.

In spring, cut back any stems that remain above soil level. The new stems can be loosely attached to the wall as they grow. In warmer areas brownish flowers appear from late spring to midsummer; shoots that have flowered should be removed in fall, leaving the new shoots to flower the following year.

PLANT PROFILE

NATURAL HABIT Sprawling, large-leaf shrubs, best grown with some support.

HARDINESS Hardy only in very mild areas, but able to regenerate after frost.

HEIGHT AND SPREAD 6ft x 4ft (2m x 1.2m); it can have a greater height and spread in areas where it overwinters successfully.

PRUNING NOTES

■ In cold areas, the plant shoots from below ground level annually—pruning is a matter of clearing away all dead material in early spring.

■ Cut back to two or three buds from the base.

Large leaves are divided into toothed leaflets

Remove any dead material

Cut back stems to near the base in spring

AIM OF PRUNING

MAKING THE CUTS

Monstera
EVERGREEN CLIMBERS
■ **Prune any time when the plant is in growth**

Monstera deliciosa

Monsteras are rampant evergreen climbers from the tropics. The most commonly grown, the Swiss cheese plant (*M. deliciosa*) should be grown indoors in cold areas since it requires a minimum temperature of 59°F (15°C). Even though a container will restrict size, plants can easily get out of hand. Main stems should be attached to sturdy supports driven into the compost to keep them upright. Variegated forms are less vigorous.

In spring, cut out shoots bearing old, damaged, or misshapen leaves. Cut back taller stems to reduce the plant's reach. Where space permits, strong stems can be trained horizontally against a wall or even overhead. Long aerial roots are produced on the stems. If these reach down to touch the compost, tuck in the tips, and they will develop as feeder roots, creating a sturdier plant.

PLANT PROFILE

NATURAL HABIT Vigorous climbers.

HARDINESS Plants will not tolerate frost and must be grown under cover in cold areas.

HEIGHT AND SPREAD 12ft x 4ft (4m x 1.2m). Plants are capable of growing bigger but can also be kept smaller with pruning.

PRUNING NOTES
■ Prune to keep plants within bounds and to reduce the number of older stems.

■ Shorten stems to encourage a bushy look.

Shorten stems to reduce size and encourage branching

Leaves are large and leathery and develop splits at the edges

Aerial roots appear on the stems

MAKING THE CUTS

Morus *Mulberry*

DECIDUOUS TREES

■ Prune in late fall to early winter

Morus alba 'Pendula'

Most mulberries are large stately trees that make excellent specimens. When mature they often have a gnarled appearance and heavy, spreading branches that may need support. Keep pruning to a minimum: any necessary work should be done in late fall to early winter to prevent the trees from bleeding sap.

The weeping *M. alba* 'Pendula' is smaller than most and ideal for a small garden. To produce a central trunk with a cascading crown, select a strong shoot, and tie this to an upright cane of the desired height. When the stem reaches the top of the cane, allow it to arch over. Sideshoots will form the canopy. Once the main stem is firm, remove the cane and any sideshoots below the crown. To extend the canopy, shorten stems to outward-facing buds. Cut back any stems that trail on the ground and any upright shoots that spoil the shape.

PLANT PROFILE

NATURAL HABIT Usually large, spreading trees with heavy branches. Weeping forms are naturally mound-forming.

HARDINESS Mainly fully hardy.

HEIGHT AND SPREAD 20ft x 15ft (6m x 5m) or more. Weeping forms can be trained to heights of 6–15ft (2–5m).

PRUNING NOTES
■ Prune only at the start of the dormant period, after the leaves have fallen.

■ Keep pruning of large trees to a minimum, and consider using an arborist if necessary.

■ Prune weeping specimens to maintain a good overall shape.

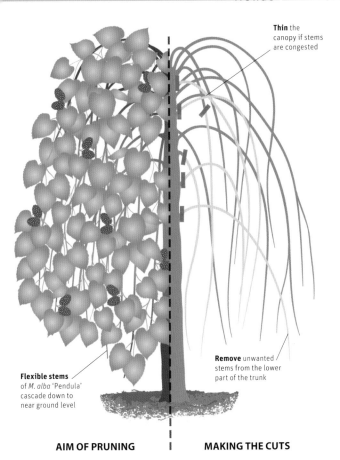

Thin the canopy if stems are congested

Flexible stems of *M. alba* 'Pendula' cascade down to near ground level

Remove unwanted stems from the lower part of the trunk

AIM OF PRUNING

MAKING THE CUTS

Myrtus *Myrtle*
EVERGREEN SHRUBS
■ **Prune in spring and summer**

Myrtus communis

Myrtles are grown for the attractive, scented white flowers that are produced between summer and fall, depending on the type. Not reliably hardy, they benefit from the shelter of a warm wall in frost-prone areas.

Prune with caution since flowers are borne on both old and new stems. In spring, when all danger of frost has passed, lightly trim to improve the shape of the plant, removing any frosted and very thin stems, because these are unlikely to bear flowers. Deadhead after the first crop of flowers to make way for new flower-bearing shoots, but avoid doing anything too drastic in late summer. Clip over wayward growth only lightly. Plants can be trained informally against a wall. Cut out awkwardly placed growth in spring, then later in the year, shorten stems that have flowered. Spring-flowering types need minimal pruning, which is best done after flowering.

PLANT PROFILE

NATURAL HABIT Dainty evergreen shrubs, usually well-covered with glossy foliage.

HARDINESS Plants generally show some vulnerability to frost and need the shelter of a warm wall in cold areas.

HEIGHT AND SPREAD 6ft x 6ft (2m x 2m), although some forms are more compact.

PRUNING NOTES
■ Cut back frost-damaged growth in spring.

■ Prune after flowering with care—the new growth may be vulnerable to winter cold.

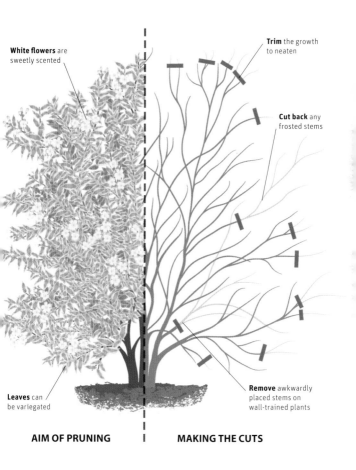

White flowers are sweetly scented

Leaves can be variegated

AIM OF PRUNING

Trim the growth to neaten

Cut back any frosted stems

Remove awkwardly placed stems on wall-trained plants

MAKING THE CUTS

Nandina *Heavenly bamboo*

EVERGREEN SHRUBS

■ **Prune in summer, immediately after flowering**

Nandina domestica

N. domestica, the only species in this group, is an elegant evergreen or semievergreen shrub that could easily be mistaken for a bamboo—until its clusters of white flowers appear in summer. In a warm situation red berries will follow. The new leaves can be bright red in spring and may redden again in fall and winter as a response to a drop in temperature.

Pruning should be kept to a minimum. If necessary, cut out dead wood and any weak shoots immediately after flowering. Trim any other shoots that spoil the overall shape of the plant, although this may be at the loss of some fall berries. To renovate neglected specimens, cut all the stems back to ground level in spring. Plants will probably not flower again until the following year.

PLANT PROFILE

NATURAL HABIT An arching shrub that freely produces new stems from ground level.

HARDINESS Hardy if grown in a sheltered spot in very cold areas.

HEIGHT AND SPREAD 6ft x 5ft (2m x 1.5m). Some varieties are more compact.

PRUNING NOTES
■ Cut out dead stems after flowering.

■ If necessary, renovate neglected specimens in spring, cutting them back to ground level.

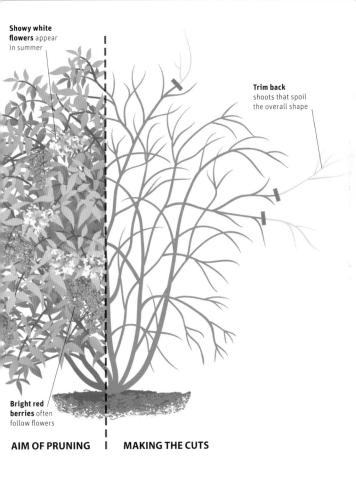

Showy white flowers appear in summer

Trim back shoots that spoil the overall shape

Bright red berries often follow flowers

AIM OF PRUNING | MAKING THE CUTS

Nerium *Oleander*

EVERGREEN TREES AND SHRUBS

■ **Prune in spring or any time when in full growth**

Nerium oleander

Commonly grown as trees in warm climates, oleanders also make excellent flowering container plants in colder areas—if given appropriate winter protection. *N. oleander* is the most widely grown, and varieties are available that bear white, pink, purple, orange, or red flowers throughout the warmer months. Some types have variegated leaves.

Plants are strongly upright. When grown as trees, they generally develop a pleasing vase shape or a rounded crown. Pruning should be kept to a minimum. As container plants they are usually kept shrubby. Tip-prune young plants to encourage them to become bushy. Shorten flowered shoots by up to one-half, and prune to neaten the shape. All parts of the plant are poisonous, so wear gloves when handling.

PLANT PROFILE

NATURAL HABIT These evergreen trees and shrubs have a strong upright look.

HARDINESS Plants will not tolerate frost.

HEIGHT AND SPREAD 20ft x 10ft (6m x 3m), when grown as a tree. Pot plants can be kept much smaller with pruning.

PRUNING NOTES
■ Prune to keep plants within bounds and to neaten the overall shape.

Cut back flowered shoots by up to one-half to restrict the size

Brightly colored flowers appear at the ends of stems

Shorten shoots to encourage bushiness

AIM OF PRUNING

MAKING THE CUTS

Nothofagus *Southern beech*

DECIDUOUS AND EVERGREEN TREES

■ **Prune in fall to mid-spring, or late spring**

Nothofagus pumilio

Whether they are grown as multi-stemmed plants or with a single trunk, these fast-growing trees make elegant specimens when mature. The bare stems of the deciduous *N. antarctica*, which grow in a herringbone formation, are particularly attractive in winter.

Their fast growth makes young beech trees vulnerable to wind damage. To grow the trees with a central leader, remove any competing upright branches as seen, otherwise they can weaken the main stem. The evergreen *N. dombeyi* tends to produce two leaders, and the weaker one should be cut back. *N. antarctica* and *N. pumilio* often develop as multi-stemmed trees, which can be more stable. Established trees need minimal pruning. Prune evergreens in late spring, after the first flush of new growth. Prune deciduous types when they are dormant between fall and mid-spring.

PLANT PROFILE

NATURAL HABIT Mainly strongly upright, fast-growing trees, sometimes developing a more spreading crown when mature.

HARDINESS Mainly hardy, although evergreens are less tolerant of freezing temperatures than deciduous types. Shelter from strong winds is desirable.

HEIGHT AND SPREAD 50ft x 30ft (15m x 10m) or more, depending on the type.

PRUNING NOTES
■ If grown with a single stem, remove any competing or strongly upright branches.

■ Remove any damaged stems, if necessary.

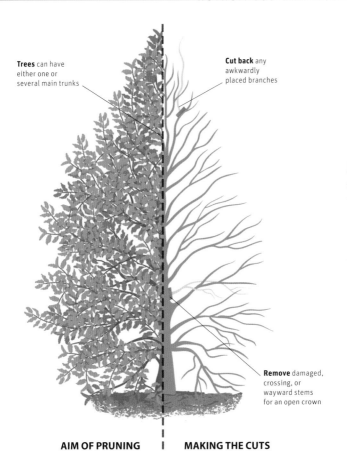

Trees can have either one or several main trunks

Cut back any awkwardly placed branches

Remove damaged, crossing, or wayward stems for an open crown

AIM OF PRUNING | **MAKING THE CUTS**

Nyssa *Tupelo*
DECIDUOUS TREES
■ Prune in fall to winter

Nyssa sylvatica

A mature nyssa is quite a sight in fall, when the leaves turn vivid shades of red, orange, or yellow before falling from the branches. In time they can form pyramids, with the branches radiating out from the central trunk in tiers. However in cold areas the main stem is often damaged, and plants develop as multi-stemmed trees. They need acid to neutral soil and are best grown away from competing trees and shrubs.

Pruning should be minimal, and any work necessary is best done between fall and winter, when plants are dormant. To develop an upright habit, stake the main stem, and remove any competing leaders. If the tip is damaged, develop the plant as a multi-stemmed tree on a short trunk no higher than 3ft (1m). On established trees, remove any strongly upright shoots on side branches that spoil the shape, and thin any congested stems.

PLANT PROFILE

NATURAL HABIT Strongly upright or multi-stemmed trees with pyramidal or rounded crowns.

HARDINESS Fully hardy, but best in areas with long, hot summers.

HEIGHT AND SPREAD Plants grow to around 30ft x 25ft (10m x 8m).

PRUNING NOTES
■ Prune when dormant.

■ Remove any strongly upright stems that spoil the outline.

■ Thin congested stems within the canopy of mature specimens.

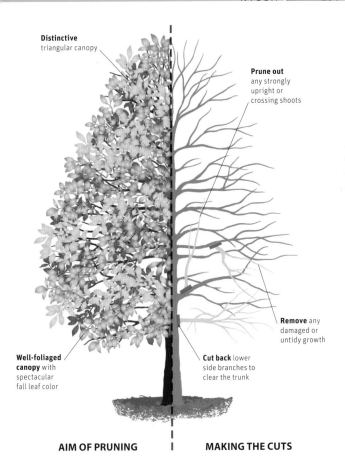

Distinctive triangular canopy

Prune out any strongly upright or crossing shoots

Well-foliaged canopy with spectacular fall leaf color

Cut back lower side branches to clear the trunk

Remove any damaged or untidy growth

AIM OF PRUNING

MAKING THE CUTS

Olearia *Daisy bush*
EVERGREEN SHRUBS
■ **Prune in spring or summer**

Olearia macrodonta

Olearias have many assets: daisylike flowers that smother the plants in spring or summer, as well as evergreen leaves that make them a splendid foil to other plants during the rest of the year. In cold areas most need a sheltered spot, but in a favorable situation some can be used for hedging. They are also tolerant of salt spray in coastal gardens.

Since they are mainly compact-growing, pruning is seldom strictly necessary. Prune spring-flowering types immediately after flowering; prune summer-flowering types in early spring, just as they are coming into growth. Remove any frosted, dead, or damaged growth. Cut back stems that spoil the outline to well within the body of the plant to strong outward-facing buds. Growth can be cut back hard to renovate if necessary. Clip hedges in summer to neaten.

PLANT PROFILE

NATURAL HABIT Mainly compact, often dome-shaped evergreen shrubs.

HARDINESS Mainly fully hardy, although some can suffer frost damage in cold areas.

HEIGHT AND SPREAD 6ft x 6ft (2m x 2m).

PRUNING NOTES
■ Prune early-flowering varieties immediately after flowering; prune late-flowering varieties in early spring.

■ Renovate plants in spring, and trim those grown as hedges in summer.

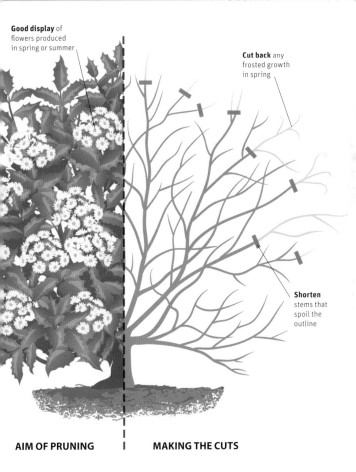

Good display of flowers produced in spring or summer

Cut back any frosted growth in spring

Shorten stems that spoil the outline

AIM OF PRUNING

MAKING THE CUTS

Osmanthus
EVERGREEN SHRUBS
■ **Prune immediately after flowering, or in spring**

Osmanthus delavayi

These handsome evergreens have sweetly fragrant, usually white flowers that are produced at various times of the year, depending on the type grown. Some varieties also have attractive leathery foliage, which can be thorny like holly leaves. Several osmanthus are suitable for hedging.

Prune early-flowering types once they have flowered, and late-flowering types in spring. Shorten the growth to improve the shape, cutting back any overlong stems to their point of origin within the body of the plant. Routinely remove any plain green shoots on variegated types. Clip over hedges once or twice in summer—this may reduce flowering potential. A later cut in cold areas is not recommended: any new growth that this stimulates will be vulnerable to frost.

PLANT PROFILE

NATURAL HABIT Slow-growing, upright to dome-shaped or spreading evergreen shrubs.

HARDINESS Mainly hardy, although some are vulnerable to frost in cold areas and should be grown in a sheltered spot.

HEIGHT AND SPREAD 10ft x 10ft (3m x 3m), or less with regular pruning.

PRUNING NOTES
■ Plants respond well to regular pruning.

■ Pruning to renovate in early spring is usually successful. Cut back into bare stems as necessary.

White flowers wreathe the branches in spring or summer

Clip over to neaten in summer, if necessary

Shorten overlong stems to within the body of the plant

Cut back older growth to near the base to renovate

AIM OF PRUNING **MAKING THE CUTS**

Paeonia *Peony*

DECIDUOUS SHRUBS

■ **Prune mainly in late winter, before new growth begins**

Paeonia
suffruticosa
'Reine Elizabeth'

Tree peonies are beautiful late-spring specimens for a sheltered part of the garden. *P. delavayi* and *P. lutea* are best treated as foliage plants since the flowers, red and yellow respectively, are small and fleeting. Types of *P. suffruticosa* bear sumptuous white, pink, red, yellow, or orange flowers, which can weigh down the stems.

When established, restrict pruning to cutting back dead shoot tips to strong buds in late winter. Cut out older stems after flowering if necessary. Plants can be encouraged to branch by pruning harder, to 6in (15cm) or less above ground level, even into apparently lifeless wood. New shoots can appear from below the soil. Many hybrids may produce suckers; cut these off at ground level.

PLANT PROFILE

NATURAL HABIT Long-lived, open, vase-shaped to spreading shrubs, usually of naturally elegant habit.

HARDINESS Fully hardy, but new growth is susceptible to frost damage in cold areas.

HEIGHT AND SPREAD To 6ft x 5ft (2m x 1.5m), depending on the form.

PRUNING NOTES

■ Prune *P. suffruticosa* when young to establish a good shape.

■ Cut out any frosted growth.

■ Hard pruning to renovate may not be successful. Cut out only very old, unproductive stems.

Heavy late-spring flowers may cause the stems to splay outward

Remove faded flowers to prevent the plant from producing seed

Cut back any shoots that have died over winter

Shorten stems to promote branching near the base if necessary

AIM OF PRUNING

MAKING THE CUTS

Parthenocissus *Virginia creeper*
DECIDUOUS CLIMBERS
■ **Prune in winter, when the stems are bare**

Parthenocissus henryana

These deciduous climbers cling to their support by means of suckering pads and are grown mainly for the rich color of their fall leaves. While they are usually used to cover walls, especially of garages and outbuildings, they can also look spectacular if allowed to scramble through a mature deciduous tree.

On planting, spread out the stems, and guide them toward the support. Once they have attached themselves no further training is required. Pruning is easiest when the branches are bare in winter. Shear over the plant to neaten it, repeating in summer if required. Cut back old plants that are bare at the base to 3ft (1m) above ground level. Pruning plants grown through trees is not usually practical.

PLANT PROFILE

NATURAL HABIT Vigorous deciduous climbers with suckering pads.

HARDINESS Fully hardy.

HEIGHT AND SPREAD Plants grow to around 30ft x 30ft (10m x 10m).

PRUNING NOTES
■ No regular pruning is required, but plants can be sheared over in winter.

■ Shorten any stray shoots in summer.

■ Plants respond well to renovative pruning.

Good coverage of foliage that colors well in fall

Shear over when dormant to neaten

Shorten any wayward or overlong shoots in summer

Remove older, unproductive stems, cutting to near ground level

AIM OF PRUNING

MAKING THE CUTS

Passiflora *Passion flower*
EVERGREEN CLIMBERS
■ **Prune in spring, when growth is strong**

Passiflora caerulea 'Constance Elliot'

The passion flowers—some of which bear edible fruit—are vigorous, mainly evergreen climbers with beautiful, showy flowers that appear over a long period in summer, and corkscrewlike tendrils. Adapted to cling onto the twiggy shoots of a host plant in the wild, they will grasp thin support wires or can be tied into a trellis.

Develop a framework of branches in the first couple of years after planting. If necessary, cut back stems on young plants to encourage new ones near the base. As the plant develops, thin and shorten vigorous growth to keep it within bounds. Once established, shorten sideshoots in spring, and reduce any wayward, over-vigorous shoots. Stems that have flowered can be shortened later on in summer. On established plants, avoid pruning stems too hard, because this can result in excessive leafy growth that will not flower.

PLANT PROFILE

NATURAL HABIT Very vigorous climbers.

HARDINESS Most will not tolerate frost but a few are hardy enough to grow outdoors in protected spots in cold areas.

HEIGHT AND SPREAD 10ft x 10ft (3m x 3m), or more in favorable climates.

PRUNING NOTES

■ Shorten sideshoots in spring, back to an established framework.

■ Very overgrown, neglected plants are best replaced since they do not respond well to hard pruning.

Flowers can be sparse but are borne over a long period

Lightly prune the growth in spring, if necessary

Cut back any tangled stems, especially if bare and woody

AIM OF PRUNING

MAKING THE CUTS

Paulownia *Foxglove tree*
DECIDUOUS TREES
■ **Prune in spring or early summer**

Paulownia tomentosa

Paulownias are shapely trees that have large, heart-shaped leaves and tall spires of purple foxglovelike flowers in late spring. The flower buds form in fall and overwinter on the plant. In very cold areas they are often damaged by winter air and frost.

While paulownias can form large trees in areas with long, hot summers, in cool climates they tend to be more shrubby. Here, particularly where flower buds are likely to perish, they can be treated as pollards or coppiced. Cut back all the previous year's stems in early spring. This results in quantities of whippy stems bearing leaves that are significantly larger than normal, but at the expense of any flowers. Coppiced paulownias are effective foliage plants in mixed borders. In warmer climates, freestanding specimens can be grown with minimal pruning in spring or early summer.

PLANT PROFILE

NATURAL HABIT Upright trees with shapely canopies, even when young.

HARDINESS Fully hardy, but flower buds are vulnerable to frost damage in cold areas.

HEIGHT AND SPREAD 25ft x 15ft (8m x 5m), although trees may not reach full height in cold areas.

PRUNING NOTES
■ Keep pruning to a minimum.

■ Remove any frosted growth.

■ Coppice or pollard in spring.

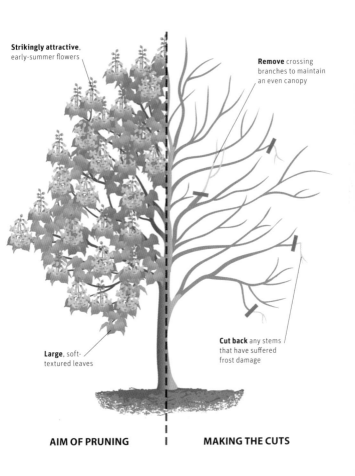

Strikingly attractive, early-summer flowers

Remove crossing branches to maintain an even canopy

Large, soft-textured leaves

Cut back any stems that have suffered frost damage

AIM OF PRUNING

MAKING THE CUTS

Perovskia *Russian sage*
DECIDUOUS SHRUBS
■ **Prune in early spring, as new growth begins**

Perovskia atriplicifolia

These low-growing shrubby plants produce quantities of gray-green leaves and blue-purple flowers from late summer to fall. The wandlike stems have white blooms. To get the full benefit of the camphor-scented foliage, place the plants near the edge of a border where you can brush past them—the aromatic oils are released on contact.

For the best stems and leaves, cut back all the previous year's growth to a low framework in late winter to early spring. The first spring after planting, cut back all the stems to 2–4in (5–10cm) from the ground. Annually thereafter, cut back the previous year's growth to strong pairs of buds near the base; cutting further up the stem will create a taller plant. In later years, as the base of the plant becomes progressively woody, cut back unproductive parts flush with the ground.

PLANT PROFILE

NATURAL HABIT Upright, sometimes scrubby subshrubs.

HARDINESS Fully hardy.

HEIGHT AND SPREAD Plants can reach 3–4ft (1–1.2m) high, and 4ft (1.2m) wide.

PRUNING NOTES
■ Cut back all the growth annually.

■ Prune some stems less drastically to produce a taller plant.

■ To renovate, cut back into the woody framework. Response is generally good.

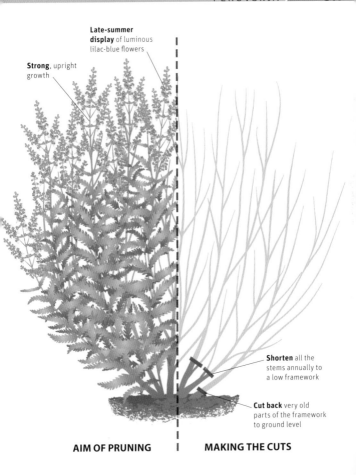

Late-summer display of luminous lilac-blue flowers

Strong, upright growth

Shorten all the stems annually to a low framework

Cut back very old parts of the framework to ground level

AIM OF PRUNING

MAKING THE CUTS

Philadelphus *Mock orange*
DECIDUOUS SHRUBS
■ **Prune in early summer, immediately after flowering**

Philadelphus
'Virginal'

The heady scent of the mock orange is a herald of summer, usually coinciding with or just preceding the first of the roses. It is the last of the hardy shrubs to flower on material produced the year before, so any pruning should be done as soon as possible after the display has finished to give the plant time to build up new growth for flowering the next year.

Prune young plants to encourage bushiness. When established, cut back stems that have flowered to strong buds. Shorten very vigorous shoots only lightly, but prune weaker ones harder. Cut older stems that are bare at the base down to near ground level. *P. coronarius* 'Aureus' is sometimes grown solely for its yellow leaves, which mature to green in summer. For a fresh crop of yellow leaves, clip over the plant in mid-spring—but this will prevent it from flowering.

PLANT PROFILE

NATURAL HABIT Mainly upright, vase-shaped or sometimes rounded shrubs.

HARDINESS Mainly fully hardy, although some types are damaged by hard frost.

HEIGHT AND SPREAD 10ft x 7ft (3m x 2.2m), or less with regular pruning. Some types are naturally more compact.

PRUNING NOTES
■ Shorten growth that has flowered.

■ Remove any crossing, dead, damaged, or diseased growth after flowering.

■ Renovative pruning in late winter to early spring is generally successful.

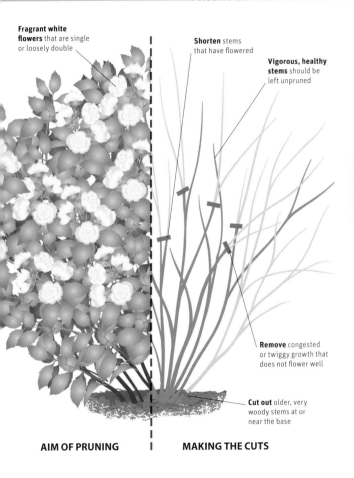

Fragrant white flowers that are single or loosely double

Shorten stems that have flowered

Vigorous, healthy stems should be left unpruned

Remove congested or twiggy growth that does not flower well

Cut out older, very woody stems at or near the base

AIM OF PRUNING

MAKING THE CUTS

Phlomis
EVERGREEN SHRUBS
■ **Prune in spring and summer, as necessary**

Phlomis fruticosa

These generally neat-growing evergreen shrubs bear gray-green leaves and whorls of flowers up the stems in summer. No routine pruning is necessary, although neglected plants can become bare at the base. To keep them well-covered in foliage, cut out weak, broken, or very old thickened shoots in spring, cutting each just above a growing point. If necessary, plants can be trimmed to shape in summer, although this may be at the loss of some late flowers. Reduce old, neglected specimens to a low framework of branches to renovate them completely. However recovery cannot be guaranteed—it may be simpler to replace the plant. Plants may not be completely hardy in all areas: the Jerusalem sage (*P. fruticosa*) with sulfur yellow flowers is one of the most reliable. *P. italica*, with lilac flowers, is daintier but needs a sheltered spot in very cold areas.

PLANT PROFILE

NATURAL HABIT Generally neat-growing shrubs, although the stems of older specimens can become bare at the base.

HARDINESS Mainly fully hardy, although some benefit from shelter in cold areas.

HEIGHT AND SPREAD To 3ft x 3ft (1m x 1m), sometimes with a broader spread.

PRUNING NOTES
■ Cut back older stems in spring to encourage new growth.

■ Shorten stems in summer to improve the overall shape, if necessary.

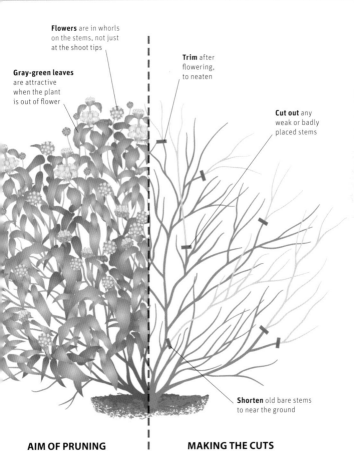

Flowers are in whorls on the stems, not just at the shoot tips

Gray-green leaves are attractive when the plant is out of flower

Trim after flowering, to neaten

Cut out any weak or badly placed stems

Shorten old bare stems to near the ground

AIM OF PRUNING

MAKING THE CUTS

Photinia

DECIDUOUS AND EVERGREEN SHRUBS

■ **Prune in winter (deciduous) or spring (evergreen)**

Photinia x fraseri 'Red Robin'

Photinias are renowned for the striking color of their leaves. Evergreen types often have bright red foliage, while deciduous specimens color up well in fall. Clusters of white flowers—borne in either spring or summer—are sometimes followed by reddish berries. Evergreen types can be used for hedging—*P.* 'Pink Marble' makes an attractive choice because its leaves are splashed with white and pink.

Pruning can be kept to a minimum. For evergreens, remove damaged shoots and any wayward or crossing stems in spring. To enhance the effect of the young leaves, shorten all the stems by up to 6in (15cm), cutting above an outward-facing bud. Shear over hedges in mid-spring and summer. Prune deciduous types in winter, cutting back overcrowded stems to strong shoots lower down. Plants can be pruned hard to renovate.

PLANT PROFILE

NATURAL HABIT Upright to rounded deciduous and evergreen shrubs.

HARDINESS Mainly fully hardy. Evergreens may be susceptible to frost damage in very cold or exposed situations.

HEIGHT AND SPREAD 10ft x 6ft (3m x 2m), or more without pruning.

PRUNING NOTES

■ For the best leaf effect on evergreens, shorten stems in spring.

■ Prune deciduous types in winter.

■ Both deciduous and evergreen specimens can be renovated by cutting back hard to a low framework of stems.

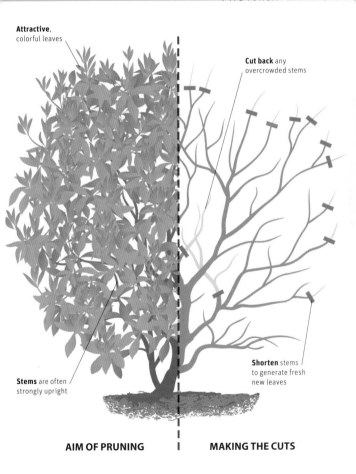

Attractive, colorful leaves

Cut back any overcrowded stems

Stems are often strongly upright

Shorten stems to generate fresh new leaves

AIM OF PRUNING

MAKING THE CUTS

Phygelius
EVERGREEN SHRUBS

■ **Prune in spring, after the worst of the frost**

*Phygelius
x rectus
'Salmon Leap'*

These low-growing shrubs produce trumpetlike bright coral red, orange, or creamy yellow flowers, which are carried over a long period in summer and into fall. They need a sunny location in the garden and should be grown against a warm wall in frost-prone areas.

In cold areas pruning is a matter of annual renovation since winter cold can often kill much of the growth. Cut back all the previous year's stems in spring to strong shoots near the base. For a larger plant, tie in a framework of stems against a wall. Shorten the sideshoots in spring, and cut back older main stems, tying in replacements as they grow. In areas where the top-growth is unimpaired, simply trim the plants as necessary in spring to shape. Thin the stems if congested, and dig up any unwanted suckers.

PLANT PROFILE

NATURAL HABIT Arching shrubs and subshrubs that shoot freely from the base.

HARDINESS Plants are vulnerable to frost in cold areas but usually produce new shoots from below ground level in spring.

HEIGHT AND SPREAD 4ft x 4ft (1.2m x 1.2m), or more, if the top-growth is not frosted.

PRUNING NOTES
■ In cold areas, cut back all stems in spring.

■ Shorten sideshoots on wall-trained plants.

■ Dig up unwanted suckers.

Profuse display of tubular flowers, flared at the tips

Cut the previous year's stems back to healthy buds

New stems appear from the base annually

AIM OF PRUNING

MAKING THE CUTS

Pieris
EVERGREEN SHRUBS
■ **Prune in mid- to late spring, after flowering**

Pieris japonica 'Blush'

Related to the rhododendrons and also requiring acidic soil, these evergreens often have bright pink or red young foliage in spring, as well as clusters of attractive bell-like white or pink flowers. They need shelter from strong winds to prevent damage to the new leaves; a location in dappled shade is ideal.

Keep pruning to a minimum. When removing faded flower clusters in late spring, cut back any straggly shoots at the same time. Routinely cut out any frost-damaged growth. To improve the shape of overgrown specimens, cut back overlong stems to strong shoots lower down. If plants have become neglected and very out of hand, they will tolerate complete renovation, but this will be at the loss of the following year's flowers. Cut all the growth back to a low framework, even into older bare wood.

PLANT PROFILE

NATURAL HABIT Rounded to upright or spreading, very shapely evergreen shrubs, becoming more open and treelike with age.

HARDINESS Generally hardy, although soft new growth is vulnerable to frost damage.

HEIGHT AND SPREAD 10ft x 6ft (3m x 2m). Dwarf varieties are much more compact.

PRUNING NOTES
■ Keep pruning to a minimum.

■ Deadhead in mid- to late spring.

■ Neglected and overgrown plants respond well to complete renovation.

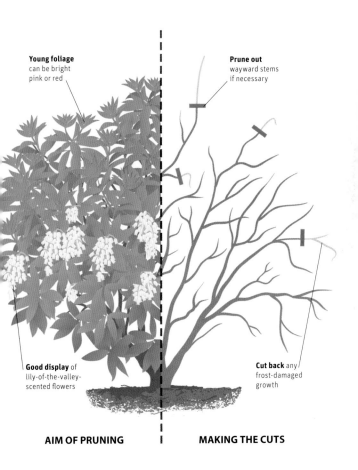

Young foliage can be bright pink or red

Prune out wayward stems if necessary

Good display of lily-of-the-valley-scented flowers

Cut back any frost-damaged growth

AIM OF PRUNING

MAKING THE CUTS

Pinus *Pine*

EVERGREEN TREES AND SHRUBS

■ Prune in late spring or in summer to fall

Pinus nigra

Pines vary from tall trees to low-growing, rounded, or spreading shrubs. Many are fine specimens in large gardens while others are wind tolerant and are excellent as wind breaks, particularly in coastal regions. The umbrella pine (*P. pinea*) sometimes branches from or near the base, developing several clear trunks with a dense, flattened crown. Dwarf pines, suitable for rock gardens, are compact and dense growing—but note that some are slow growing rather than dwarf, staying neat in the short term but ultimately becoming large trees.

Pruning is seldom strictly necessary apart from the removal of atypical or wayward growth that spoils the outline. To restrict size, shorten all the new growth by up to half its length in late spring. This will be at the expense of cone production. Light pruning to shape may be done in late summer to early fall.

PLANT PROFILE

NATURAL HABIT Extremely variable, depending on the type grown.

HARDINESS Mainly hardy. Young plants are more vulnerable than established specimens.

HEIGHT AND SPREAD Varies enormously. Up to 100ft x 30ft (30m x 10m), but many forms are dwarf or prostrate.

PRUNING NOTES
■ Keep pruning to a minimum.

■ Cut back any growth that spoils the outline.

■ Shorten the new growth to restrict size.

■ Frequent clipping will result in a denser, more bushy plant.

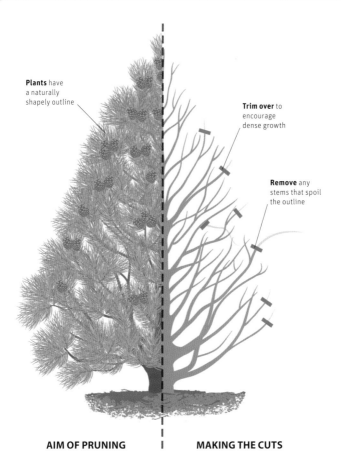

Plants have a naturally shapely outline

Trim over to encourage dense growth

Remove any stems that spoil the outline

AIM OF PRUNING

MAKING THE CUTS

Pittosporum
EVERGREEN SHRUBS
■ **Prune in mid- to late spring**

Pittosporum tenuifolium

These evergreens are mainly grown for their attractive leaves, which are often leathery with wavy edges and may be green, yellow, or purple, depending on the variety. The small flowers are sometimes fragrant and are borne in late spring and early summer. Colorful berries often follow in fall. Most are compact and neat-growing, and some make suitable hedging material. Not all are reliably hardy however, and even those that tolerate frost need a sheltered location in cold areas.

To maintain an even shape, shorten any straggly shoots in mid- to late spring, and remove any frost-damaged growth. Clip over hedging plants after planting to encourage bushiness. Once established, shear them over in spring and summer. Note that clipped hedges will not flower and fruit prolifically. Cut back any plain shoots on variegated forms as seen.

PLANT PROFILE

NATURAL HABIT Mainly upright, neat-growing evergreens.

HARDINESS All show some vulnerability to frost. Some are unsuitable for growing outdoors in cold climates.

HEIGHT AND SPREAD 12ft x 10ft (4m x 3m). Some varieties are more compact.

PRUNING NOTES
■ Prune in mid- to late spring after all risk of frost has passed in cold areas.

■ Cut back wayward or damaged shoots.

■ Prune hard to a low framework in mid-spring to renovate. Plants usually recover well.

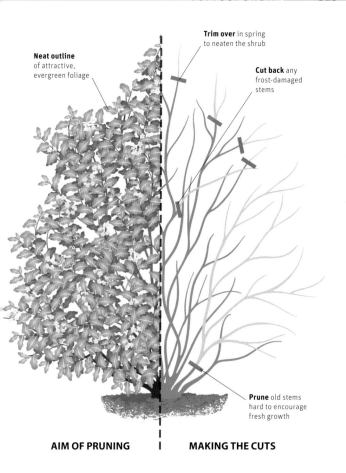

Trim over in spring to neaten the shrub

Cut back any frost-damaged stems

Neat outline of attractive, evergreen foliage

Prune old stems hard to encourage fresh growth

AIM OF PRUNING

MAKING THE CUTS

Platanus *Sycamore*
DECIDUOUS TREES
■ **Prune in fall to winter**

Platanus x hispanica

Tolerant of urban pollution, sycamores have attractive bark and are commonly planted as street trees in towns and cities. They are often subjected to regular pruning to restrict size and keep them safe, a practice to which they respond well. With more limited pruning they make majestic trees with heavy branches.

Trees are usually grown with a clear trunk of 6–10ft (2–3m). Lower branches of the London plane (*P. x hispanica*) can be retained and allowed to sweep to the ground; remove side branches to clear the trunk to 4ft (1.2m) only. If the lower stems are not already downward-growing, trim them back lightly to buds on the underside. *P. orientalis* occasionally produces side branches in pairs or clusters as it develops—prune to achieve an evenly balanced crown. All major work on established trees should be done by a qualified arborist only.

PLANT PROFILE

NATURAL HABIT Stately, upright-growing deciduous trees with heavy branches.

HARDINESS Mainly hardy but some are vulnerable to frost, especially when young.

HEIGHT AND SPREAD 80ft x 60ft (25m x 18m), or less with appropriate pruning. Variegated forms are naturally less vigorous.

PRUNING NOTES
■ Keep pruning to a minimum.

■ Remove any plain shoots on variegated varieties as soon as you spot them.

■ Leave all major work on established trees to an arborist.

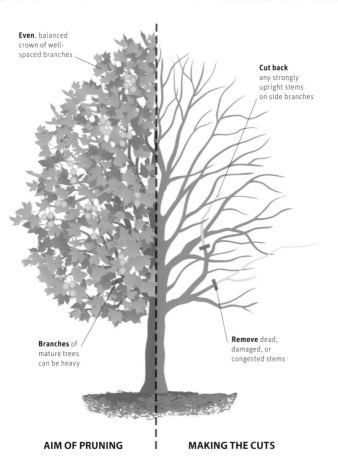

Even, balanced crown of well-spaced branches

Cut back any strongly upright stems on side branches

Branches of mature trees can be heavy

Remove dead, damaged, or congested stems

AIM OF PRUNING

MAKING THE CUTS

Plumeria *Pagoda tree*
DECIDUOUS TREES
■ Prune in early spring, just before new growth begins

Plumeria rubra

Plumerias are plants of the tropics and produce their richly scented flowers mainly in summer and fall. In frost-free areas where they can be grown outdoors, they form large shrubs or trees, and pruning can be minimal. In cooler areas they make excellent container plants and are suitable for a large sunroom.

They are best grown as densely branched trees on a short trunk: 3ft (1m) or less. The crown branches naturally. Prune annually in early spring to restrict size, shortening the previous year's stems by one-half to two-thirds. Multiple branches will develop from the cuts. To ease congestion as the plant develops, prune branches back hard to the main trunk, and remove any crossing stems. Stems bleed an irritant sap if cut or broken during the growing season.

PLANT PROFILE

NATURAL HABIT Small trees or shrubs that naturally form a dense canopy.

HARDINESS Plants will not survive freezing temperatures and must be overwintered in frost-free conditions.

HEIGHT AND SPREAD 20ft x 20ft (6m x 6m). Plants can be kept smaller with pruning.

PRUNING NOTES
■ Soft growth is prone to rot when cut, so restrict pruning to firmer material.

■ Prune before the plants come into growth.

■ Pruning to renovate is usually tolerated.

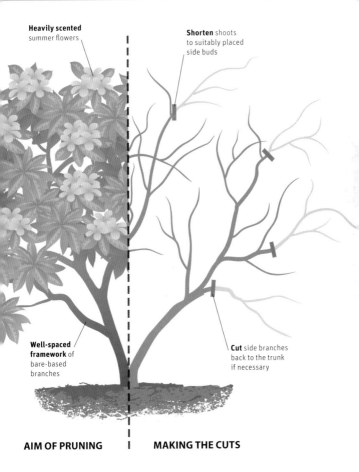

Heavily scented summer flowers

Shorten shoots to suitably placed side buds

Well-spaced framework of bare-based branches

Cut side branches back to the trunk if necessary

AIM OF PRUNING

MAKING THE CUTS

Populus *Poplar*
DECIDUOUS TREES
■ **Prune in summer to fall, or as required**

Populus x jackii 'Aurora'

These fast-growing, deciduous trees have a number of uses. The stiffly upright Lombardy poplar (*P. nigra* var. *italica*) is often planted as a privacy hedge. Other varieties are planted as street trees and sometimes pollarded to reduce size. Most are best trained with a central leader when young, so remove lower side branches and any competing stems as the plant grows. Retain the lower stems on upright types such as *P. alba* 'Pyramidalis', as well as the Lombardy poplar. Cut back suckers on sight.

P. x *jackii* 'Aurora' has leaves that are generously marked with pink and cream, and no two are identical. For the best foliage effect and to restrict growth, it can be pollarded at a height of around 10ft (3m)—cut all the stems back annually. New leaves may not show the characteristic markings on opening, but remove any that have clearly reverted to plain green by midsummer.

PLANT PROFILE

NATURAL HABIT Fast-growing, often strongly upright deciduous trees.

HARDINESS Fully hardy.

HEIGHT AND SPREAD 30–43ft (10–13m) high, with a spread of 20–30ft (6–10m), depending on the species. Upright forms are much narrower; pollarded trees are smaller.

PRUNING NOTES
■ Established trees need little pruning. Any essential work can be done between summer and fall. Consider employing a tree surgeon if necessary.

■ Pollard in late winter to early spring.

Poplars often develop a naturally balanced outline

Remove any stems with plain green leaves

Even coverage of healthy foliage

Cut back suckers or unwanted shoots from the bare trunk

AIM OF PRUNING

MAKING THE CUTS

Potentilla *Cinquefoil*
DECIDUOUS SHRUBS
■ **Prune in early to mid-spring, then again in fall**

Potentilla fruticosa 'Goldfinger'

Shrubby potentillas flower for a long period from late spring to mid-fall. They make excellent groundcover in full sun or can be used to create a low, billowing hedge. The attractive, often cup-shaped flowers are borne in shades of white, pink, red, yellow, and orange. Although the plants are normally neat-growing and well-covered with foliage, older specimens can occasionally develop twiggy or untidy patches.

No regular pruning is necessary. If the plants begin to look untidy, shorten overlong shoots in early spring. Cut back any older growth and any weak, twiggy stems. Prune with caution however, as further pruning at this time may delay the onset of flowering. Trim over plants after flowering in fall to neaten and deadhead, as required.

PLANT PROFILE

NATURAL HABIT Low-growing, mound-forming to spreading, often twiggy shrubs.

HARDINESS Fully hardy.

HEIGHT AND SPREAD Plants grow to around 18–36in (45–90cm) high, spreading about 4ft (1.2m).

PRUNING NOTES
■ Prune as necessary in spring, and trim over plants in fall to deadhead and neaten.

■ Cut all stems down to a low framework in early to mid-spring to renovate. Recovery isn't certain, and old plants may be best replaced.

Flowers may cover the plant in spring and summer

Cut off faded flowers

Shorten overlong sideshoots to neaten in early spring

Cut old, woody stems hard to the base

AIM OF PRUNING

MAKING THE CUTS

Prunus *Cherry*
DECIDUOUS TREES AND SHRUBS
■ Prune in midsummer during dry, settled weather

Prunus
'Shirofugen'

Apart from the types that are grown for fruit—peaches, apricots, plums, and cherries (see pp.442–451)—this is a vast group of mainly spring-flowering deciduous trees and shrubs. *P. serrula* is also grown for the winter appeal of its shining brown bark. The plants have an elegant shape and do best with minimal pruning. To reduce the risk of silver leaf disease, which is carried in rainwater, any essential pruning should be done during settled, warm, dry weather in summer, when the plant will heal most rapidly.

P. cerasifera makes an excellent flowering hedge. To encourage branching from near the base, shorten the main stem in the first summer after planting. Once established, prune after flowering. The shrubby *P. glandulosa* benefits from hard pruning annually after flowering to strong buds near the base of the plant.

PLANT PROFILE

NATURAL HABIT Often large trees with spreading, vase-shaped, or rounded crowns. Some are upright, while a few are shrubby.

HARDINESS Mainly hardy, although early flowers can be vulnerable to frost damage.

HEIGHT AND SPREAD Plants grow to 30ft x 20ft (10m x 6m), depending on the type.

PRUNING NOTES
- ■ Keep pruning as minimal as possible.
- ■ Prune established hedges after flowering.
- ■ Cut back flowered stems on *P. glandulosa*.
- ■ Renovation is seldom successful.
- ■ For evergreen prunus, see pp.336–337.

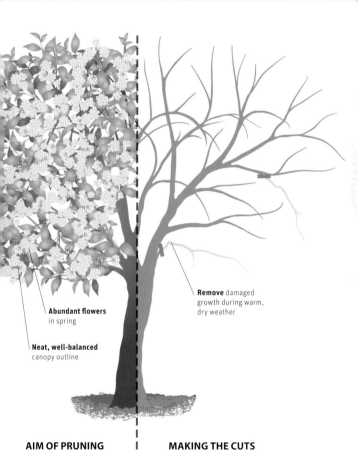

Abundant flowers in spring

Neat, well-balanced canopy outline

Remove damaged growth during warm, dry weather

AIM OF PRUNING

MAKING THE CUTS

Prunus *Cherry*
EVERGREEN TREES AND SHRUBS
■ Prune in late spring to summer, during dry weather

Prunus laurocerasus 'Otto Luyken'

With their handsome leathery leaves, evergreen prunus make valuable additions to shrub borders or form dense billowing hedges. They are more tolerant of pruning than deciduous types (see pp.334–335).

Both the cherry laurel (*P. laurocerasus*) and the Portugal laurel (*P. lusitanica*) can be grown with minimal pruning as specimens, becoming treelike at maturity. To restrict size, cut back overlong shoots in late spring or early summer. Cut out plain green shoots on variegated varieties. Overgrown shrubs can be cut back to a low framework of branches, even into old bare wood. When cutting hedges, trim over the plants during a period of warm dry weather. Specimens of *P. lusitanica* can be clipped to shape as required.

PLANT PROFILE

NATURAL HABIT Mound-forming to billowing evergreens that become treelike.

HARDINESS Mainly hardy, but *P. lusitanica* can show some sensitivity to hard frost.

HEIGHT AND SPREAD 15ft x 15ft (5m x 5m) or more, but plants can be kept smaller with regular pruning. Dwarf forms are smaller.

PRUNING NOTES
■ Prune during a period of dry, settled weather in the growing season.

■ Plants generally respond well to renovative pruning during late spring or summer.

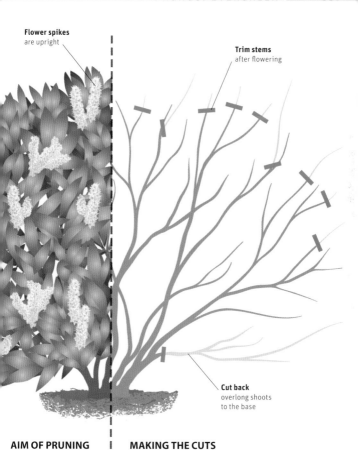

Flower spikes are upright

Trim stems after flowering

Cut back overlong shoots to the base

AIM OF PRUNING | **MAKING THE CUTS**

Pyracantha *Firethorn*
EVERGREEN SHRUBS
■ Prune in spring, then again in summer

Pyracanthas are tough, versatile evergreens with two seasons of interest: early summer, when they are covered with creamy white flowers, then fall, when red, orange, or yellow berries ripen. Use them in shrub borders, as a hedge, or trained against a wall.

Freestanding shrubs can be grown with minimal pruning. Cut out any damaged or awkwardly placed shoots in mid-spring. Shear over hedges in spring and summer—three or four trims can be made, though this will be at the loss of some flowers and fruits.

Pyracantha 'Mohave'

To train plants against a wall, tie in a framework of main stems, shortening badly placed shoots in spring. Older stems can be cut out entirely if necessary; guide in strong replacements. In summer, shorten any new stems that grow out from the framework and hide the berries.

PLANT PROFILE

NATURAL HABIT Often dense, thorny, stiffly upright or spreading shrubs.

HARDINESS Generally fully hardy—some can suffer frost damage in very cold winters.

HEIGHT AND SPREAD Plants grow to around 10ft x 10ft (3m x 3m), but can be kept within bounds with regular pruning.

PRUNING NOTES
■ Freestanding plants need minimal pruning.

■ Clip over hedges three or four times a year.

■ Prune wall-trained pyracanthas in spring and summer, as necessary.

■ Wear thick gloves to protect against thorns.

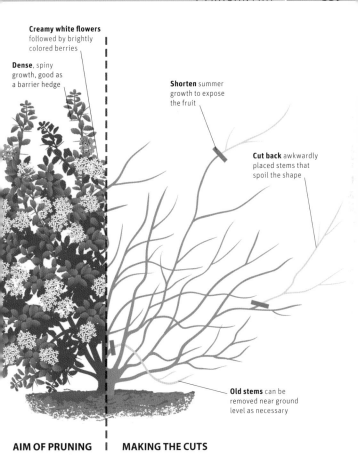

Creamy white flowers followed by brightly colored berries

Dense, spiny growth, good as a barrier hedge

Shorten summer growth to expose the fruit

Cut back awkwardly placed stems that spoil the shape

Old stems can be removed near ground level as necessary

AIM OF PRUNING | **MAKING THE CUTS**

Pyrus *Pear*
UPRIGHT DECIDUOUS TREES
■ **Prune in late winter to early spring**

Pyrus calleryana 'Chanticleer'

Although pears are usually grown for their edible fruits, a few varieties are valued for their ornamental qualities because their fruits are small, brown, and unpalatable. They have several seasons of interest since they bear masses of cup-shaped white flowers in spring and the fall leaf color can be spectacular, depending on the variety.

A popular choice that makes an attractive alternative to ornamental cherries (*Prunus*) and crabapples (*Malus*), is *P. calleryana*. Some types—such as 'Capital' and 'Chanticleer'—are particularly suitable for smaller gardens. Prune in the dormant period between winter and early spring. On young trees, remove any side branches that spoil the overall shape of the crown. Established trees need little further pruning beyond the removal of broken, crossing, or weak-growing branches. For weeping types, see pp.342–343.

PLANT PROFILE

NATURAL HABIT Conical to upright trees.

HARDINESS Fully hardy, though flowers may be damaged by late frost.

HEIGHT AND SPREAD Plants grow to 25ft x 15ft (8m x 5m) or more.

PRUNING NOTES
■ Keep pruning to a minimum.

■ Only cut branches during the dormant period if absolutely necessary.

■ Remove any badly placed stems on young plants between winter and early spring.

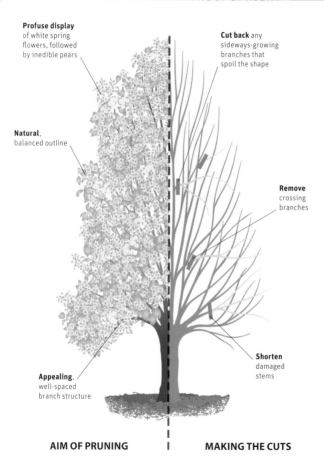

Profuse display of white spring flowers, followed by inedible pears

Cut back any sideways-growing branches that spoil the shape

Natural, balanced outline

Remove crossing branches

Appealing, well-spaced branch structure

Shorten damaged stems

AIM OF PRUNING

MAKING THE CUTS

Pyrus *Pear*

WEEPING DECIDUOUS TREES

■ **Prune between late fall and early spring**

Pyrus salicifolia 'Pendula'

Among the ornamental pears (see also pp.340–341), the weeping willow-leaf pear, *P. salicifolia* 'Pendula', has particular value. The silver-gray leaves borne on stems that hang down like curtains provide a long season of interest, and its generally compact shape makes it a top choice as a specimen in a lawn. Trees are normally grown on a trunk no taller than 10ft (3m).

Growth often becomes congested. In winter when the branches are bare, cut back any upward-growing shoots that spoil the domed shape at the top of the canopy. Shorten stems that trail on the ground back to outward-facing buds. Thin any congested stems as necessary, cutting back to suitably placed buds. To extend the spread of the canopy, cut back to a bud on the upper surface of the branch. New growth can be thinned, if necessary, in late summer.

PLANT PROFILE

NATURAL HABIT Small to medium-sized deciduous trees with a broad, domed canopy of weeping branches.

HARDINESS Fully hardy.

HEIGHT AND SPREAD Plants can grow to 15ft x 12ft (5m x 4m), although they can be kept smaller with pruning and training.

PRUNING NOTES
■ Prune to thin congested growth.
■ Shorten stems that trail on the ground.
■ Remove any stems that spoil the outline.

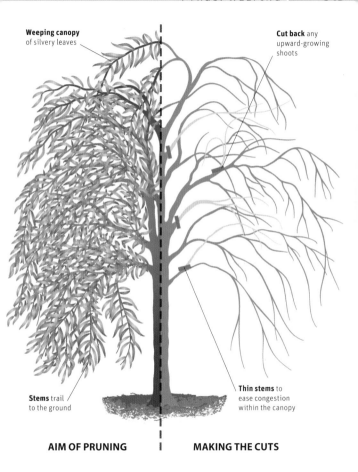

Weeping canopy of silvery leaves

Cut back any upward-growing shoots

Stems trail to the ground

Thin stems to ease congestion within the canopy

AIM OF PRUNING

MAKING THE CUTS

Quercus *Oak*
DECIDUOUS AND EVERGREEN TREES
■ **Prune between fall and spring**

Quercus robur

Oaks are magnificent trees that can live to a ripe old age. They usually develop large, spreading crowns, and deciduous types can have spectacular fall leaf color. Some forms grow narrowly upright, while some of the evergreens are suitable for hedging.

No formal pruning is required. Any necessary work should be done when the trees are dormant, between fall and spring. On young trees, remove lower lateral branches if necessary to clear the stem and encourage upright growth. Remove any obviously dead growth on older trees. Large, mature specimens sometimes suffer wind or snow damage during fall and winter. Any work needed to restore them is best done by an arborist, and recovery is nearly always excellent. Shear over evergreen hedges a couple of times between spring and summer.

PLANT PROFILE

NATURAL HABIT Usually large, spreading trees that are occasionally upright.

HARDINESS Mainly hardy, but evergreens are less tolerant of frost until well established.

HEIGHT AND SPREAD Plants grow to around 30ft x 20ft (10m x 6m), although some may be larger on maturity.

PRUNING NOTES
■ Keep pruning to a minimum.

■ Prune during the dormant period between fall and spring.

■ Shear over evergreen hedges twice from spring to midsummer.

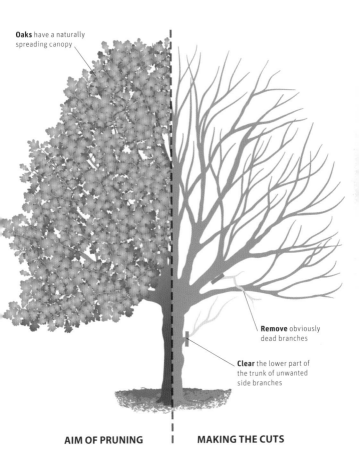

Oaks have a naturally spreading canopy

Remove obviously dead branches

Clear the lower part of the trunk of unwanted side branches

AIM OF PRUNING

MAKING THE CUTS

Rhododendron *Azalea*
DECIDUOUS SHRUBS
■ Prune immediately after flowering, if necessary

Rhododendron luteum

While most rhododendrons are evergreen (see pp.348–349), some are deciduous. They bear funnel-shaped, sometimes scented flowers in shades of white, pink, red, yellow, orange, and purple in late spring to early summer. The flowers give way to attractive fall leaf color.

Deciduous rhododendrons become open, elegant shrubs that usually need little pruning, although young plants can be pruned to promote bushiness, if necessary. Established plants can be deadheaded after flowering, and this is also the ideal time to remove any congested stems and shorten unproductive shoots back to strong buds. Pruning to restrict size is not recommended. Plants that have become straggly can be renovated in spring—shorten all stems to around 12in (30cm) from ground level. Normal flowering will not resume until the following year at the earliest.

PLANT PROFILE

NATURAL HABIT Often open, upright to spreading, dome-shaped shrubs that can become treelike with age.

HARDINESS Fully hardy.

HEIGHT AND SPREAD Around 10ft x 10ft (3m x 3m), depending on the variety.

PRUNING NOTES
■ Deadhead after flowering, if necessary.

■ Cut back any older stems that have become bare at the base.

■ Renovate straggly plants in spring.

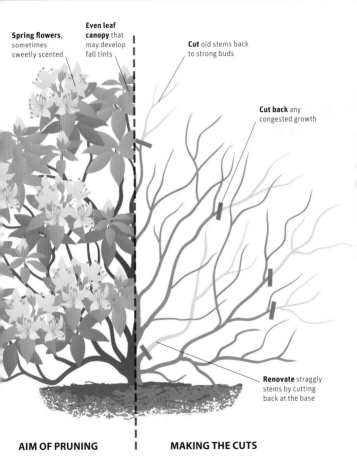

Spring flowers, sometimes sweetly scented

Even leaf canopy that may develop fall tints

Cut old stems back to strong buds

Cut back any congested growth

Renovate straggly stems by cutting back at the base

AIM OF PRUNING

MAKING THE CUTS

Rhododendron *Azalea*

EVERGREEN SHRUBS

■ **Prune in spring, after flowering**

Rhododendron 'Polar Bear'

Evergreen rhododendrons vary dramatically in size, from compact, neat-growing dwarfs that are ideal for rock gardens to much larger plants that can assume treelike proportions with a spreading crown. Their beautiful, showy blooms range in color from pure white to vivid oranges and purples.

Rhododendrons do not generally need regular pruning beyond the removal of wayward shoots that spoil the outline. This job can be carried out in spring at the same time as deadheading. Large plants may develop asymmetrically or suffer snow or wind damage. To correct this, remove any dead or damaged growth in mid-spring. You may need a saw to cut back very thick stems. Avoid planting large types in shade: they can become leggy with age, which may not be easy to rectify.

PLANT PROFILE

NATURAL HABIT Evergreen rhododendrons vary greatly in habit.

HARDINESS Mainly hardy, although some early-flowering varieties benefit from shelter to prevent frost damage to the flowers.

HEIGHT AND SPREAD To 10ft x 10ft (3m x 3m). Dwarfs will be much more compact.

PRUNING NOTES

■ Old plants can be cut back hard, although they may not achieve a good shape when they recover.

■ Larger-growing specimens are most likely to need pruning.

■ For deciduous types see pp.346–347.

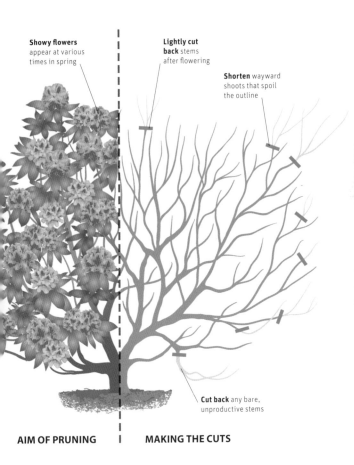

Showy flowers appear at various times in spring

Lightly cut back stems after flowering

Shorten wayward shoots that spoil the outline

Cut back any bare, unproductive stems

AIM OF PRUNING

MAKING THE CUTS

Rhus *Sumac*
DECIDUOUS SHRUBS AND TREES
■ **Prune in spring or late summer**

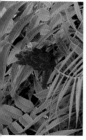

Rhus typhina

These open trees and shrubs have velvety, antler-like branches and large leaves, which turn rich shades of orange and red before falling in fall. They spread using suckers, and many are potentially invasive. The trees tend to lose their leaders early and develop low, spreading crowns. Varieties with finely cut leaves are usually less vigorous.

Pruning can be kept to the minimum. Suckers should be routinely removed—they may appear some distance away from the plant. To produce the best foliage display from cut-leaf types, prune all the stems back to near ground level in early spring. Wear gloves when pruning since contact with the sap can cause allergic skin reactions. Any other pruning is best done in late summer, when the sap will flow less freely.

PLANT PROFILE

NATURAL HABIT Spreading, open, often invasive deciduous trees and shrubs.

HARDINESS Fully hardy.

HEIGHT AND SPREAD 15ft x 20ft (5m x 6m) or more. Trees will be taller; cut-leaf types are generally more compact.

PRUNING NOTES
■ Remove all suckers to restrict spread.

■ Prune cut-leaf types to a low framework of branches each spring.

■ Renovative pruning is generally successful but may result in quantities of thin stems. Thin these, as necessary.

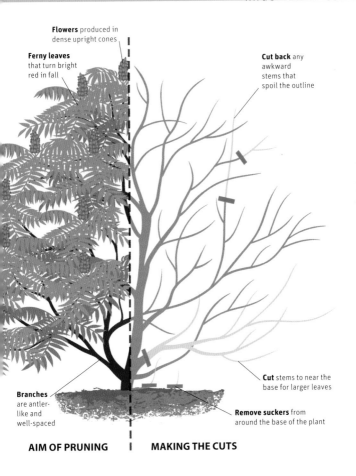

Flowers produced in dense upright cones

Ferny leaves that turn bright red in fall

Cut back any awkward stems that spoil the outline

Cut stems to near the base for larger leaves

Branches are antler-like and well-spaced

Remove suckers from around the base of the plant

AIM OF PRUNING

MAKING THE CUTS

Ribes *Flowering currant*
DECIDUOUS SHRUBS
■ **Prune in spring, after flowering**

Ribes sanguineum 'Pulborough Scarlet'

Among the first of the shrubs to bloom in spring, these deciduous plants bear dangling racemes of flowers, usually in shades of pink, at the same time as their soft green leaves. They are excellent when used to create an informal flowering hedge.

Prune immediately after flowering. Young, healthy stems can be left unpruned or lightly clipped back to neaten the appearance, but older stems can be cut back to outward-facing buds lower down. Remove very old stems completely, especially if they are bare at the base. It can be more practical to do this part of the job in winter, when it is easier to identify—and gain access to—thickened stems. However this inevitably leads to the loss of any flowers that may have formed at the stem tips.

PLANT PROFILE

NATURAL HABIT Upright to arching shrubs that can become untidy if neglected.

HARDINESS Mainly hardy.

HEIGHT AND SPREAD Plants grow to around 6ft x 4ft (2m x 1.2m).

PRUNING NOTES
■ The aim is to refresh the plant by reducing older, less productive growth and allowing new stems to take its place.

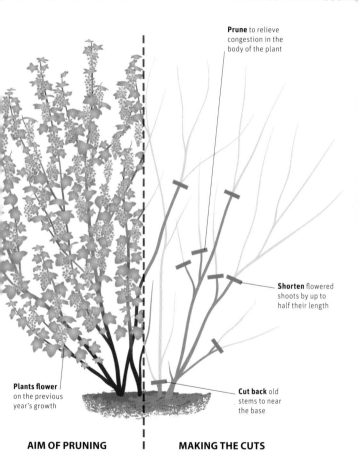

Prune to relieve congestion in the body of the plant

Shorten flowered shoots by up to half their length

Plants flower on the previous year's growth

Cut back old stems to near the base

AIM OF PRUNING

MAKING THE CUTS

Robinia *Locust*
DECIDUOUS TREES AND SHRUBS
■ **Prune in late summer to early fall**

Robinia pseudoacacia 'Frisia'

These elegant open trees and shrubs are grown for their foliage and wisterialike flowers, although some types do not always flower reliably. Pruning can be kept to a minimum and is best done in late summer to early fall to prevent the plants from bleeding sap. Simply shorten any broken or crossing stems as necessary.

In cool climates branches are often brittle and prone to damage from strong fall storms—badly affected specimens are best replaced. Types such as *R. pseudoacacia* can be pollarded to produce a small tree with a dense, compact crown that is likely to be more wind resistant, although it will not flower. Shrubby *R. hispida* can be wall trained. Some plants produce suckers, which should be removed on sight.

PLANT PROFILE

NATURAL HABIT Upright to spreading trees and shrubs that often produce suckers.

HARDINESS Mainly fully hardy, although shelter from strong winds is essential.

HEIGHT AND SPREAD 30ft x 15ft (10m x 5m), or more in favorable locations.

PRUNING NOTES

■ Prune only to remove damaged growth.

■ Cut back all unwanted suckers on sight.

■ Shorten the sideshoots of wall-trained plants in late summer.

■ Employ an arborist if necessary.

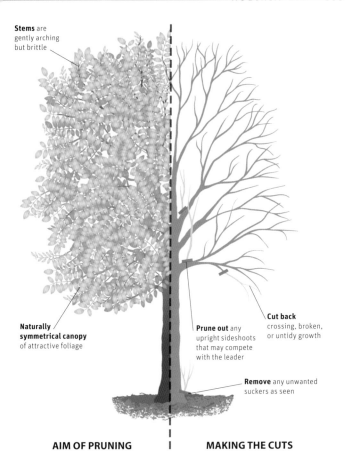

Stems are gently arching but brittle

Naturally symmetrical canopy of attractive foliage

Prune out any upright sideshoots that may compete with the leader

Cut back crossing, broken, or untidy growth

Remove any unwanted suckers as seen

AIM OF PRUNING

MAKING THE CUTS

Rosa *Rose*

SHRUB AND OLD GARDEN ROSES

■ **Prune in winter to early spring, and after flowering**

Rosa
JACQUELINE DU
PRE ('Harwanna')

Old roses and those that don't fit into other categories often become large shrubs. Many bear flowers in a single flush in early summer, but some are repeat-flowering. Unlike other bush roses, they don't need a rigorous annual prune.

The first spring after planting, cut back any weak or badly placed stems, and allow the plant to grow unpruned. Once established, aim to refresh the plant by periodically removing old stems in late winter or early spring. Varieties that bear a single flush of flowers should be pruned once these fade to reduce congestion. Shorten stems to balance the growth, as necessary. Deadhead repeat-flowering types to encourage further flowering. Roses grown for their fall hips such as *R. rugosa* and *R. moyesii* should not be deadheaded.

PLANT PROFILE

NATURAL HABIT Mainly upright to arching but sometimes more compact deciduous shrubs.

HARDINESS Mainly fully hardy.

HEIGHT AND SPREAD Plants grow to around 5ft x 5ft (1.5m x 1.5m). Some varieties are taller, others more spreading.

PRUNING NOTES

■ Cut out older, unproductive stems at the base of the plant, and remove any twiggy, weak-growing stems.

■ Shorten any stems that spoil the shape.

■ Deadhead the plants after flowering unless fall hips are required.

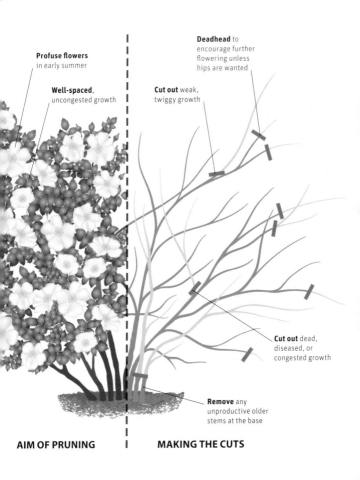

Profuse flowers in early summer

Well-spaced, uncongested growth

Deadhead to encourage further flowering unless hips are wanted

Cut out weak, twiggy growth

Cut out dead, diseased, or congested growth

Remove any unproductive older stems at the base

AIM OF PRUNING

MAKING THE CUTS

Rosa *Rose*

FLORIBUNDA AND HYBRID TEA ROSES

■ Prune in early spring, as new growth begins

Rosa ICEBERG ('Korbin')

An invaluable component of the summer flower garden, these roses vary in habit from compact shrubs to larger plants that can be used as specimens or at the back of a border. The flowers are usually produced either in two flushes, with the second continuing into fall, or sporadically over a long period.

Annual pruning is essential. In late winter to early spring, shorten all the previous year's stems. Cut thick old stems back to the base, and remove any thin, twiggy, crossing, or frosted growth. Prune the remaining stems to create a vase-shaped plant, cutting to outward-facing buds. Shorten vigorous stems only slightly, but cut weaker ones harder. Remove faded flowers in summer, cutting to a growth bud to encourage further flowering. In exposed areas, lightly shorten stems in fall to stabilize plants over winter.

PLANT PROFILE

NATURAL HABIT Often upright, usually vase-shaped deciduous shrubs, generally with thorny stems.

HARDINESS Mainly hardy, although a few types show some vulnerability to late frost.

HEIGHT AND SPREAD Plants grow to 5ft x 3ft (1.5m x 1m); some are more compact.

PRUNING NOTES

■ Cut out older stems, remove twiggy growth, and shorten all other stems.

■ Renovative pruning is effective, although flowers the following year may not be abundant.

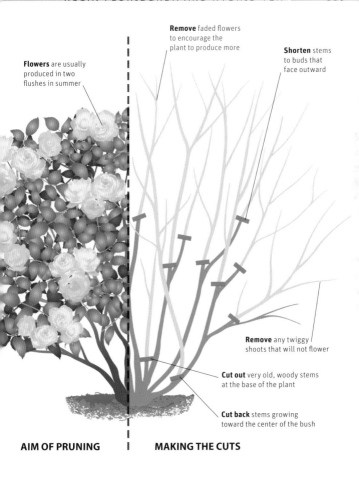

Remove faded flowers to encourage the plant to produce more

Shorten stems to buds that face outward

Flowers are usually produced in two flushes in summer

Remove any twiggy shoots that will not flower

Cut out very old, woody stems at the base of the plant

Cut back stems growing toward the center of the bush

AIM OF PRUNING

MAKING THE CUTS

Rosa *Rose*
GROUNDCOVER, MINIATURE, AND PATIO ROSES
■ Prune in early spring, and in summer as necessary

These compact roses are neat-growing, robust, hardy, and generally disease resistant. They can be grown in containers, as groundcover, or even as a low hedge. They should be pruned annually but less strictly than other roses. Clip them over in early spring, shortening the stems by one-third to one-half. To develop a larger plant, trim them back by no more than one-quarter of their length.

Patio roses occasionally have a very vigorous stem, and this should be taken back to its point of origin. Long, arching stems on groundcover roses may be pinned to the ground to extend the coverage. Most can be clipped over again in summer after the first flush of flowers to encourage further flowering. Some groundcover types have bright red fall hips, and summer pruning is not necessary; to enjoy both flowers and hips, deadhead selectively.

Flowers are usually small but often cover the plant

Rosa 'Northamptonshire'

Plants produce quantities of growth from near the base

AIM OF PRUNING

PLANT PROFILE

NATURAL HABIT Sometimes twiggy, usually thorny, compact to dense-growing deciduous shrubs.

HARDINESS Mainly fully hardy.

HEIGHT AND SPREAD 3ft x 4ft (1m x 1.2m); some are naturally smaller.

PRUNING NOTES
- Prune annually to restrict growth.
- Remove any overly vigorous shoots.
- Deadhead the plants selectively if fall hips are desired.
- Renovative pruning is usually successful.

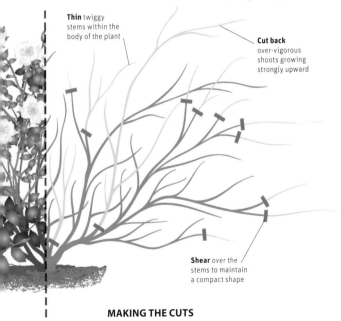

Thin twiggy stems within the body of the plant

Cut back over-vigorous shoots growing strongly upward

Shear over the stems to maintain a compact shape

MAKING THE CUTS

Rosa *Rose*
CLIMBING ROSES
■ **Prune in early spring, as growth begins**

Rosa 'Maigold'

Climbing roses can be compact, miniature types with small flowers or much larger growing. They are usually repeat-flowering—either producing their blooms in two distinct flushes or intermittently during the summer and into early fall. Deadhead to extend the display.

When wall training, create a framework, training the stems as horizontally as possible—the branches may be very stiff. When training plants up a pergola or obelisk, wrap the stems in a spiral. In spring, shorten sideshoots growing from the framework stems to outward-facing buds, and cut back any unproductive framework stems to the base. Tie in strong new shoots to replace them. Plants respond well to renovation, but on those that are closely related to bush roses, such as *R*. 'Climbing Iceberg', hard pruning should be staggered over a few years to prevent the plant from reverting to a shrubby habit.

PLANT PROFILE

NATURAL HABIT Usually extremely vigorous climbers with stiffly upright to arching or very flexible stems.

HARDINESS Mainly hardy, although some are best given the shelter of a warm wall.

HEIGHT AND SPREAD 12ft x 12ft (4m x 4m). Miniature climbers are much smaller.

PRUNING NOTES
■ Prune annually to refresh the plant.

■ Cut back older, unproductive stems.

■ Deadhead after flowering.

■ Renovation is almost always successful.

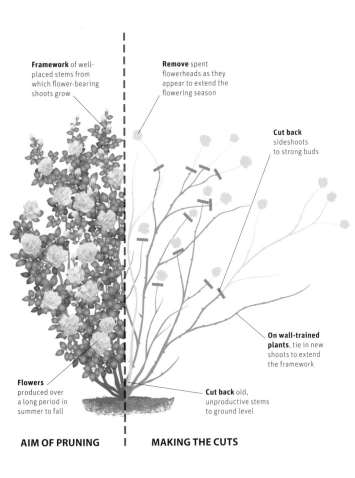

Framework of well-placed stems from which flower-bearing shoots grow

Remove spent flowerheads as they appear to extend the flowering season

Cut back sideshoots to strong buds

Flowers produced over a long period in summer to fall

On wall-trained plants, tie in new shoots to extend the framework

Cut back old, unproductive stems to ground level

AIM OF PRUNING

MAKING THE CUTS

Rosa *Rose*

RAMBLING ROSES

■ **Prune in midsummer, immediately after flowering**

Rosa
'Wedding Day'

Rambling roses are very vigorous plants that usually bear their flowers in a single spectacular flush in early summer. The stems are usually very flexible when young and easy to train horizontally, producing a plant with a spread that exceeds its height. Wrap them in a spiral if upright growth is needed on a pergola or obelisk.

Guide stems as they grow to create a framework. Flowers are produced on sideshoots from these main branches. After flowering, shorten the flowered sideshoots, then cut out older, unproductive branches at the base. It can be easier to remove them in sections from the plant. Ramblers also look attractive grown through established trees. Wrap the stems around the trunk until they reach the canopy, then leave them to grow unimpeded.

PLANT PROFILE

NATURAL HABIT Very vigorous, often thorny plants that shoot freely from the base.

HARDINESS Mainly fully hardy.

HEIGHT AND SPREAD Around 20ft x 15ft (6m x 5m), depending on the variety.

PRUNING NOTES

■ Prune plants during summer, immediately after they have flowered.

■ Complete renovation of old plants in late winter or early spring is generally successful, but at the loss of the following year's flowers.

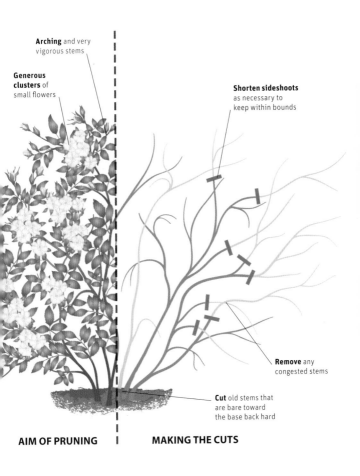

Arching and very vigorous stems

Generous clusters of small flowers

Shorten sideshoots as necessary to keep within bounds

Remove any congested stems

Cut old stems that are bare toward the base back hard

AIM OF PRUNING

MAKING THE CUTS

Rosa *Rose*
STANDARD ROSES
■ **Prune in spring before growth begins, then in fall**

Rosa 'The Fairy'

Standard roses are created by grafting one variety onto a tall stem of another, vigorous one. In spring, prune any weak growth hard, and shorten vigorous shoots only lightly, even if this creates asymmetry in the short term. Remove crossing shoots, and cut back older stems. The remaining stems should be evenly distributed around the top of the plant; the aim of pruning is to create a rounded, balanced head. Deadhead in summer to encourage additional flowers. Trim all the growth lightly in fall to reduce the weight of the crown.

Groundcover and rambling roses are used to create weeping standards. Begin regular pruning only when the crown is well-developed, around two years after planting. Thin congested growth, cutting older stems back to upward-facing buds near the graft union. Shorten overlong stems as necessary.

PLANT PROFILE

NATURAL HABIT Dainty plants with rounded or weeping heads.

HARDINESS Mainly hardy, although plants are very vulnerable to wind damage.

HEIGHT AND SPREAD 5ft x 4ft (1.5m x 1.2m), depending on the height of the main stem and the grafted variety.

PRUNING NOTES
■ Prune to create a balanced framework.

■ Hard, renovative pruning may be successful, but a good result is not guaranteed.

■ Rub out any shoots that appear on the main stem below the graft union during the growing season.

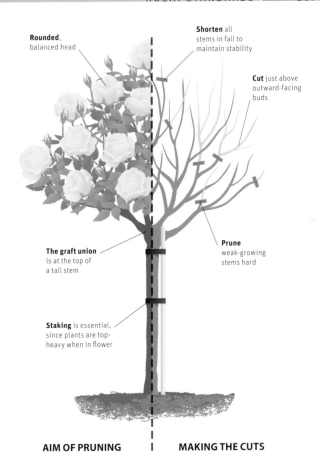

Rounded, balanced head

Shorten all stems in fall to maintain stability

Cut just above outward-facing buds

The graft union is at the top of a tall stem

Prune weak-growing stems hard

Staking is essential, since plants are top-heavy when in flower

AIM OF PRUNING

MAKING THE CUTS

Rosmarinus *Rosemary*

EVERGREEN SHRUBS

■ **Prune in spring and summer as required**

Rosmarinus officinalis

A common garden herb, rosemaries produce blue, purple, or white blooms that are very attractive to bees. They flower from late spring and into early summer, then often again in late summer to fall. They vary from prostrate to more upright types, and some are suitable for hedging.

In spring, cut back any frost-damaged growth to healthy wood. Stems on overgrown plants can be shortened by half their length or more, but this will be at the loss of the early flowers. In summer after the first flowering, shorten any lanky stems, and trim over plants to neaten. For an informal flowering hedge, clip once annually in summer, when the blooms have faded. To create a crisper finish, cut again in summer—but at the loss of late flowers. Old plants that have become bare at the base are best replaced.

PLANT PROFILE

NATURAL HABIT Usually upright, sometimes spreading, evergreen subshrubs.

HARDINESS Fully hardy when grown in a well-drained soil.

HEIGHT AND SPREAD Plants grow to 6ft x 4ft (2m x 1.2m), or less with regular pruning.

PRUNING NOTES
■ Cut out any frost-damaged growth.

■ Trim over after flowering.

■ Plants that are bare at the base generally do not respond well to renovative pruning.

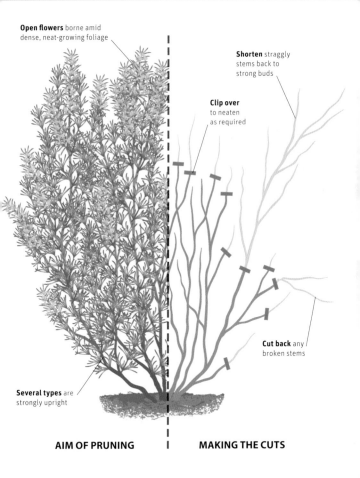

Open flowers borne amid dense, neat-growing foliage

Shorten straggly stems back to strong buds

Clip over to neaten as required

Cut back any broken stems

Several types are strongly upright

AIM OF PRUNING

MAKING THE CUTS

Rubus *Ornamental Raspberry*
DECIDUOUS SHRUBS
■ **Prune in late winter to early spring**

Rubus cockburnianus

Ornamental raspberries are sometimes grown for their summer flowers, but there are others, such as *R. biflorus*, *R. cockburnianus*, and *R. thibetanus*, whose winter stems are of greater interest. Known as "ghost brambles," these shrubs have arching stems that are covered in a whitish bloom and rise up from the bare earth to make a strong statement during the darker months. The shrubs combine well with snowdrops and early hellebores but, like all the brambles, they can be invasive.

Pruning is a matter of ruthlessly cutting back all the stems—either right to the ground or to a low framework—in early spring; this job is most easily done with loppers. Regular cutting not only maintains the production of young stems, but also prevents the plants from spreading. Wear gloves to protect your hands from the vicious thorns.

PLANT PROFILE

NATURAL HABIT Arching, colonizing shrubs that will form new plants where the shoot tips meet the ground.

HARDINESS Mainly hardy.

HEIGHT AND SPREAD 4ft x 4ft (1.2m x 1.2m), with annual pruning.

PRUNING NOTES
■ Prune to maximize the number of young stems that will make most impact in winter.

■ Pruning will also prevent unwanted spread of the plant.

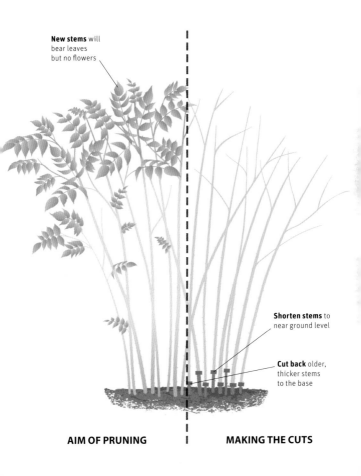

New stems will bear leaves but no flowers

Shorten stems to near ground level

Cut back older, thicker stems to the base

AIM OF PRUNING

MAKING THE CUTS

Salix *Willow*
DECIDUOUS TREES WITH WEEPING HABITS
■ Prune in winter, when stems are bare

Salix caprea 'Kilmarnock'

Weeping types of willow are elegant specimens. The true weeping willow (*S. x sepulcralis*) looks particularly attractive near a lake or stream if its stems trail in the water. The much smaller Kilmarnock willow (*S. caprea* 'Kilmarnock') is an ideal specimen for a small garden.

Allow weeping willows to develop unpruned. Once they are established, branches within the crown can be thinned to ease congestion. The Kilmarnock willow benefits from annual pruning, a job most easily tackled in winter. Cut out any older stems entirely as well as any upward-growing shoots. Shorten any branches that cross or rub against each other. To maintain the weeping look, cut back to downward-facing buds. To extend the spread of the canopy, cut back to well-placed, upward-facing buds—new shoots will grow upward initially, then arch over to create the characteristic outline.

PLANT PROFILE

NATURAL HABIT Often elegant, sometimes large and asymmetrical trees with whippy, trailing stems.

HARDINESS Fully hardy.

HEIGHT AND SPREAD Plants can grow to 50ft x 50ft (15m x 15m). The Kilmarnock willow is much smaller.

PRUNING NOTES
■ Cut out older stems in winter.

■ Shorten rubbing and congested stems.

■ Consider employing a professional arborist for large specimens.

■ For upright willows, see pp.374–375.

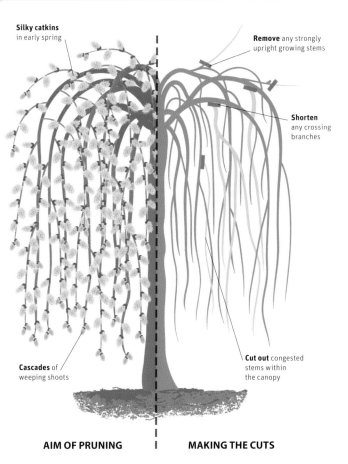

Silky catkins in early spring

Remove any strongly upright growing stems

Shorten any crossing branches

Cascades of weeping shoots

Cut out congested stems within the canopy

AIM OF PRUNING

MAKING THE CUTS

Salix *Willow*
DECIDUOUS TREES AND SHRUBS WITH UPRIGHT SHAPES
■ **Prune in early spring, as new growth begins**

Salix alba
var. vitellina
'Britzensis'

Willows are trees and shrubs of varying habits (for weeping types, see pp.372–373). Grown as trees, they are excellent for stabilizing damp ground and are often kept small by coppicing or pollarding, bearing quantities of often brightly colored stems that have great appeal in winter. Most shrubby types are grown for their early-spring catkins and stems; a few are creeping and make excellent groundcover.

Willows grown for their colorful stems, such as *S. daphnoides* and many types of *S. alba*, should be entirely cut back to a low framework in spring. For catkins, cut back only some of the stems, allowing others to mature and bear flowers. The twisted willow (*S. babylonica* var. *pekinensis* 'Tortuosa') is a multi-stemmed bush with contorted stems; cut back any straight stems. Creeping types seldom require pruning.

PLANT PROFILE

NATURAL HABIT Usually upright, sometimes creeping trees and shrubs.

HARDINESS Fully hardy.

HEIGHT AND SPREAD 25ft x 20ft (8m x 6m), depending on the type. Many are much smaller and all larger-growing types can be kept within bounds with regular pruning.

PRUNING NOTES
■ For brightly colored winter stems, prune all the growth hard annually.

■ For catkins, leave plants unpruned, or cut back only a portion of stems.

■ Renovative pruning is generally successful.

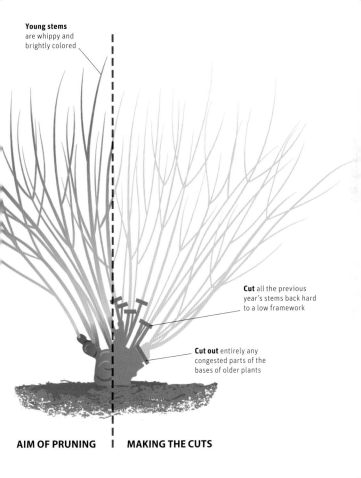

Young stems are whippy and brightly colored

Cut all the previous year's stems back hard to a low framework

Cut out entirely any congested parts of the bases of older plants

AIM OF PRUNING | **MAKING THE CUTS**

Salvia *Sage*
EVERGREEN SHRUBS
■ **Prune in spring, and as required in summer**

Salvia officinalis

Shrubby sages belong with lavenders and rosemaries in a herb or Mediterranean garden. The light purple summer flowers of *S. officinalis* and its forms are secondary to the foliage; these plants are grown for their leaves, which can be gray green (*S. officinalis*), yellow ('Aurea'), purple ('Purpurascens'), or marked with cream and purple ('Tricolor'). They are often used in cooking.

Regular harvesting of the leaves throughout the growing season generally keeps plants neat and bushy. Otherwise, shorten all the stems annually in spring, and remove any dead growth entirely.

On older plants stems become woody at the base and splay out sideways, opening up bare patches. Cut them back hard in spring to stimulate new growth. However, old plants with quantities of dead material are best replaced.

PLANT PROFILE

NATURAL HABIT Low-growing, mound-forming evergreens.

HARDINESS Mainly hardy, although some types will not survive freezing weather.

HEIGHT AND SPREAD Plants will usually grow to around 32in x 36in (80cm x 90cm), depending on the type.

PRUNING NOTES
■ Shorten new growth to keep plants bushy.

■ Harvest leaves as needed.

■ Cut back old, woody stems to the base.

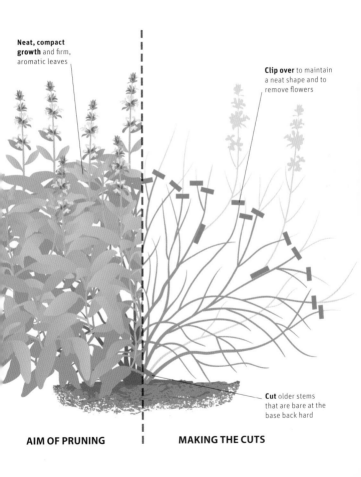

Neat, compact growth and firm, aromatic leaves

Clip over to maintain a neat shape and to remove flowers

Cut older stems that are bare at the base back hard

AIM OF PRUNING

MAKING THE CUTS

Sambucus *Elder*
DECIDUOUS SHRUBS
■ **Prune in late winter to early spring**

Sambucus nigra 'Guincho Purple'

While elders can be a pernicious weed in some gardens, cultivated forms are highly desirable, often with striking foliage that makes a splendid foil to the creamy white flowerheads that appear in late spring. In full leaf but out of flower, they are sometimes mistaken for Japanese maples. Elders naturally branch from the base, but over time can become excessively woody and oversized. Fortunately, the plants are very tolerant of pruning. In late winter to early spring, cut any thickened, older branches back to ground level. Shorten the remaining branches by up to half their length. Prune very vigorous stems only lightly, because hard pruning will stimulate further strong growth. Types with colored or lacy leaves, such as *S. nigra* 'Guincho Purple' or *S. laciniata*, can be pruned hard each year in late winter, but this will be at the expense of the flowers.

PLANT PROFILE

NATURAL HABIT Usually open, airy shrubs that become less productive near the base.

HARDINESS Fully hardy, although forms with lacy leaves benefit from protection against strong winds.

HEIGHT AND SPREAD Plants grow to around 10ft x 10ft (3m x 3m).

PRUNING NOTES
■ Each year, remove some of the oldest stems at ground level, and shorten the remainder.

■ Prune harder for improved foliage effect—this will result in the loss of the flowers.

■ Deadhead the plant after flowering to prevent it from self-seeding.

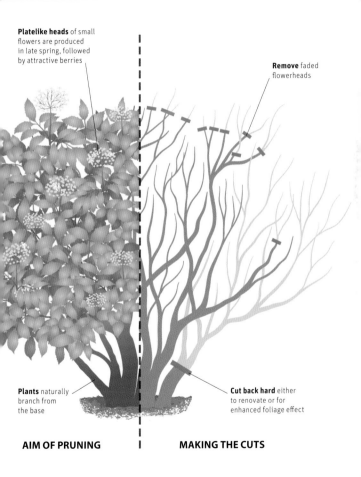

Platelike heads of small flowers are produced in late spring, followed by attractive berries

Remove faded flowerheads

Plants naturally branch from the base

Cut back hard either to renovate or for enhanced foliage effect

AIM OF PRUNING

MAKING THE CUTS

Santolina *Cotton lavender*
EVERGREEN SHRUBS
■ **Prune in spring and after flowering**

Santolina chamae-cyparissus 'Lemon Queen'

Unlike several other gray-leaf plants, cotton lavenders have attractive buttonlike summer flowers ranging from white to yellow, depending on the type. They are naturally neat plants and form low mounds—ideal for edging a sunny border or as a dwarf hedge.

Shorten all the growth in the first spring after planting to encourage a bushy habit. Thereafter, prune annually in spring, reducing the previous year's stems by up to three quarters in length. Clip lightly after flowering to deadhead and neaten. Older plants tend to splay out to reveal the bare lower portions of stems—cut back into old wood to encourage new growth from near the base. Clip low hedges three or four times in spring and summer to neaten; this will be at the loss of the flowers.

PLANT PROFILE

NATURAL HABIT Low-growing, spreading, mound-forming evergreen shrubs.

HARDINESS Mainly hardy, if grown in well-drained soil in cool climates.

HEIGHT AND SPREAD Plants grow to around 20in x 36in (50cm x 90cm); some forms are more compact.

PRUNING NOTES
■ Prune when young to promote bushiness.

■ Remove faded flowers in summer.

■ Cut back older, unproductive stems; replace individual plants that are very bare.

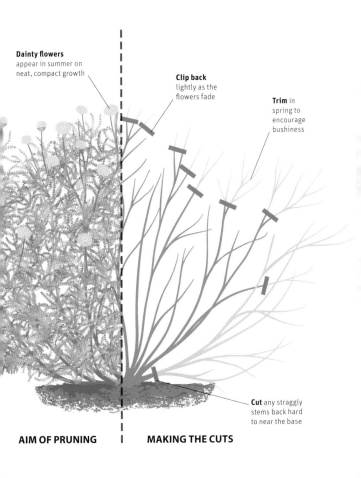

Dainty flowers appear in summer on neat, compact growth

Clip back lightly as the flowers fade

Trim in spring to encourage bushiness

Cut any straggly stems back hard to near the base

AIM OF PRUNING

MAKING THE CUTS

Sarcococca *Sweetbox*

EVERGREEN SHRUBS

■ **Prune in spring, after flowering**

These low-growing evergreens are among the few shrubs that thrive in the shade beneath deciduous trees. The scent of the small white flowers is sweet and powerful; they are borne along the stems in the depths of winter and are largely hidden by the glossy leaves. The plants bear shiny black or sometimes red berries that ripen in fall.

All sarcococcas are slow growing, and pruning can be kept to a minimum. If necessary, shorten any wayward growth in spring immediately after flowering—this will be at the loss of some of the berries. Some types can be used to create an informal hedge, while types such as *S. hookeriana* are suckering and thicket-forming, making an excellent choice for groundcover. Remove unwanted suckers from around the base of groundcover types to restrict their spread.

Sarcococca humilis

Good coverage of pointed, glossy, evergreen leaves

Powerfully scented winter flowers

AIM OF PRUNING

PLANT PROFILE

NATURAL HABIT Sometimes suckering, mainly low-growing evergreen shrubs.

HARDINESS Mainly hardy, although some are vulnerable to very low temperatures.

HEIGHT AND SPREAD Plants can grow to 3ft x 4ft (1m x 1.2m), depending on the type.

PRUNING NOTES
- Keep pruning to a minimum.
- Remove any unwanted suckers from suckering types as necessary.
- Hard pruning is unlikely to be necessary.

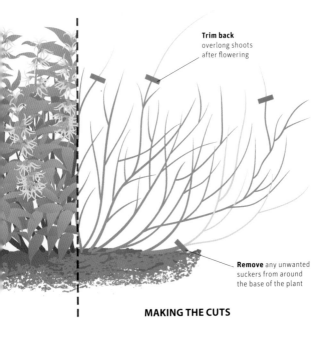

Trim back overlong shoots after flowering

Remove any unwanted suckers from around the base of the plant

MAKING THE CUTS

Skimmia

EVERGREEN SHRUBS

■ **Prune in spring, immediately after flowering**

Skimmia japonica

For long-lasting bright red winter berries skimmias rival the hollies and have the added advantage of conical heads of scented, usually white flowers in spring. Berrying skimmias are female and need a nearby male to ensure pollination, although some forms are hermaphrodite. Most are rounded, compact shrubs that develop a good shape without extensive pruning. The male type *S. japonica* 'Rubella' is weak-growing and sparsely leaved, an issue that pruning cannot rectify; it does not berry but forms large heads of pink flowerbuds in winter that are very attractive. Skimmias tolerate lime, but produce their best foliage in acid to neutral soils.

Pruning is seldom required. If necessary, shorten wayward growth in spring—this may be at the loss of some of the berries. Also remove any frost-damaged growth.

PLANT PROFILE

NATURAL HABIT Usually mound-forming, compact evergreen shrubs.

HARDINESS Fully hardy.

HEIGHT AND SPREAD 3–6ft (1–2m) in both directions, depending on the type.

PRUNING NOTES

■ Shorten growth after flowering, in spring.

■ Renovative pruning may not be successful.

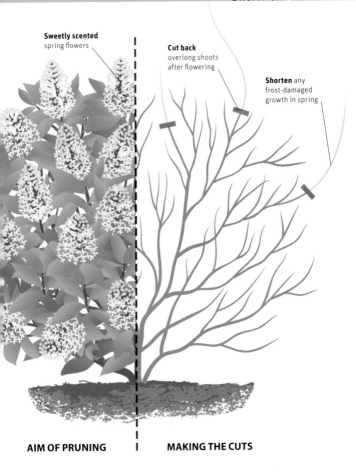

Sweetly scented spring flowers

Cut back overlong shoots after flowering

Shorten any frost-damaged growth in spring

AIM OF PRUNING

MAKING THE CUTS

Solanum *Potato vine*
EVERGREEN CLIMBERS
■ **Prune in spring and summer**

Solanum laxum 'Album'

The potato family is a varied group, including several shrubs and climbers, not all of them hardy. Most commonly grown are the hardy, evergreen climbers. They do not tolerate severe pruning, but wayward and overlong sideshoots can be shortened in spring. If you need to thin the growth, cut out the older, thicker stems, retaining the newer ones. The flexible stems lend themselves to horizontal training. Wear gloves when pruning since the sap in the stems can cause an allergic reaction.

Commonly grown examples include *S. laxum* 'Album', which produces abundant clusters of pure white flowers during summer and into fall, and the pale blue-flowered *S. crispum*. Both are fragrant and excellent for wall training. Against a low wall or fence, established plants can have the appearance of a hedge.

Scrambling branches are well-covered with leaves

AIM OF PRUNING

PLANT PROFILE

NATURAL HABIT A scrambling evergreen climber with stems that have to be tied in to their support.

HARDINESS Grow plants against a wall—they may not be hardy in the coldest areas.

HEIGHT AND SPREAD 6ft x 10ft (2m x 3m); more in warmer climates.

PRUNING NOTES

■ Prune to reduce congestion within the body of the plant.

■ Trim lightly, since plants do not tolerate severe pruning.

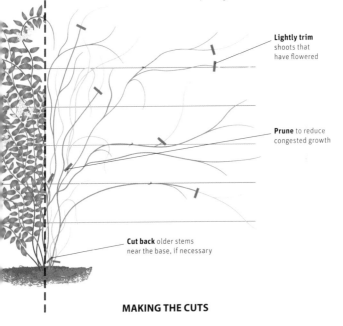

Lightly trim shoots that have flowered

Prune to reduce congested growth

Cut back older stems near the base, if necessary

MAKING THE CUTS

Sophora *Kowhai*
DECIDUOUS AND EVERGREEN TREES AND SHRUBS
■ Prune in midsummer, during warm, dry weather

Sophora japonica

Sophoras are trees and shrubs grown for their spring or summer flowers—which are produced reliably only in areas with long hot summers—and also for their attractive foliage. The trees can have a single trunk or be multi-stemmed and shrubby. One popular example, weeping *S. japonica* 'Pendula', is often spreading, developing gnarled, twisting branches that are vulnerable to wind damage. It rarely flowers but is valued for its overall appearance. A strong leader is essential for stability. Shrubs are suitable for wall training.

The plants are mainly slow growing, and pruning is best kept to a minimum. Cut stems bleed sap, so any necessary work should be carried out in midsummer during warm, dry weather. To train against a wall, tie in suitably placed stems to the support. Cut back wayward stems and any growing toward or away from the wall.

PLANT PROFILE

NATURAL HABIT Rounded to spreading, deciduous and evergreen trees and shrubs.

HARDINESS Mainly hardy, although some types show varying tolerance to frost.

HEIGHT AND SPREAD Trees grow to around 20ft x 15ft (6m x 5m). Shrubby types are smaller.

PRUNING NOTES
■ Keep pruning to a minimum, and employ an arborist if necessary.

■ Prune during warm dry periods in summer.

■ Hard pruning to renovate is likely to be successful only in warm climates.

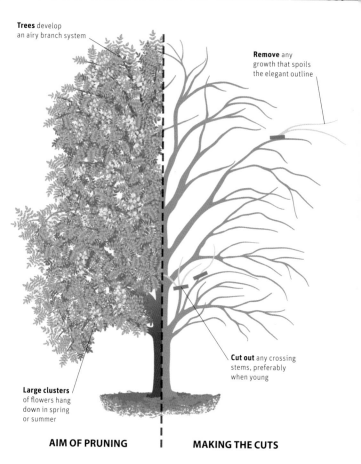

Trees develop an airy branch system

Remove any growth that spoils the elegant outline

Cut out any crossing stems, preferably when young

Large clusters of flowers hang down in spring or summer

AIM OF PRUNING

MAKING THE CUTS

Sorbus
DECIDUOUS TREES
■ **Prune in fall to winter, while dormant**

Sorbus aria 'Lutescens'

Sorbus make an excellent choice of tree for a small garden. With mainly upright-growing crowns they cast little shade and have a dual season of interest—white spring flowers are followed by white, pink, or red berries that ripen as the leaves turn yellow or red in fall and provide an excellent food source for birds over the winter. Some varieties prefer acid to neutral soil.

Most produce a good shape without any particular pruning. Cut out any damaged growth when trees are dormant between fall and winter. Any dead branches can be removed in summer, during a dry period. On very upright varieties, such as *S. aucuparia* 'Sheerwater Seedling', it is important to establish a balanced framework when young. Cut back any side branches that are too close together so that the remainder are evenly distributed around the trunk.

PLANT PROFILE

NATURAL HABIT Mainly upright to rounded, deciduous trees and shrubs.

HARDINESS Mainly fully hardy.

HEIGHT AND SPREAD To 30ft x 25ft (10m x 8m); shrubby types are smaller.

PRUNING NOTES
■ Keep pruning to a minimum.

■ Shrubby types, such as *S. vilmorinii*, usually respond well to renovative pruning.

Balanced, even canopy of well-spaced branches

Remove crossing or awkwardly placed branches

Clear the lower trunk of any unwanted side branches

AIM OF PRUNING

MAKING THE CUTS

Spiraea
DECIDUOUS SHRUBS
■ **Prune in early spring, or after flowering**

Spiraea japonica 'Anthony Waterer'

Spiraeas flower either in spring on the previous year's growth or in summer on the current year's growth. Invaluable in borders, they are planted mainly for their white, pink, yellow, or purple flowers, although some also have colored leaves. All benefit from regular pruning. Prune spring-flowering types after flowering. Cut out older, unproductive stems at the base, and remove any thin, twiggy growth. Shorten remaining stems, cutting back to strong growth buds. Spiraeas that flower in summer should be pruned in early spring. Cut any weak and older, very thick stems back to ground level. Shorten the rest to two or three buds from the base. For a larger plant, leave healthy, very vigorous stems unpruned, or trim them only slightly. Prune dwarf forms of *S. japonica* more lightly. Deadhead after flowering.

PLANT PROFILE

NATURAL HABIT Usually rounded, although sometimes arching or twiggy deciduous shrubs.

HARDINESS Mainly fully hardy, but new growth is vulnerable to frost in cold areas.

HEIGHT AND SPREAD Around 5ft x 5ft (1.5m x 1.5m), depending on the type.

PRUNING NOTES
■ Prune spring-flowering types immediately after they have flowered; prune summer-flowering types in early spring.

■ Renovative pruning is generally successful, although some may recover slowly.

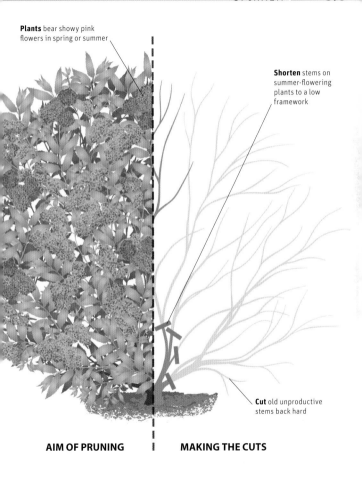

Plants bear showy pink flowers in spring or summer

Shorten stems on summer-flowering plants to a low framework

Cut old unproductive stems back hard

AIM OF PRUNING

MAKING THE CUTS

Stachyurus
DECIDUOUS SHRUBS
■ Prune in spring, immediately after flowering

Stachyurus praecox

This small group of deciduous shrubs are grown for their pale greenish yellow flowers that dangle in small clusters from bare branches in early spring. They need neutral to acidic soil. Best in light dappled shade and ideal for a woodland garden, they are suitable for wall training in areas where late frost might otherwise damage the flower buds. Types with variegated leaves are less vigorous.

Freestanding stachyurus can be grown with minimal pruning. After flowering, remove any damaged or crossing stems. To refresh older plants, cut back unproductive stems to ground level. Cut out badly placed growth on wall trained specimens. Shorten older stems as necessary, and tie in replacement shoots.

PLANT PROFILE

NATURAL HABIT Spreading deciduous shrubs with arching stems, often shooting freely from the base.

HARDINESS Fully hardy, although some shelter from cold winter winds is desirable.

HEIGHT AND SPREAD Plants grow to around 10ft x 10ft (3m x 3m).

PRUNING NOTES
■ Keep pruning to a minimum.

■ If necessary, hard pruning to renovate is usually successful.

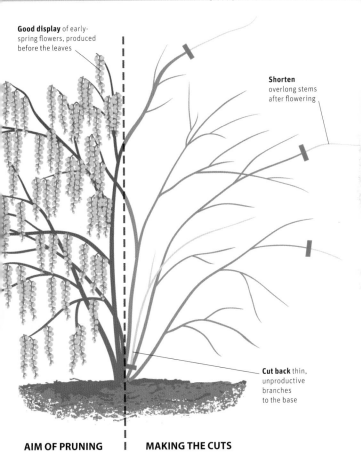

Good display of early-spring flowers, produced before the leaves

Shorten overlong stems after flowering

Cut back thin, unproductive branches to the base

AIM OF PRUNING | MAKING THE CUTS

Styrax
DECIDUOUS OR EVERGREEN TREES AND SHRUBS
■ **Prune between fall and spring**

Styrax japonicus

These dainty trees and shrubs can be deciduous or evergreen. They bear clusters of scented, bell-like, white or pink flowers in summer, and deciduous types often have good fall leaf color. They make delightful specimens in a spot sheltered from cold winter winds but must have neutral to acidic soil. Remember that plants can be slow to establish and may not flower until some years after planting.

Plants have varied shapes: *S. americanus* develops a spreading, open crown; *S. japonicus* has fanlike branches; others can be more upright. All dislike pruning, so keep it to the absolute minimum. Any necessary work to remove damaged or wayward branches should take place during the dormant period between fall and early spring. Avoid cutting too hard—any whippy new stems will be vulnerable to frost damage.

PLANT PROFILE

NATURAL HABIT Rounded to upright or spreading, deciduous or evergreen trees and shrubs.

HARDINESS Mainly hardy. Young plants may be vulnerable to frost damage.

HEIGHT AND SPREAD 25ft x 18ft (8m x 6m) or less, depending on the type grown.

PRUNING NOTES
■ Pruning should be kept to a minimum.

■ Renovative pruning is not recommended.

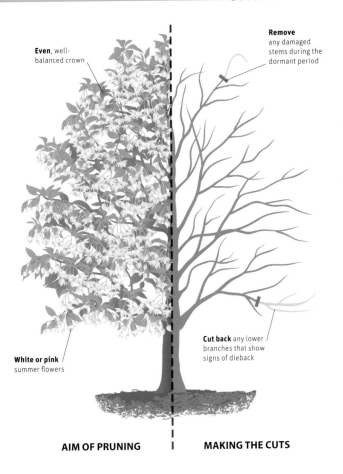

Even, well-balanced crown

White or pink summer flowers

Remove any damaged stems during the dormant period

Cut back any lower branches that show signs of dieback

AIM OF PRUNING

MAKING THE CUTS

Syringa *Lilac*
DECIDUOUS SHRUBS
■ **Prune immediately after flowering**

Syringa vulgaris 'Madame Lemoine'

Delicate lilac flowers carry the defining scent of late spring. They are deciduous shrubs and can become large and treelike as they mature. Lilacs are generally of good vaselike shape but have a tendency to develop several thick stems that may become bare at the base.

The plants flower on the previous year's wood, so perform any general pruning after flowering has finished. Deadhead carefully since they flower so late in spring that the following year's flowering shoots will already be forming. More extensive pruning involves removing the following year's flowers, so this should not be an annual practice. Renovate plants in stages over several years, or cut neglected specimens back hard to a low framework of stems all at once. They recover well but will probably not flower again for at least three years.

PLANT PROFILE

NATURAL HABIT Open, vaselike shrubs or small trees. Mature specimens will become bare at the base of their stems.

HARDINESS Fully hardy.

HEIGHT AND SPREAD Plants grow to around 10ft (3m) tall, with a narrower spread.

PRUNING NOTES
■ Prune carefully after flowering, removing congested and damaged growth.

■ Deadhead plants carefully so as not to remove the following year's flowering shoots.

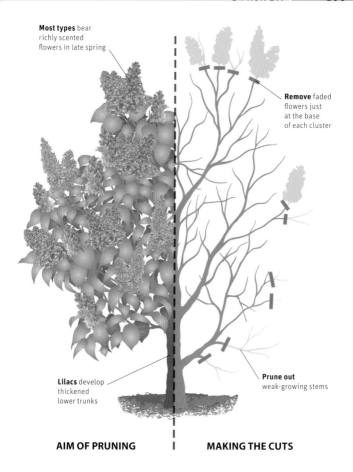

Most types bear richly scented flowers in late spring

Remove faded flowers just at the base of each cluster

Lilacs develop thickened lower trunks

Prune out weak-growing stems

AIM OF PRUNING

MAKING THE CUTS

Tamarix *Tamarisk*
DECIDUOUS SHRUBS
■ **Prune in spring, or after flowering**

Tamarix ramosissima

Often recommended for coastal gardens, tamarisks are airy, mainly deciduous shrubs that bear plumes of pink flowers in mid- to late spring or late summer to fall, depending on the type grown. They are occasionally treelike, and some can also be used to create an informal, billowing hedge. All respond well to regular pruning.

To encourage young plants to become bushy, shorten all the growth immediately after planting, then again the following spring. Once established, prune early-flowering types immediately after flowering. Cut back flowered shoots to strong buds, and take out older stems at the base. On late-flowering plants, cut back all the stems to a low framework in early spring. Trim hedges and treelike specimens at the time of year appropriate to the flowering season to keep them to size and shape.

PLANT PROFILE

NATURAL HABIT Usually upright to spreading deciduous shrubs with whippy, sometimes arching branches.

HARDINESS Plants are fully hardy and very tolerant of wind.

HEIGHT AND SPREAD Plants can grow to around 10–15ft (3–5m) in both directions.

PRUNING NOTES
■ Pruning time depends on the type grown.

■ Prune young plants to create bushiness, or leave unpruned to develop a treelike habit.

■ Renovative pruning is often successful, but plants may not flower again for a few years.

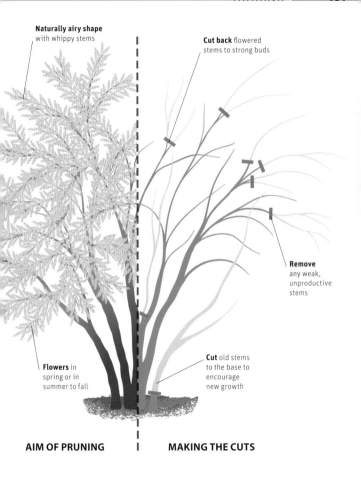

Naturally airy shape with whippy stems

Cut back flowered stems to strong buds

Remove any weak, unproductive stems

Flowers in spring or in summer to fall

Cut old stems to the base to encourage new growth

AIM OF PRUNING

MAKING THE CUTS

Taxus *Yew*
EVERGREEN TREES AND SHRUBS
■ **Prune in spring and summer to restrict size**

Taxus baccata 'Fastigiata'

Yew is the classic choice for evergreen hedging and large topiary. To shape and keep the plants within bounds, clip them at least twice during the year, in mid-spring and late summer. For a really sharp appearance, cut twice more within that period. If you are growing yew as a tall hedge, it should be pruned to slope outward slightly at the base—otherwise the lower part may die back if the upper portion of the hedge casts it into shade.

Unpruned plants have a feathery outline when young, developing as trees with a single trunk and an impressive crown as they age. The Irish yew (*T. baccata* 'Fastigiata') is a noble upright, whose pillarlike form can be enhanced by running wires around the plant. Yew is one of the few conifers that responds well to regular pruning.

PLANT PROFILE

NATURAL HABIT Potentially large trees, often with a spreading crown.

HARDINESS Fully hardy.

HEIGHT AND SPREAD Unpruned, 30ft (10m) or more. With regular pruning, plants can be kept within 10ft (3m).

PRUNING NOTES
■ To keep within bounds, prune at least twice a year during the growing season.

■ Plants respond well to hard pruning, even when cut back to old, bare wood.

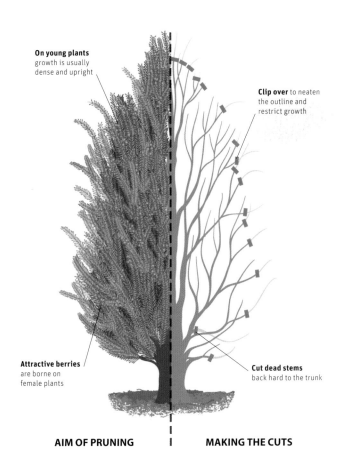

On young plants growth is usually dense and upright

Clip over to neaten the outline and restrict growth

Attractive berries are borne on female plants

Cut dead stems back hard to the trunk

AIM OF PRUNING

MAKING THE CUTS

Tilia *Linden*
DECIDUOUS TREES
■ **Prune in midsummer; coppice or pollard in late winter**

Tilia x europaea

Lindens are often found lining the driveways of stately homes. Long-lived, they make excellent shade trees with the advantage of sweetly scented, although inconspicuous, summer flowers. To reduce the size and create an attractive feature, some can be pleached, coppiced, or pollarded, although this will be at the loss of the flowers. Selected forms of *T. platyphyllos* can have red or yellow young stems that can be a strong feature when bare in winter.

The trees are naturally shapely and require minimal pruning. Any necessary work should be done from midsummer onward, since lindens bleed sap if pruned in spring. Cut back stems of pollarded and coppiced trees in late winter. Pollarded limes are prone to produce suckers around the base; cut these back to the ground with pruners. Remove unwanted shoots on the trunk promptly.

PLANT PROFILE

NATURAL HABIT Elegant, potentially large, sometimes slow-growing trees with upright to rounded crowns.

HARDINESS Fully hardy.

HEIGHT AND SPREAD 70ft x 45ft (20m x 15m), or less, depending on the type grown. Pollarded trees will be smaller.

PRUNING NOTES
■ Prune only as necessary during warm dry periods in summer with pruners.

■ Remove suckers from around the base of trees and from the trunks.

■ Consider employing an arborist for large specimens in need of pruning.

Trees are naturally shapely with a rounded crown

Remove lower branches to produce a clear trunk

Cut back any suckers around the base of the tree

AIM OF PRUNING

MAKING THE CUTS

Trachelospermum *Jasmine*
EVERGREEN CLIMBERS
■ **Prune in spring, when plants are in full growth**

Trachelospermum jasminoides

Producing one of the most potent scents in the garden, these evergreen climbers benefit from a sheltered spot in cold areas. The small white flowers are produced over a long period in summer and into early fall. As a response to a drop in temperature the leaves redden in winter. The stems climb by twining so require a system of wires or canes if the plant is to cover a wall or fence.

Guide the stems of young plants into their support, fanning them out as they grow. Plants are naturally dense and well-covered with leaves, and no regular pruning is needed. If any stems twine around each other and become congested, cut back the older ones in spring. Shorten any stems that exceed the allotted space. Shoots that grow outward away from the support are usually flexible enough to be trained in to fill any gaps in the coverage.

PLANT PROFILE

NATURAL HABIT Woody, evergreen climbers with twining stems.

HARDINESS The plants are hardy, although they need the protection of a warm wall in frost-prone districts.

HEIGHT AND SPREAD Plants grow to around 15ft x 10ft (5m x 3m).

PRUNING NOTES
■ No regular pruning is required.

■ Thin stems in spring if necessary.

■ To renovate, shorten only a portion of stems in the first year; prune the remainder in the following year, if recovery is good.

Small, sweetly fragrant flowers produced over a long period

Good coverage of green leaves that often turn reddish in winter

Remove or shorten any excessive growth

AIM OF PRUNING

MAKING THE CUTS

Ulex *Gorse*
EVERGREEN SHRUBS
■ Prune in spring; prune hedges in summer

Ulex europaeus

Tough, hardy, and tolerant of wind, gorse makes an excellent choice for hedging in coastal areas and can also be an attractive addition to a border. These shrubs have green, spiny stems, and their dense habit of growth makes them appear evergreen, though in fact they are virtually leafless. The honey-scented yellow flowers appear mainly in spring but can also be produced at other times of the year.

Plants tend to become straggly and benefit from pruning to keep them neat. Shorten all the stems immediately after planting to encourage bushiness. Thereafter, clip them over in late spring, after flowering—this will also prevent unwanted seed formation. For a dense hedge, trim over again in summer; this may be at the loss of late flowers. Wear gloves when pruning to protect against the spiky stems.

PLANT PROFILE

NATURAL HABIT Tough, dense evergreen shrubs with spiny stems.

HARDINESS Fully hardy and very tolerant of exposed locations.

HEIGHT AND SPREAD Plants can grow to around 5–8ft (1.2–2.2m) in both directions; less with regular pruning.

PRUNING NOTES
■ Clip over the plants as necessary in spring and summer.

■ Cut back old, leggy plants to within 6in (15cm) of the ground to renovate.

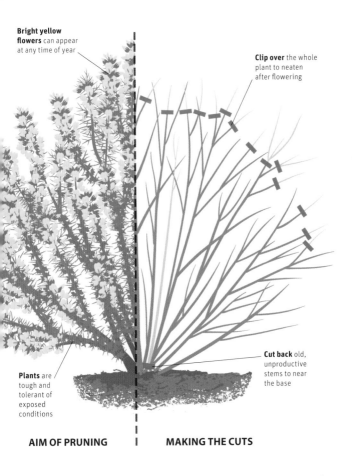

Bright yellow flowers can appear at any time of year

Clip over the whole plant to neaten after flowering

Plants are tough and tolerant of exposed conditions

Cut back old, unproductive stems to near the base

AIM OF PRUNING

MAKING THE CUTS

Ulmus *Elm*

DECIDUOUS TREES

■ **Prune in fall to winter**

Ulmus glabra 'Camperdownii'

Before the ravages of Dutch elm disease in the 20th century, elms were widely planted as street trees and in public parks. Happily, several modern varieties show resistance to the problem, although they are not immune. Most become long-lived, stately trees, but some are more shrubby or upright and suitable for small gardens or as hedging. *U. glabra* 'Camperdownii' is weeping.

Freestanding trees need little pruning. Any work should be done in fall to winter. Narrowly upright varieties can be trimmed to reduce the spread and accentuate the outline. Clip over hedging plants two or three times a year to keep the growth dense. Thin congested stems of *U. glabra* 'Camperdownii' during winter to balance the canopy. To extend the spread, shorten strong stems back to upward-facing buds. New shoots will grow upward initially, then arch over.

PLANT PROFILE

NATURAL HABIT Stately, usually deciduous trees with rounded to spreading, occasionally upright crowns.

HARDINESS Fully hardy.

HEIGHT AND SPREAD 30ft x 20ft (10m x 6m). Mature specimens of some types may be bigger; some are much smaller.

PRUNING NOTES

■ Keep pruning to a minimum; employ a tree surgeon if necessary.

■ Prune to accentuate the form of upright varieties such as the yellow-leaf *U. x hollandica* 'Dampieri Aurea'.

■ Clip over hedges in spring and summer.

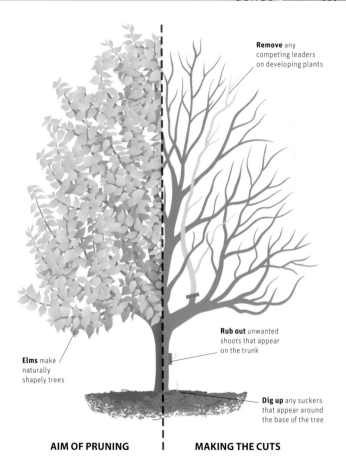

Remove any competing leaders on developing plants

Rub out unwanted shoots that appear on the trunk

Dig up any suckers that appear around the base of the tree

Elms make naturally shapely trees

AIM OF PRUNING

MAKING THE CUTS

Viburnum
DECIDUOUS SHRUBS
■ **Prune in spring, immediately after flowering**

Viburnum x
bodnantense
'Dawn'

Deciduous viburnums are mainly spring flowering, with heads of white or pink flowers that are sometimes fragrant. There are many commonly grown varieties: *V. opulus* has bright red fall berries and is often used as a component of a wildlife hedge; *V.* x *bodnantense* is a group of hybrids that produce clusters of scented flowers in shades of pink in the depths of winter; *V. plicatum* has a very distinctive look, with main stems held in horizontal tiers.

Allow young plants to grow without pruning in the early years. Once established, prune after flowering to remove older or damaged growth as necessary. On *V. plicatum*, cut back to their point of origin any strongly upright-growing stems that spoil the outline. This species can also be wall-trained. Prune *V. opulus* with care to avoid losing too many of the fall fruit.

PLANT PROFILE

NATURAL HABIT Upright to rounded or spreading shrubs, sometimes with a horizontally tiered shape.

HARDINESS Fully hardy.

HEIGHT AND SPREAD Plants grow to around 6ft x 6ft (2m x 2m) in either direction, depending on the type grown.

PRUNING NOTES
■ Prune only when necessary, once the plants are established, removing any stems that spoil the outline.

■ Most can be pruned hard to renovate, though may not respond well.

■ For evergreen viburnums see pp.414–415.

Fragrant flowers in winter or spring

Remove awkwardly placed stems within the body of the plant

A vase-shaped habit is typical of *V. x bodnantense*

Cut out old and weak stems at the base

AIM OF PRUNING

MAKING THE CUTS

Viburnum
EVERGREEN SHRUBS
■ **Prune in spring, after flowering**

Viburnum tinus

Evergreen viburnums are valuable shrubs with a number of uses. *V. x burkwoodii* makes a handsome specimen with fragrant white flowers in spring. *V. tinus* is tough and suitable for hedging; its white flowers are produced in winter and occasionally at other times. *V. davidii* is low-growing and spreading, making excellent groundcover. It has handsome, pleated leaves, and its small spring flowers are succeeded by metallic blue berries, but only where plants of both sexes are grown.

Types of *V. x burkwoodii* are naturally shapely, and any necessary pruning can be done after flowering. *V. tinus* can be trimmed to shape at intervals during the growing season or grown more informally with minimal pruning in early summer. Cut back wayward stems on *V. davidii* in spring. Deadhead male plants since these will not form berries.

PLANT PROFILE

NATURAL HABIT Upright to dome-shaped, spreading, or low-growing evergreens.

HARDINESS Mainly fully hardy, though a hard frost may scorch the leaves.

HEIGHT AND SPREAD Plants grow to around 10ft x 6ft (3m x 2m); some are more spreading or low growing.

PRUNING NOTES

■ Most shrubs need minimal pruning.

■ Clip hedges twice in spring–summer.

■ To renovate, cut all stems back to a low framework in early spring.

■ For deciduous viburnums, see pp.412–413.

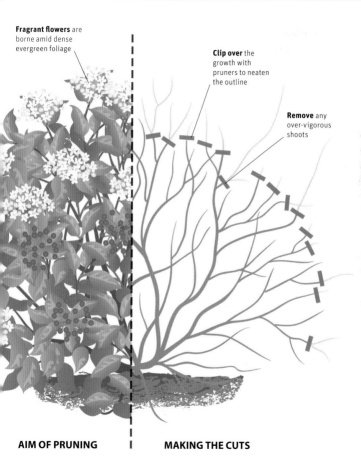

Fragrant flowers are borne amid dense evergreen foliage

Clip over the growth with pruners to neaten the outline

Remove any over-vigorous shoots

AIM OF PRUNING

MAKING THE CUTS

Vinca *Periwinkle*

EVERGREEN SHRUBS

■ **Prune from spring onward**

Vinca difformis

Periwinkles are very versatile plants: they can provide useful groundcover in shady areas, but their trailing style also makes them ideal for softening the edges of large containers. The flowers, which are never produced in abundance, are white, "periwinkle" blue, or purple. There are large-leaf and small-leaf species, both with less vigorous variegated forms.

The stems root freely where they touch the ground and will rapidly form dense evergreen mats. You can encourage young plants to spread by pinning down the stems, which are flexible enough to bend down to ground level. Plants used to cover large patches of ground can be clipped over with shears. On small plants, thin the stems as necessary in spring to reduce congestion and to keep them within bounds.

Flowers are produced most profusely in summer

Stems have a trailing habit

AIM OF PRUNING

PLANT PROFILE

NATURAL HABIT Low-growing, soft-stemmed evergreen shrubs with a tendency to creep and form groundcover.

HARDINESS Mainly fully hardy.

HEIGHT AND SPREAD 18in x 18in (45cm x 45cm); less with frequent clipping.

PRUNING NOTES
- Plants respond well to being clipped over at virtually any time during the growing season.
- Prune out congested stems in spring.

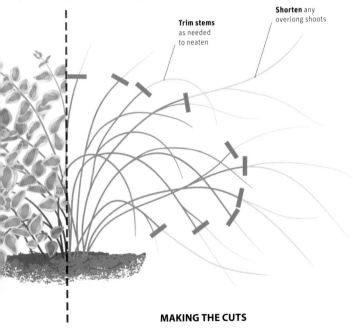

Shorten any overlong shoots

Trim stems as needed to neaten

MAKING THE CUTS

Vitis *Grape*
DECIDUOUS CLIMBERS
■ **Prune by midwinter, while plants are fully dormant**

Vitis coignetiae

Apart from the types grown for their grapes, there are several vines of purely ornamental value with stunning fall leaf color. They are often planted to cover archways and pergolas to create shade in the summer. Once established, these vigorous climbers need annual pruning to keep them within bounds. They climb using tendrils, so are best supported on a system of wires.

Most pruning should be done by midwinter to prevent the cuts from bleeding sap. Use two or three of the strongest new stems to start the framework—tie them in horizontally against a wall or fence, or spiral them around the upright of a pergola. Remove the growing tip of young plants to encourage branching. Once established, shorten the sideshoots back to two or three buds. These will thicken in time to become spurs. If plants get out of hand, clip back during a dry spell in midsummer.

Large leaves
color well in fall

AIM OF PRUNING

PLANT PROFILE

NATURAL HABIT Very vigorous deciduous tendril climbers.

HARDINESS Fully hardy.

HEIGHT AND SPREAD Plants grow to around 30ft x 20ft (10m x 6m), although they can be kept smaller with regular pruning.

PRUNING NOTES

■ Prune when plants are dormant, by midwinter, to prevent the sap from bleeding.

■ Reduce new growth in summer, as needed.

■ To renovate, cut back all stems to near ground level. Recovery is usually good.

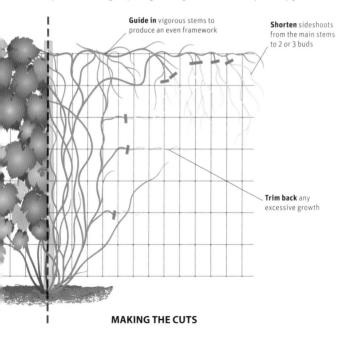

Guide in vigorous stems to produce an even framework

Shorten sideshoots from the main stems to 2 or 3 buds

Trim back any excessive growth

MAKING THE CUTS

Weigela
DECIDUOUS SHRUBS
■ **Prune in early summer, immediately after flowering**

Weigela florida

These popular deciduous shrubs have an upright to arching shape but can appear rather shapeless, especially if they are shaded by other plants. The trumpetlike flowers open in late spring, usually in shades of white, pink, or ruby red, although some species, such as *W. middendorffiana*, have pale yellow blooms. Some varieties are grown for their foliage, which can be ruby red, yellow, or boldly variegated with white, cream, or yellow.

Prune after flowering, and shorten stems that have flowered by up to one-third. Cut back overlong or badly placed shoots to their point of origin—to the base of the plant, if necessary. If they are congested, thin stems in the body of the plant, retaining the younger ones. Varieties grown for their foliage can be cut back harder, which will result in a fresh crop of leaves.

PLANT PROFILE

NATURAL HABIT Upright to spreading shrubs that can become unruly.

HARDINESS Fully hardy.

HEIGHT AND SPREAD About 5ft x 5ft (1.5m x 1.5m), depending on the species.

PRUNING NOTES
■ The aim is always to improve next year's flowering and neaten the shape. This is achieved by cutting out older stems entirely and shortening flowered stems.

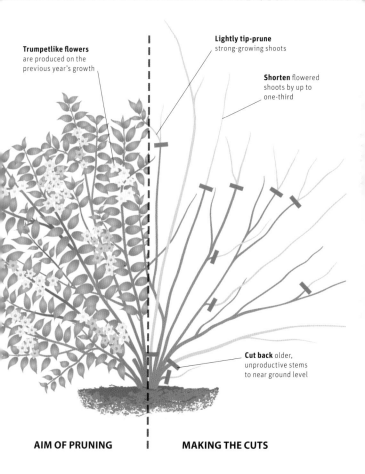

Trumpetlike flowers are produced on the previous year's growth

Lightly tip-prune strong-growing shoots

Shorten flowered shoots by up to one-third

Cut back older, unproductive stems to near ground level

AIM OF PRUNING

MAKING THE CUTS

Wisteria
DECIDUOUS CLIMBERS
■ **Prune in late summer and again in late winter**

Wisteria floribunda

Wisterias are long-lived climbers that have a late spring display of beautiful pendulous flowers in dark or pale shades of purple, or white. The plants are fully hardy, but for prolific flowering in cold areas they are best trained against a warm wall. They can also be trained over arches or pergolas or grown through trees.

The plants are naturally very vigorous, and annual pruning diverts their energy from new stem production into flowering. For a curtain of flowers, develop a framework of strong horizontal branches from which the blooms will dangle from stubby sideshoots. Between spring and summer, tie in vigorous stems as they grow. In late summer, shorten any that have outgrown their space. Also shorten whippy sideshoots to five or six leaves to encourage the shoot to thicken. Shorten these again in late winter, usually to two or three buds.

PLANT PROFILE

NATURAL HABIT Extremely vigorous, long-lived, twining climbers.

HARDINESS Fully hardy, but plants need a warm situation in cold areas to flower reliably.

HEIGHT AND SPREAD Plants grow to around 30ft x 20ft (10m x 6m). The spread of wall-trained plants can exceed the height.

PRUNING NOTES

■ For the best flowering, prune twice a year.

■ Lower portions become treelike with age. If necessary, renovate in stages, cutting back only some of the stems in the first year.

■ Remove any thin shoots that appear near the base of the plant.

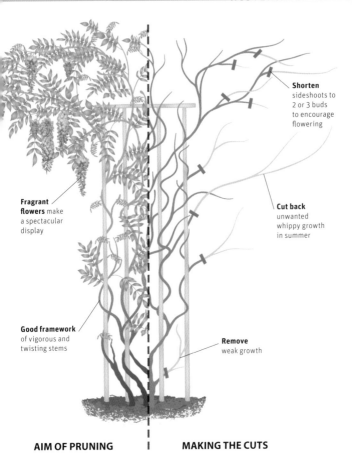

Shorten sideshoots to 2 or 3 buds to encourage flowering

Fragrant flowers make a spectacular display

Cut back unwanted whippy growth in summer

Good framework of vigorous and twisting stems

Remove weak growth

AIM OF PRUNING

MAKING THE CUTS

PRUNING
Fruit trees and soft fruit

Why fruit is different

Fruit trees and bushes generally need a stricter pruning regime than the ornamental plants gardeners value exclusively for their flowers because they are also expected to produce an edible crop. But the extra attention is worth it—few things compare to the taste of fruit picked fresh from the plant, still warm from the heat of the sun.

THE IMPORTANCE OF PRUNING

Most fruiting plants are hybrids bred to produce abundant crops of large, tasty fruits, and many are sold grafted onto dwarfing rootstocks to create smaller, neat-growing plants. Unlike ornamentals, which often perform well without pruning, nearly all tree and bush fruits benefit from attention at least once a year, and often at other times as well.

Correct pruning not only maximizes the crop and ensures fruit will be at a suitable height for picking, but also helps you plan your plot. Regular pruning keeps plants within strict boundaries and enables you to predict almost exactly how much room a mature plant will require. When planting in tight rows this allows you to calculate how many different fruits—or varieties of a single fruit—you can fit into your space.

Some fruits can be grown with minimal pruning. Medlars (*Mespilus germanica*), quinces (*Cydonia oblonga*), and crabapples (*Malus*) all make attractive additions to orchards. Mulberries (*Morus nigra*) and nut trees such as walnuts (*Juglans regia*) and chestnuts (*Castanea sativa*) are generally allowed to grow as large ornamentals—their crop is incidental.

FRUIT IN THE GARDEN

Strictly trained fruit trees have a beauty of their own; they complement ornamental plants that are grown alongside and add structure to the garden. As espaliers on a system of posts and wires, apples may be used as a screen to separate different areas; as step-overs you can create an interesting substitute for a low boxwood hedge.

Small fruit trees and bushes are suitable for containers but generally will not crop as freely as plants in the open ground. Figs are the exception—restricting the roots diverts the plant's energies into fruiting.

Blueberries are produced on one of the most attractive fruiting plants. A whitish bloom on the fruit indicates that they are nearly ready for harvesting.

Common fruit forms

It is possible to train fruit trees and bushes into almost any shape, but a number of forms have been developed to suit different situations and meet the need for compact plants. In general the aim is to exploit the plant's natural habit and encourage reliable crops in a relatively small patch of ground. If you are planting fruit in rows, keep in mind the ultimate width of each plant when judging planting distances and how much space to leave between rows. Most fruit trees and bushes can be bought ready-trained and usually flower and fruit in the first year after planting. It can be very rewarding to train your own, but you should not expect the plants to crop until the third year.

Standard and semi-dwarf trees have a spreading crown and a clear trunk—for standards this is usually around 6ft (2m); on semi-dwarfs, 4ft (1.2m). It can be difficult to gather fruit from the topmost branches.

Pyramids are dainty trees with a strong central leader. The tapered shape ensures fruits at the base are exposed to the sun and ripen evenly. Staking is necessary. Pears and plums are commonly trained this way.

Espaliers have side branches that are trained strictly horizontally, either against a wall or on wires stretched between posts. They are decorative and highly productive but need regular, careful pruning. Freestanding espaliers make effective screens.

Fans are also trained using a system of horizontal wires. This method is particularly suitable for fruits that are not commonly grown on dwarfing rootstocks—such as peaches and apricots—as well as those that benefit from wall protection in cold areas.

Cordons are vigorous uprights that have been trained at an angle; they are suitable for many varieties of apples and pears. Ideal where space is limited, cordons are grown on wires, either against a wall or freestanding.

Step-overs are a variation of cordons and may be used to create low edging to beds in kitchen gardens, making the maximum use of a limited space. They are suitable for apples on a dwarfing rootstock.

Raspberry canes are suckering plants that produce new upright stems from below ground each year. Pruning is a matter of annual renewal: older stems are removed to make way for the new. The timing of pruning depends on when the plant bears its crop.

Blackberry canes are very vigorous plants with a naturally arching habit. Training on wires keeps plants from becoming congested —and the berries difficult to harvest—and stops the tips from touching the ground, where they would root to form new plants.

Bushes are an excellent form for any garden, especially where a number of fruit trees have to be accommodated. Bushes are grown on dwarfing rootstocks and have a short trunk, 3ft (1m) or less, making harvesting easy. Compact types may be grown in containers.

Multi-stemmed bushes are a form used for many soft fruit bushes such as black currants, most of which regularly produce new growth from near the ground. Some are also grown on a short leg or trunk, about 4in (10cm) high.

Basic techniques

Unless you buy them ready trained, fruit trees will need formative pruning when planting, as will nearly all fruit bushes. This is generally at the cost of fruit formation during the first season or two but greatly increases productivity in subsequent years.

ESTABLISHING FRUITING PLANTS

Plants are available in containers or as bare-root plants when dormant. Trees are sold either as "whips" (see p.24) or with a branching crown on an established trunk. Lightly prune the roots before planting to ensure good root development, and shorten broken stems in the top growth.

Plant bare raspberry canes in rows in well-prepared, weed-free soil. Keep them well watered when new leafy growth emerges in spring, then cut back the old canes to the ground (below, left to right).

FORMATIVE PRUNING

Nearly all fruit trees need pruning at first to encourage a balanced, branching framework of fruiting stems. Ideally stems will be sturdy enough to bear the crops without dragging on the ground, fruits will have even exposure to light and warmth, and there will be free movement of air within the body of the plant to reduce the risk of mildew or airborne fungal diseases.

Leave soft fruits unpruned to establish. For compact plants, reduce the number of stems in the first winter and shorten the rest.

Stake young fruit trees, and attach them with a rubber tie that can be loosened as the trunk thickens. For a tree with a framework of side branches, the stake should reach to just beneath the crown.

Fruit trees will need staking. Many are sold as maiden whips with a single upright stem and a scattering of sideshoots. To train as a standard or half-standard, leave the main stem unpruned until it reaches just beyond the desired height, then shorten it. Three years after planting, start to clear the trunk of lower branches.

For a pyramid, in the first winter after planting cut the main stem to 20–30in (50–75cm). Develop lower branches first, cutting them back to outward-facing buds on the undersides to encourage sideways growth. As the tree grows, tie in a replacement leader to the stake (see p.24). Prune suitably placed upper side branches in the same way as the lowest tier.

To train into a bush, reduce the height of the leader to around 3ft (1m) to encourage branching. In winter, select the strongest side branches as the framework; cut back the rest. Shorten branches to outward-facing buds to develop an open center.

DEVELOPING SPURS

Many fruit trees and bushes produce their best crops if sideshoots from the main branches are regularly pruned to produce "spurs." This keeps the plant compact and diverts its energies into producing flowers and fruit instead of leafy growth. It also improves the stability of the plant—the fruit is carried on thicker branches that are less likely to bend or snap under their weight. Shorten sideshoots from the main branches in winter—see individual crops for detailed advice. If spur systems become congested, cut out older parts in winter.

It is often beneficial to thin fruit as they develop, resulting in a smaller crop, but giving larger fruit of better quality. Unthinned, fruit can rub against one another, ripen unevenly, and rot if crowded. In early summer, remove two or more fruit in each cluster to give the rest room to grow. Many apple and pear trees shed a portion of fruit naturally in summer.

MAINTAINING FRUITING PLANTS

Keep a look out for any dead, diseased, or damaged growth, and remove it promptly, cutting back to healthy buds or into bare wood in winter if necessary. On grafted plants, cut back suckers from the rootstock that appear around the base of the plant. In winter or early spring, cut out old stems that did not fruit well the previous year, back to the ground if necessary. This may result in the loss of some of the next year's crop, but replacement growth stimulated by pruning will fruit the year after that.

Old soft fruit bushes and grapevines that are not performing well often gain a new lease on life after hard pruning to renovate.

In late winter to early spring: cut down all stems to within 4in (10cm) of the ground. If the bush has a short trunk, cut the framework branches back to 4in (10cm) from the trunk. Thereafter prune as for a new plant to re-establish the shape. Flowering and fruiting usually resumes after a couple of years. If the plant does not recover well, replace it.

Trees are more difficult to renovate. Thick branches can be removed entirely or shortened, but this usually results in quantities of whippy upright stems that are generally not fruit bearing. These should be cut back at an early stage. Old, unproductive trees are best replaced.

Pruning to develop spurs greatly increases the plant's fruiting potential, encouraging high yields in a limited space. For the best crops, thin the young fruit as they develop.

Cut back older, unproductive stems right to the base in winter. The younger, vigorous replacement stems will be more productive, and should fruit the following year.

Training fruit on wires

The aim of training on a system of horizontal wires is to encourage the production of side branches, which flower and fruit more prolifically than upright stems. Training also supports plants and keeps them within a height of 6ft (2m), making harvesting much easier. This system is useful if you do not have a lot of space. Plants that are trained against a warm wall will also receive some protection from frost.

TRAINING TREES AND BUSHES

Create your support system before planting. Choose an appropriate gauge of rust-proof wire that is sturdy enough to bear the weight of the stems. Against a wall, stretch wires horizontally between vine eyes that are either drilled or hammered into the mortar. These should

Tie young flexible stems into the wires as they grow; the aim is to produce a well-spaced and balanced spread of well-ventilated branches.

hold the wires around 6in (15cm) away from the wall—the gap between the wires and the wall allows for good air circulation around the branches, reducing the risk of fungal diseases. The wires should be spaced 12–18in (30–45cm) apart.

To train freestanding plants, run wires between sturdy posts firmly anchored into the ground about 6ft (2m) apart. Thread wires through holes drilled in the posts, or pin them, stretching them as tight as possible. Attach growing stems loosely with raffia, twine, or rubber-coated wire.

ESPALIERS, FANS, AND CORDONS

To create espaliers and fans, stems need to be trained progressively while they are growing and still flexible; for cordons you will need to establish the desired angle when planting.

Train an espalier from a whip. The first winter after planting, cut this back to a strong bud just above the lowest wire.

Of the new shoots that appear in spring, select the strongest as the leader, and tie it to an upright cane lashed to the wires. Select two strong side branches, and attach them to canes tied diagonally across the wires. In winter, pull these branches down to the horizontal, and tie in to the lowest wire. Shorten the leader to just above the second wire up. Subsequent tiers are formed in the same way.

For a fan, choose a young plant with several strong side branches. On planting, cut all of these back apart from two that are suitably placed for training diagonally. Tie these to canes lashed diagonally to the

The tiers of this espaliered apple tree were developed over a four-year period. Once established, fruiting is prolific.

wires. Shorten the leader to just above the upper "arm." As strong shoots emerge from the arms, tie them to the wires, aiming for even coverage on both sides.

For a cordon, select a young tree with a flexible main stem that has well-spaced side branches along its whole length. Tie a cane to the stem, then attach this to the wires at an angle—the more oblique the angle, the better the fruiting potential. Shorten longer sideshoots if necessary to encourage them to form spurs.

MAINTAINING FRUIT ON WIRES

Regular pruning is needed throughout the year to keep trained plants healthy and productive, and within their allotted space. Once the uppermost tier has been created on espaliers, cut back new growth on the central leader and all the main side branches to one bud each year in late spring or summer. On fans, shorten overlong growth on the main arms in the same way. For cordons, when the main stem has reached the top wire, cut it back to a weak shoot just below the wire to discourage excessive growth.

On all trained plants, trim back new growth in summer to maintain the form and expose the ripening fruits to the sun.

Shorten any overlong shoots that are unsuitable for training in. On wall-trained plants, cut back shoots growing toward the wall as well as any others that are awkwardly placed. After harvesting the fruit, shorten the stems that carried them to one or two leaves from the base. On fans, tie in suitably placed new shoots for flowering and fruiting next year.

Winter is a good time to assess the structure of your plants. On fans, cut out any congested stems. Thin older, congested spurs on both espaliers and fans. Cut out thickened, older stems that are no longer fruiting well. Train in suitably placed vigorous stems as replacements during the next growing season.

Remove outward-growing shoots and any others that are awkwardly placed, cutting back to two leaves from the base.

Thin apple fruitlets as they develop to prevent them from becoming overcrowded and to encourage the largest possible fruit.

TRAINING SOFT FRUIT

Some soft fruit—such as currants and gooseberries—is suitable for fan training, but most fruit bushes are grown in rows as freestanding shrubs. Vigorous, sprawling raspberries and blackberries however, are regularly grown on system of posts and wires to keep their stems off the ground and to promote good ventilation.

Create a support by driving sturdy uprights into the ground every 3–6ft (1–2m) and stretching wires between them at intervals of 4–6in (10–15cm). For fall-fruiting raspberries, which fruit on newly produced stems, simply attach these stems to the wires in a loose fan as they grow.

Summer-fruiting raspberries and blackberries fruit on stems produced the previous year. On raspberries, tie in new stems loosely as they grow, making sure they do not crowd the older stems that are carrying the crop. Blackberries are usually more vigorous. Depending on their flexibility, either arch the stems over, or weave them into the wires the first year after planting.

In the following year, allow the new stems to grow upright, and tie them in a loose bundle against the wires. Cut the old stems back after fruiting then untie the new stems from the bundle, spread them out, and train them in as replacements for fruiting the following year.

Raspberries and blackberries are often grown against wire and post supports. If the new stems reach above the uppermost wire, bend them over and tie them in to prevent wind damage over the winter.

Apples
Malus domestica
■ **Prune mainly in winter**

Apples are usually grown on dwarfing rootstocks as semi-dwarfs, bushes, or cordons. Some carry their fruit at the ends of stems produced the previous year —these are known as "tip-bearing." More often though, plants are "spur-bearing," holding their fruit on short sideshoots on branches that are two years old or more.

Prune both types in winter. On freestanding plants, remove damaged growth, and thin congested stems. On tip-bearers, cut back a few of the older stems to allow room for replacements—this will reduce cropping the following year. On spur-bearers, lightly shorten the year's growth on the main branches, cutting back weak stems by up to a half. Cut back sideshoots on what remains to 4–6 buds. For cordons, shorten new growth in summer, thin congested spur systems in winter, and cut any new growth from the main stem back to a weak bud in spring.

FRUIT PROFILE

FLOWERING TIME Spring.

HARVEST Pick fruit when ripe in summer to fall, depending on the variety.

HARDINESS Fully hardy.

HEIGHT AND SPREAD 12ft x 12ft (4m x 4m), depending on the rootstock and training.

FORMATIVE PRUNING Train freestanding plants as semi-dwarfs or bushes. Some varieties are suitable as cordons or for other training methods on wires.

ESTABLISHED PRUNING Prune mainly in winter. Hard pruning of mature branches results in unproductive, whippy shoots.

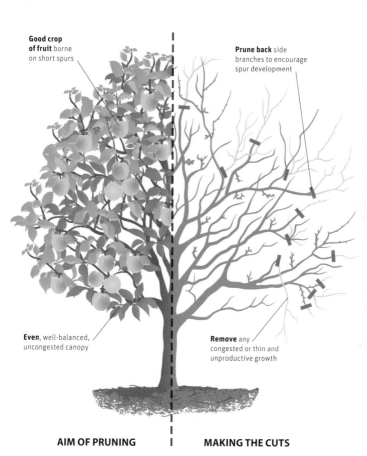

Good crop of fruit borne on short spurs

Prune back side branches to encourage spur development

Even, well-balanced, uncongested canopy

Remove any congested or thin and unproductive growth

AIM OF PRUNING

MAKING THE CUTS

Pears
Pyrus communis
■ Prune in winter and summer

Pears are usually grafted onto dwarfing rootstocks and grown as small trees or bushes or as fans or cordons. They fruit best in long, hot summer; in cool climates they can be wall trained. Most fruit on sideshoots, or "spurs," on growth that is two years old or more.

Prune established plants twice a year. In winter, remove crossing or congested branches, and cut back any strongly upright stems to maintain the form. Older branches can be cut back to the main stem— new replacement stems will develop from dormant buds on the trunk the following spring. Thin congested spurs. In summer, shorten the new growth on the main side branches. Also shorten the fruit-bearing sideshoots, retaining three leaves of the new growth. Cut back new non-fruiting sideshoots to one leaf beyond the cluster of leaves at the shoot base.

FRUIT PROFILE

FLOWERING TIME Spring.

HARVEST Pick while hard from late summer to fall. Ripen indoors for 6–8 weeks.

HARDINESS Fully hardy.

HEIGHT AND SPREAD 12ft x 12ft (4m x 4m). Rootstocks and training methods vary.

FORMATIVE PRUNING Train freestanding plants as a pyramid, bush, or standard. On wires, train as a cordon or espalier.

ESTABLISHED PRUNING Prune mainly in winter. Hard pruning of mature branches can result in unproductive, whippy growth. Thin any congested fruit in summer.

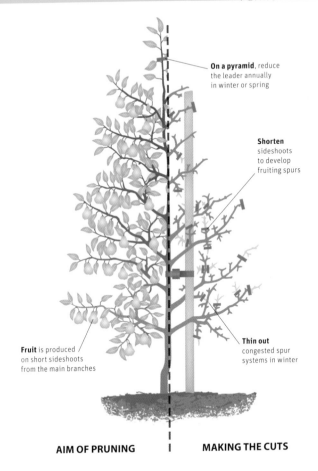

On a pyramid, reduce the leader annually in winter or spring

Shorten sideshoots to develop fruiting spurs

Thin out congested spur systems in winter

Fruit is produced on short sideshoots from the main branches

AIM OF PRUNING

MAKING THE CUTS

Plums
Prunus domestica
■ Prune during warm weather in spring or summer

Plums are deciduous trees or shrubs that are usually grown as freestanding bushes or small trees. Crops are produced along stems that are two years old or more and are often heavy. For the best results the crop should be thinned in early summer.

All pruning should be done during warm, dry periods in spring and summer to minimize the risk of infection. Once the shape of the plant is established, prune out congested stems within the crown, even if they are fruit-bearing. Check the developing fruit, and remove any that touch, will touch when ripe, or that are not exposed to the sun since these may not ripen properly. On old plants the lower branches may need support to prevent them from dragging on the ground under the weight of the fruit. Left unsupported, they may split from the trunk and create large wounds.

FRUIT PROFILE

FLOWERING TIME Spring.

HARVEST In mid- to late summer, when fruit is fully ripe.

HARDINESS Fully hardy.

HEIGHT AND SPREAD 12ft x 12ft (4m x 4m); less if trained on wires.

FORMATIVE PRUNING Grow freestanding plants as a tree or bush or train on wires as a fan.

ESTABLISHED PRUNING Thin growth as necessary in summer, and reduce the number of fruits. On fans, remove older stems, and tie in replacements. Shorten shoots after harvest.

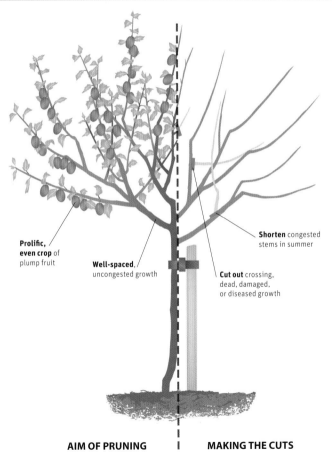

Prolific, even crop of plump fruit

Well-spaced, uncongested growth

Shorten congested stems in summer

Cut out crossing, dead, damaged, or diseased growth

AIM OF PRUNING

MAKING THE CUTS

Sweet cherries
Prunus avium
■ **Prune in warm, dry weather in spring to summer**

Cherries are potentially large plants. In small gardens varieties grafted onto dwarfing rootstocks can be grown as semi-dwarfs, bushes, pyramids, or fans. If you only have space for one, choose a self-pollinating variety.

To reduce the risk of infection, prune in warm, dry spells in spring to early summer. In the first two years, prune freestanding plants to create an open-centered crown with a balanced framework of main branches. Cherries fruit on wood that is two years old or more, so pruning thereafter should be minimal. As plants mature, cut back poorly fruiting stems to ease congestion. Fans are often sold ready-trained but need regular pruning. Remove old, unproductive branches, and tie in vigorous replacements. Cut back any badly placed shoots that cannot be tied in. Shorten sideshoots to five or six leaves; after harvesting, shorten them further to three leaves.

Even coverage of well-spaced branches

AIM OF PRUNING

FRUIT PROFILE

FLOWERING TIME Spring.

HARVEST In summer, when fully ripe.

HARDINESS Fully hardy.

HEIGHT AND SPREAD 12ft x 12ft (4m x 4m), or less on a dwarfing rootstock or if trained on horizontal wires.

FORMATIVE PRUNING Prune freestanding trees to create a trunk of at least 30in (75cm).

ESTABLISHED PRUNING Shorten new growth that is not fruit-bearing in summer. On fans, thin crowded growth, and shorten new shoots to maintain the framework.

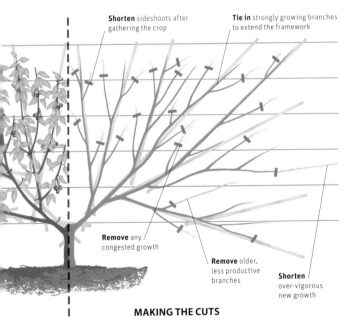

Shorten sideshoots after gathering the crop

Tie in strongly growing branches to extend the framework

Remove any congested growth

Remove older, less productive branches

Shorten over-vigorous new growth

MAKING THE CUTS

Tart cherries
Prunus cerasus
■ **Prune during dry weather in spring or summer**

Tart cherries are too sour to eat raw but are delicious cooked. Unlike sweet cherries they fruit only on one-year-old stems, so should be pruned accordingly. All work should be done during dry periods in spring and summer when wounds will heal most rapidly.

Prune in the early years to create an open-centered plant with a well-balanced framework. In subsequent years, cut back unproductive stems to suitably placed sideshoots, and remove any congested growth. After harvesting, shorten overlong branches, and thin the remaining growth as required—remembering that most of the new growth should be retained. On fans, in spring, cut back older stems that did not grow well the previous year, as well as any awkwardly placed growth. After fruiting, remove older stems if there is suitable new growth to replace them.

FRUIT PROFILE

FLOWERING TIME Spring.

HARVEST When fully ripe, in summer.

HARDINESS Fully hardy.

HEIGHT AND SPREAD Plants can grow to 12ft x 12ft (4m x 4m), less if on a dwarfing rootstock. Fan-trained plants are smaller.

FORMATIVE PRUNING Prune a semi-dwarf or bush to create a clear trunk of 30in (75cm) or train as a fan on a short leg.

ESTABLISHED PRUNING Prune in summer only to thin the growth, and remove older stems. Cut back awkwardly placed growth on fans.

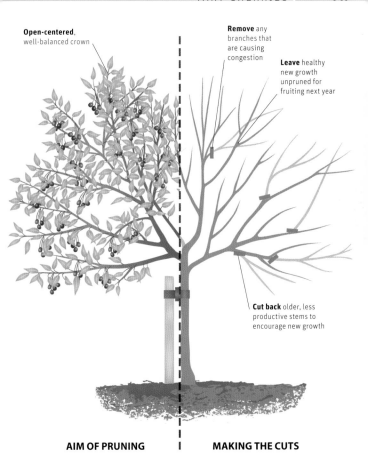

Open-centered, well-balanced crown

Remove any branches that are causing congestion

Leave healthy new growth unpruned for fruiting next year

Cut back older, less productive stems to encourage new growth

AIM OF PRUNING

MAKING THE CUTS

Peaches and nectarines
Prunus persica
■ **Prune during dry weather in summer**

Peaches and nectarines are closely related and are pruned and trained in the same way. Depending on the variety, peaches may have white or yellow flesh, and all have a characteristically fuzzy skin. Some peach varieties are genetic dwarfs and suitable for small gardens and containers. Nectarines are similar, although their slightly smaller fruit have a smooth skin. The fruits need a long, warm summer to ripen fully; in cold areas trees can be wall trained.

Prune during dry periods in summer to maintain an open-centered crown. Thin the fruit if necessary, particularly on dwarf trees. On wall-trained plants, shorten any new growth that shades the fruit; after harvesting, cut back the fruited branches, and tie in replacements. Remove and burn leaves affected by peach leaf curl as soon as they are noticed in early spring.

FRUIT PROFILE

FLOWERING TIME Early to mid-spring.

HARVEST When ripe in mid- to late summer.

HARDINESS Fully hardy, but flowers are vulnerable to frost damage in cold areas.

HEIGHT AND SPREAD 20ft x 15ft (6m x 5m); less if trained on wires.

FORMATIVE PRUNING Train freestanding plants with an open crown of up to ten main branches. Train as a fan or espalier.

ESTABLISHED PRUNING Prune in summer to thin the growth and reduce the number of fruits. Cut back fruited stems on fans, and tie in replacements.

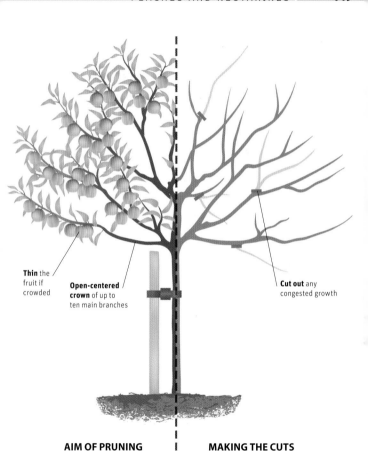

Thin the fruit if crowded

Open-centered crown of up to ten main branches

Cut out any congested growth

AIM OF PRUNING

MAKING THE CUTS

Apricots
Prunus armeniaca
■ **Prune in spring**

Apricots are deciduous trees that produce their attractive blossoms on bare branches. Long, hot summers are needed if the fruit—oval, orange-yellow, and with a distinctive smoky flavor—is to ripen fully. In cool climates they can be trained against a warm wall, although the flowers may still need protection in spring from late frost. Dwarf varieties are suitable for containers.

Pruning and training of young trees is best done in spring. For a bush or tree, aim to retain three or four main branches with an open center on a clear trunk at least 30in (75cm) tall. In warm climates where crops can be heavy, thin the fruits in early summer.

Plants can also be fan-trained on horizontal wires. On established fans, remove any leafy growth that shades the developing fruit in summer. After harvesting, cut back the fruited shoots to suitable replacements, and tie these in.

Balanced crop of fruit, allowed to ripen on the plant

Even framework of branches on fans, tied to horizontal wires

AIM OF PRUNING

FRUIT PROFILE

FLOWERING TIME Late winter to spring.

HARVEST When ripe, in late summer.

HARDINESS Fully hardy, but flowers are vulnerable to frost damage.

HEIGHT AND SPREAD 20ft x 20ft (6m x 6m); dwarf varieties are smaller.

FORMATIVE PRUNING Prune freestanding plants with 3–4 main branches; train fans on wire supports.

ESTABLISHED PRUNING Prune in summer to remove unproductive growth and to thin and expose ripening fruits. On fans, cut back fruited shoots to suitable replacements.

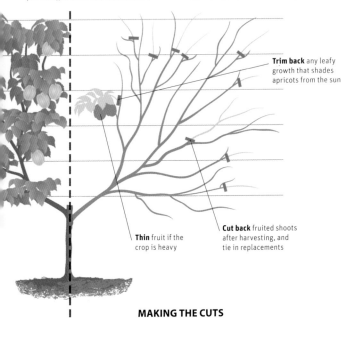

Trim back any leafy growth that shades apricots from the sun

Thin fruit if the crop is heavy

Cut back fruited shoots after harvesting, and tie in replacements

MAKING THE CUTS

Figs
Ficus carica
■ **Prune in late winter and summer**

Figs crop most freely when grown in pots or brick-lined "fig pits." Restricting the roots diverts the plant's energy into its fruit. This "fruit" is actually inverted flowerheads, filled with a mass of tiny female flowers. Plants are best wall trained in cool climates.

In warm climates, plants will produce two or three crops annually; in cool climates, only one crop will ripen fully. Small figs that develop toward the end of the growing season will overwinter and ripen the following year. In summer, remove any newly formed fruit because it won't have time to ripen. At the same time, cut back any leafy growth that is shading the swelling figs. Stems cut during the growing season bleed white sap so pruning is best done in late winter when plants are dormant. Remove older branches on wall-trained plants, and tie in suitable replacements.

FRUIT PROFILE

FLOWERING TIME Intermittently, throughout the growing season.

HARVEST When ripe, in late spring and midwinter or in late summer to fall.

HARDINESS Fully hardy, but a warm, sheltered location is needed in cold areas to ripen fruit fully.

HEIGHT AND SPREAD 10ft x 12ft (3m x 4m); pot-grown or wire-trained plants are smaller.

FORMATIVE PRUNING Prune to create an open-centered plant. To train on wires, tie in vigorous stems, and shorten the remainder.

ESTABLISHED PRUNING Cut out older, unproductive stems.

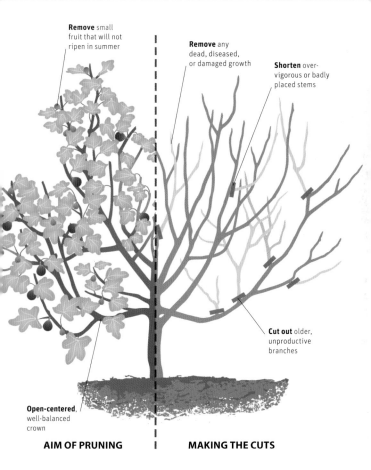

Remove small fruit that will not ripen in summer

Remove any dead, diseased, or damaged growth

Shorten over-vigorous or badly placed stems

Cut out older, unproductive branches

Open-centered, well-balanced crown

AIM OF PRUNING

MAKING THE CUTS

Citrus fruit
Citrus species and hybrids
■ **Prune in late winter to early spring**

The citrus group includes lemons, limes, sweet and bitter oranges, grapefruit, and others of hybrid origin. All evergreen, they can be trees of varying sizes. Most flower intermittently throughout the year. The fruit, which in some cases may take up to nine months to ripen, can be produced at any time, often simultaneously with the next crop of flowers. Fruit is only produced in abundance in warm climates.

Trees need little pruning, although stems of young plants can be shortened in late winter to early spring to encourage bushiness. Remove the lower branches of types that produce heavy fruit, such as grapefruit, to prevent fruit from touching the ground. This can lead to rotting. Dwarf forms of clementine, tangerine, and mandarin need little pruning.

FRUIT PROFILE

FLOWERING TIME Mainly in spring and summer but also at other times of year.

HARVEST When ripe, at any time of year—depending on the climate and the type grown.

HARDINESS Most will not withstand frost.

HEIGHT AND SPREAD 15ft x 15ft (5m x 5m), more or less. Plants in containers can be kept smaller; some varieties are dwarf.

FORMATIVE PRUNING Prune to create a clear 12in (30cm) trunk and a bushy shape.

ESTABLISHED PRUNING Prune to restrict size, if necessary.

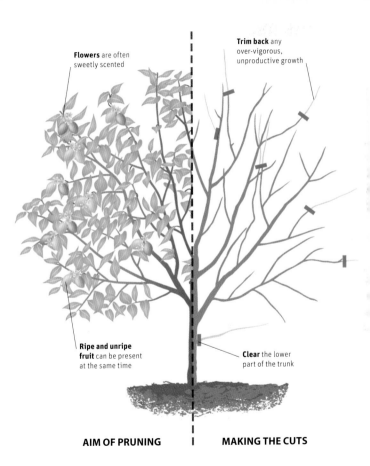

Flowers are often sweetly scented

Trim back any over-vigorous, unproductive growth

Ripe and unripe fruit can be present at the same time

Clear the lower part of the trunk

AIM OF PRUNING

MAKING THE CUTS

Olives
Olea europea
■ **Prune in fall and winter, after harvest**

Olives are slow-growing but exceptionally long-lived evergreen trees. Old specimens develop very thick, gnarled trunks with rounded to spreading crowns. They fruit reliably only in areas where summers are long, hot, and dry but need periods of freezing weather in winter if they are to achieve their full potential. Olives are popularly grown in cool climates for the ornamental appearance of their firm, gray-green leaves, which are silvery on the undersides. Although plants flower, they will not produce edible fruits.

Olives can be grown as multi-stemmed or standard trees. Clip over standards in summer to neaten the outline as required. For multi-stemmed trees, prune the leader of young plants to encourage branching; once established, lightly shorten stems after harvesting in late fall to winter to encourage a compact shape.

FRUIT PROFILE

FLOWERING TIME Early spring.

HARVEST Late fall to winter. Fruit can be stored long term in oil or brine.

HARDINESS Mature trees withstand freezing temperatures.

HEIGHT AND SPREAD 30ft x 30ft (10m x 10m); less with pruning.

FORMATIVE PRUNING Grow as multi-stemmed trees or standards.

ESTABLISHED PRUNING Shorten the growth after harvesting the crop.

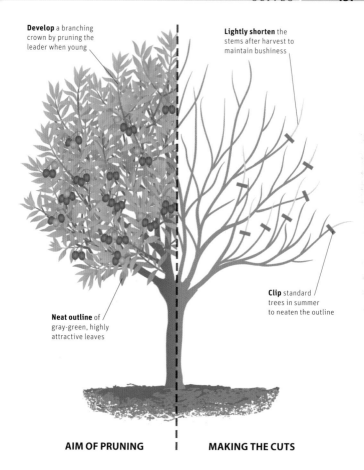

Develop a branching crown by pruning the leader when young

Lightly shorten the stems after harvest to maintain bushiness

Neat outline of gray-green, highly attractive leaves

Clip standard trees in summer to neaten the outline

AIM OF PRUNING

MAKING THE CUTS

Summer-fruiting raspberries
Rubus idaeus
■ **Prune after harvesting in late summer**

Summer-fruiting raspberries flower and fruit on stems (canes) that grew during the previous season, so a crop will not be not produced until the second year after planting. They do best in a sheltered spot in cool areas, and annual pruning will help to keep them productive.

Summer-fruiting varieties often produce taller stems than fall types, and may need support. Grow them against a "ladder" of horizontal wires that are attached every 4in (10cm) up sturdy upright posts. Space the plants 18in (45cm) apart. As the new stems grow, attach them loosely to the wires. If the stems grow beyond the top wire, bend them over and tie them in to avoid wind damage. After the first crop, cut back to the ground all the older stems that have borne fruit. Space out and reattach the remaining stems to the support, shortening them in winter to 6in (15cm) above the wire.

FRUIT PROFILE

FLOWERING TIME Spring.

HARVEST When ripe, in midsummer.

HARDINESS Fully hardy.

HEIGHT AND SPREAD Plants can grow to around 5ft x 3ft (1.5m x 1m).

FORMATIVE PRUNING Shorten all the canes immediately after planting.

ESTABLISHED PRUNING Cut all the fruited canes back to ground level after harvesting the crop.

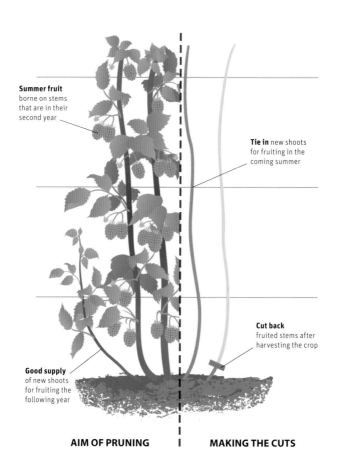

Summer fruit borne on stems that are in their second year

Tie in new shoots for fruiting in the coming summer

Cut back fruited stems after harvesting the crop

Good supply of new shoots for fruiting the following year

AIM OF PRUNING

MAKING THE CUTS

Fall-fruiting raspberries
Rubus idaeus
■ **Prune in spring**

Fall raspberries fruit for a longer period than summer types, often producing berries until the first frost. They can be grown without support in a very sheltered garden but are generally best planted against a system of horizontal wires. Because of their fruiting habit, the plants may crop in their first season.

At the end of the first winter after planting, cut all stems back to ground level. New shoots will appear from below the soil in early spring. If the growth is very soft before it reaches the lowest wire, tie the stems loosely together with string to keep them upright. Attach them to the wires as they grow upward. In following years after harvesting, stems can be left unpruned over the winter. All growth should be cut to ground level in spring. At this time, dig out unwanted suckers from around the base of plants—these can be used to replace older plants.

FRUIT PROFILE

FLOWERING TIME Spring.

HARVEST When ripe, in fall.

HARDINESS Fully hardy.

HEIGHT AND SPREAD Plants can grow to around 5ft x 3ft (1.5m x 1m).

FORMATIVE PRUNING Cut all stems to the base the first winter after planting.

ESTABLISHED PRUNING Cut all growth down to ground level annually in spring.

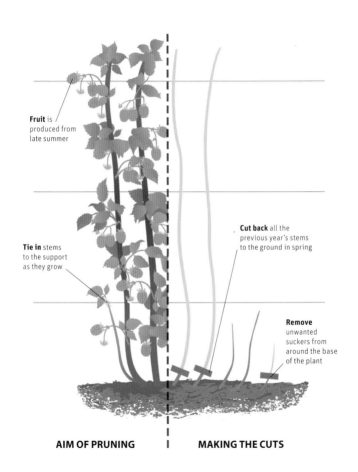

Fruit is produced from late summer

Tie in stems to the support as they grow

Cut back all the previous year's stems to the ground in spring

Remove unwanted suckers from around the base of the plant

AIM OF PRUNING

MAKING THE CUTS

Blackberries and hybrid berries
Rubus fruticosus; *Rubus* hybrids
■ **Prune after harvest, in late summer to fall**

Blackberries are succulent fruit that are commonly found growing wild in fields across the US. Many hybrids have been produced to create plants with larger fruit; often these are blackberry-raspberry crosses. They extend the berry season into fall and cope well in cool, damp climates where summer rains are common.

Plants are best trained on horizontal wires. Shorten the canes when planting. The shoots that develop in the first year will not fruit until the following year. As they grow, weave them into the wires, pulling them as close to horizontal as possible. The following year, allow new canes to grow upright, tying them loosely to the upper wires. After fruiting, cut back the older horizontally trained fruited stems to the base, untie the newer upright canes, then weave these onto the wires for fruiting the following year.

FRUIT PROFILE

FLOWERING TIME Late spring.

HARVEST When fruit is ripe, in late summer to fall.

HARDINESS Fully hardy.

HEIGHT AND SPREAD Plants grow to around 5ft x 5ft (1.5m x 1.5m).

FORMATIVE PRUNING Shorten all the stems when planting.

ESTABLISHED PRUNING Cut fruited stems to the base after harvesting.

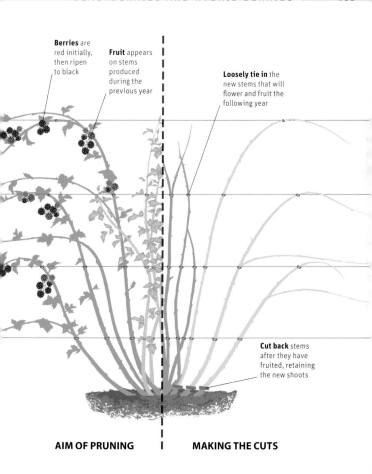

Berries are red initially, then ripen to black

Fruit appears on stems produced during the previous year

Loosely tie in the new stems that will flower and fruit the following year

Cut back stems after they have fruited, retaining the new shoots

AIM OF PRUNING

MAKING THE CUTS

Black currants
Ribes nigrum
■ **Prune in mid- to late winter**

An excellent source of vitamin C, black currants are round, dull black fruit with a very tart flavor. The plants are neat-growing, twiggy, deciduous shrubs that benefit from annual pruning. They like fertile soil but are tough plants and will tolerate a range of conditions.

Plant new plants slightly deeper than they were in the pot to encourage a multi-stemmed form, and cut all stems down to within 4in (10cm) of the base. Growth produced in the first year will not fruit. The following winter, remove straggly stems and others as necessary to create an open-centered bush—the unpruned stems will flower and fruit the following year. From then on, in mid- to late winter, remove up to one-third of the fruited stems. Old bushes can be renovated by hard pruning, but this will be at the expense of the following year's fruit.

FRUIT PROFILE

FLOWERING TIME Mid-spring.

HARVEST When ripe, in summer.

HARDINESS Fully hardy.

HEIGHT AND SPREAD Plants grow to around 4ft x 5ft (1.2m x 1.5m).

FORMATIVE PRUNING Cut back all stems to a low framework on planting. Prune to create an open-centered bush.

ESTABLISHED PRUNING Cut out some of the older stems annually.

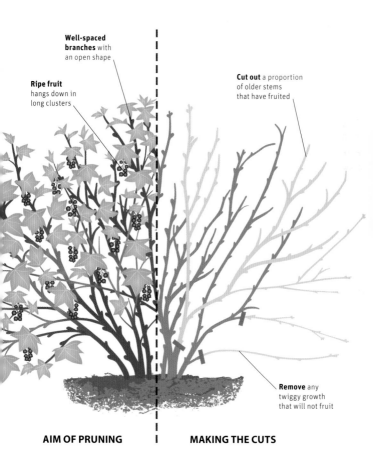

Well-spaced branches with an open shape

Ripe fruit hangs down in long clusters

Cut out a proportion of older stems that have fruited

Remove any twiggy growth that will not fruit

AIM OF PRUNING

MAKING THE CUTS

Red currants and white currants
Ribes rubrum
■ **Prune in winter, once the plant is established**

There is no clear botanical distinction between red currants and white currants, which are twiggy, deciduous shrubs that fruit well in areas with cool summers. Careful pruning greatly enhances productivity.

A young plant should have three or four strong stems on a short trunk. The first winter after planting, shorten these by half. Allow shoots to develop without pruning in spring and summer—initially they will not flower or fruit. The following winter, reduce these to eight to ten main branches, aiming to produce a balanced, open-centered bush. These stems form the main framework; shoots that emerge from these will carry the crop. Each winter, cut back all the shoots that grow from the framework stems to one bud from the base to develop a system of spurs. Remove older framework branches that are not fruiting well—cut back to suitably placed shoots.

FRUIT PROFILE

FLOWERING TIME Spring.

HARVEST When ripe, in midsummer.

HARDINESS Fully hardy.

HEIGHT AND SPREAD Plants grow to around 6ft x 6ft (2m x 2m).

FORMATIVE PRUNING Shorten strong stems by up to half when planting; cut back any weak ones at this time.

ESTABLISHED PRUNING Cut back the previous year's fruited sideshoots to one bud from the base; remove older, unproductive framework branches.

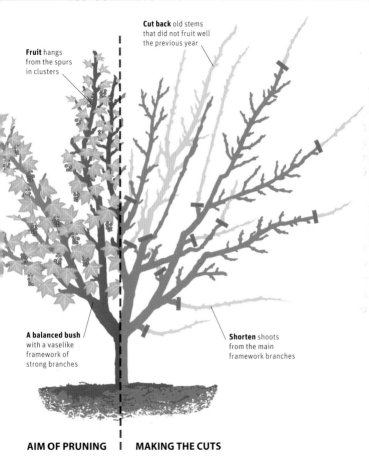

Cut back old stems that did not fruit well the previous year

Fruit hangs from the spurs in clusters

A balanced bush with a vaselike framework of strong branches

Shorten shoots from the main framework branches

AIM OF PRUNING | **MAKING THE CUTS**

Gooseberries
Ribes uva-crispa
■ **Prune in late winter**

Gooseberries produce translucent oval fruits that are mostly too tart to eat raw. The fruits are most commonly bright green, although some varieties are red or yellow. The plants are often very thorny and fruit well in areas with cool summers.

In late winter, shorten the growth of new plants to create a bush on a short stem about 4in (10cm) high, with two or three strong side branches. Of the shoots that develop from these during the following growing season, select eight to ten to create a balanced framework with an open center. These shoots will fruit the following year. Once established, older branches should be removed entirely each winter. For smaller crops of larger fruits, thin the developing crop by up to half in late spring to early summer. Thinning also helps to control the spread of gooseberry mildew.

FRUIT PROFILE

FLOWERING TIME Spring.

HARVEST When ripe, in summer.

HARDINESS Fully hardy.

HEIGHT AND SPREAD Plants grow to around 6ft x 6ft (1.8m x 1.8m).

FORMATIVE PRUNING Shorten the stems on new plantings.

ESTABLISHED PRUNING In winter, remove old branches entirely. To develop a spur system, shorten all the sideshoots that have fruited to one bud from the base.

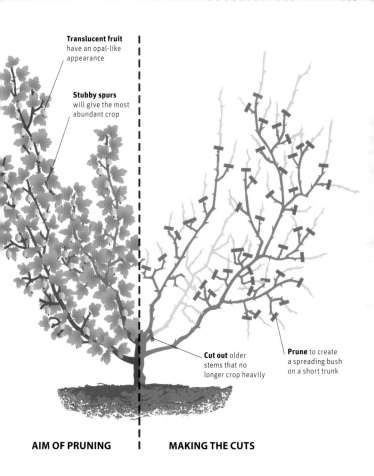

Translucent fruit have an opal-like appearance

Stubby spurs will give the most abundant crop

Cut out older stems that no longer crop heavily

Prune to create a spreading bush on a short trunk

AIM OF PRUNING

MAKING THE CUTS

Blueberries
Vaccinium corymbosum
■ Prune in late winter to early spring

Blueberries are valued not only for their delicious blue berries, which are high in vitamins and can be eaten raw or cooked in desserts, but also for their overall appearance—with bell-like white flowers in spring and glowing red leaves in fall. They need acidic soil but can be grown very successfully in large containers filled with acidic soil mix and added grit or sharp sand.

Blueberries flower on the previous season's wood, so any strong shoots that appear between spring and summer can be left unpruned for fruiting the following year. In late winter to early spring, shorten fruited stems to allow for new growth, cutting back to strong, outward-facing buds. Remove any twiggy shoots. Cut older, unproductive shoots to the base. Thin stems in the middle of the plant to allow room for any strong new shoots and to create an open-centered bush.

FRUIT PROFILE

FLOWERING TIME Mid-spring.

HARVEST In midsummer to fall, depending on the variety.

HARDINESS Fully hardy.

HEIGHT AND SPREAD Plants grow to around 5ft x 5ft (1.5m x 1.5m).

FORMATIVE PRUNING The first winter after planting, remove straggly stems and others as necessary to produce an open-centered bush.

ESTABLISHED PRUNING Prune annually in winter to thin congested growth; remove some of the oldest branches entirely.

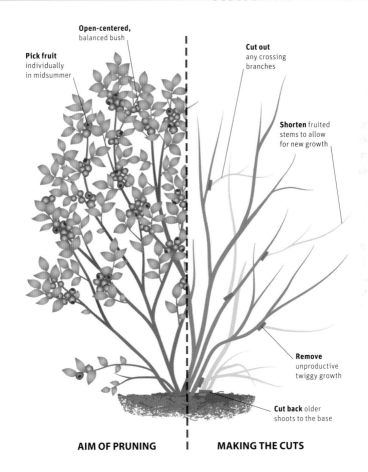

Open-centered, balanced bush

Pick fruit individually in midsummer

Cut out any crossing branches

Shorten fruited stems to allow for new growth

Remove unproductive twiggy growth

Cut back older shoots to the base

AIM OF PRUNING

MAKING THE CUTS

Grapevines
Vitis vinifera

■ **Formative pruning of a cordon in winter and spring**

Grapevines are long-lived, vigorous, deciduous tendril climbers that produce large quantities of new growth each year. Careful pruning and training diverts their energy into fruit production. Plants are hardy, but the fruit needs long, warm summers to ripen fully.

One of the simplest training methods is to grow the plant as a cordon on a system of horizontal wires. The aim is to develop an upright main stem with stubby sideshoots, or "spurs," from which fruit-bearing stems grow. Rigorous pruning in the early years encourages thick, sturdy growth. Since cut stems bleed sap copiously, main pruning is best done in midwinter, when the plants are dormant.

When planting, shorten the main stem to 6in (15cm). Allow a single, strong shoot to develop from this, and tie it to a vertical cane attached to the wires. Shorten sideshoots to five leaves, and cut back any shoots that emerge from the sideshoots to one leaf. In winter—and the winter after—reduce the main stem by two-thirds, and cut back the remaining side branches to one bud. In summer, tie in a new leader, and shorten the sideshoots to five leaves. Remove any flower buds that form.

Once established, clusters of new shoots emerge from the spurs in spring. Reduce the number to two per spur by pinching or rubbing out the rest. Tie in the stronger of the two to the wire, and pinch back the other to two leaves—it will provide replacement growth if the selected stem is damaged at a later stage.

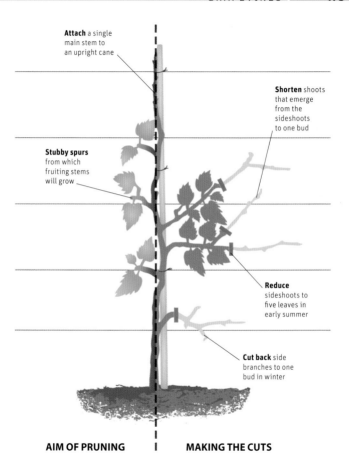

Attach a single main stem to an upright cane

Shorten shoots that emerge from the sideshoots to one bud

Stubby spurs from which fruiting stems will grow

Reduce sideshoots to five leaves in early summer

Cut back side branches to one bud in winter

AIM OF PRUNING   **MAKING THE CUTS**

Grapevines

■ **Pruning an established cordon in summer and winter**

In summer, tie in the central leader as it grows, and continue to tie in the sideshoots. Shorten any sideshoots that are not flower-bearing to five leaves. Shorten sideshoots with flowers to two leaves beyond the flower truss farthest from the main stem. Reduce the number of flower trusses to one per sideshoot for dessert grapes and one per 12in (30cm) for wine grapes.

For dessert grapes, as the crop begins to develop, reduce the number of grapes within each cluster by about one-third, cutting out smaller fruit so the remainder have room to swell. This encourages the plant to channel its energy into producing larger fruit. This is not necessary for wine grapes. Pinch back any leafy growth shading the bunches.

Each winter, cut back the leader as necessary to maintain the cordon —cut to a strong bud just below the highest horizontal wire. Cut back the sideshoots to one bud, and thin any congested stems as necessary.

FRUIT PROFILE

FLOWERING TIME Late spring to summer.

HARVEST When ripe, in fall.

HARDINESS Fully hardy, but fruit needs a warm exposure to ripen fully.

HEIGHT AND SPREAD Plants can grow to 6ft x 6ft (2m x 2m), when trained as a cordon.

FORMATIVE PRUNING Cut back most of the growth when planting, and develop a strong central stem with evenly spaced sideshoots.

ESTABLISHED PRUNING Trim sideshoots annually. Thin the grapes as they swell. Each winter, cut back the leader to one or two buds.

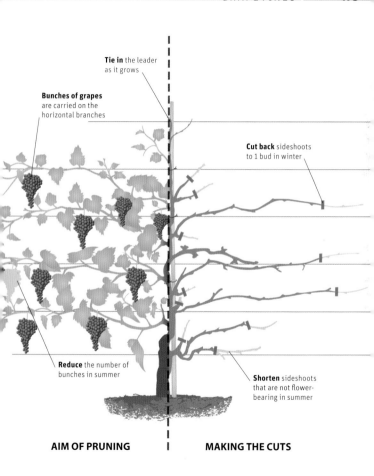

Tie in the leader as it grows

Bunches of grapes are carried on the horizontal branches

Cut back sideshoots to 1 bud in winter

Reduce the number of bunches in summer

Shorten sideshoots that are not flower-bearing in summer

AIM OF PRUNING

MAKING THE CUTS

Index

A

Abelia 36
Abeliophyllum 38
Abies 40
Abutilon 42
Acacia 44
Acer 46
Actinidia 48
Aesculus 50
Akebia 52
Alder (Alnus) 54
Alnus 54
Aloysia 56
Amelanchier 58
Angels' trumpets
 (Brugmansia) 82
Apples (Malus domestica) 438
Apricots
 (Prunus armeniaca) 450
Aralia 60
Arbutus 62
Aronia 64
Artemisia 66
Aucuba 68
Azalea (Rhododendron)
 346–349
Azara 70

B

Barberry (Berberis) 72–75
Bay tree (Laurus) 256
Beautyberry (Callicarpa) 90
Beautybush (Kolkwitzia) 248
Beech (Fagus) 186
Berberis
 deciduous 72
 evergreen 74

Betula 76
Birch (Betula) 76
Bittersweet (Celastrus) 112
Black currants
 (Ribes nigrum) 464
Blackberries
 (Rubus fruticosus) 462
Bluebeard (Caryopteris) 102
Blueberries (Vaccinium
 corymbosum) 470
Bottlebrush (Callistemon) 92
Bougainvillea 78
Boxwood (Buxus) 88
Brachyglottis 80
Broom
 (Cytisus) 162
 (Genista) 204
Brugmansia 82
Buckeye (Aesculus) 50
Buddleja
 early-flowering 84
 late-flowering 86
Butterfly bush
 (Buddleja) 84–87
Buxus 88

C

Calico bush (Kalmia)
 244
Callicarpa 90
Callistemon 92
Calluna 94
Camellia 96
Campsis 98
Carpinus 100
Caryopteris 102
Catalpa 104

Ceanothus
 deciduous 106
 evergreen 108
Cedar (Cedrus) 110
Cedrus 110
Celastrus 112
Celtis 114
Cercis 116
Cestrum 118
Chaenomeles 120
Cherry (Prunus)
 deciduous ornamental 334
 evergreen ornamental 336
 sweet 444
 tart 446
Chimonanthus 122
Chocolate vine (Akebia) 52
Choisya 124
Chokeberry (Aronia) 64
Cinquefoil (Potentilla) 332
Cistus 126
Citrus fruit (Citrus species and
 hybrids) 454
Clematis
 Group 1 128
 Group 2 130
 Group 3 132
Clerodendrum 134
Clethra 136
Clianthus 138
Colutea 140
Cornus
 shrubs 144
 trees 142
Corylopsis 146
Corylus 148
Cotinus 150

Acknowledgments

Author's thanks

This book would not have been possible without the constant vigilance and care shown by the editorial and design team at Dorling Kindersley. Rebecca Tennant gave particular attention to the accuracy of the artwork (beautifully drawn by Debbie Maizels, Martine Collings, and all at the Peter Bull Art Studio) besides laying out the book so attractively. Becky Shackleton did a sterling job of tidying up the text and proved very adept at interpreting my handwriting. Simon Maughan at the RHS made several helpful suggestions, both at the planning stage and later on. Lastly, Helen Fewster and Jo Doran, who supervised the whole project, remaining unfailingly polite and unflappable, made sure it stayed on track at all stages. All were a pleasure to work with.

Publisher's acknowledgments

Dorling Kindersley would like to thank Suefa Lee for editorial assistance; Vicky Read, Alison Shackleton, and Aastha Tiwari for design assistance, and Anurag Trivedi for DTP assistance.

The publisher would like to thank the following for their kind permission to reproduce their photographs: (Key: a-above; b-below/bottom; c-center; f-far; l-left; r-right; t-top)

10 Dorling Kindersley: Alan Buckingham (br). **34 GAP Photos**: Visions. **62 GAP Photos**: Geoff Kidd (tl). **76 GAP Photos**: Howard Rice (tl). **126 Dorling Kindersley**: The Chesea Physic Garden, London (tr). **156 Getty Images**: DEA / S.Montanari (tl). **208 GAP Photos**: Jan Smith (tl). **212 GAP Photos**: Howard Rice (tl). **246 Getty Images**: Ron Evans (tl). **308 Getty Images**: Visuals Unlimited, Inc. / Consumer Institute / NSIL (tl). **326 Dorling Kindersley**: Tony Russell (tl). **344 Getty Images**: DEA / Dani-Jeske (tl). **424 Getty Images**: Joff Lee. **431 Dorling Kindersley**: Alan Buckingham (bl,bc,br). **432 Dorling Kindersley**: Alan Buckingham (tl). **433 Dorling Kindersley**: Alan Buckingham (bl). **435 Dorling Kindersley**: Alan Buckingham (t). **437 Dorling Kindersley**: Alan Buckingham (tr, br). **440 Dorling Kindersley**: Alan Buckingham (tl). **442 Dorling Kindersley**: Alan Buckingham (tl). **444 Dorling Kindersley**: Alan Buckingham (tr). **446 Dorling Kindersley**: Alan Buckingham (tl). **450 Dorling Kindersley**: Alan Buckingham (tr). **452 Dorling Kindersley**: Alan Buckingham (tl). **460 Dorling Kindersley**: Alan Buckingham (tl). **462 Dorling Kindersley**: Alan Buckingham (tl). **464 Dorling Kindersley**: Alan Buckingham (tr). **466 Dorling Kindersley**: Alan Buckingham (tl). **468 Dorling Kindersley**: Alan Buckingham (tl). **470 Dorling Kindersley**: Alan Buckingham (tl).

All other images © Dorling Kindersley
For further information see: www.dkimages.com

About the author

A graduate of London University, **Andrew Mikolajski** worked first as a music critic before entering publishing. He is the author of over 30 gardening titles, including *Plants for Shade*, *An Encyclopedia of Garden Plants*, *1001 Garden Questions Answered*, and the *Encyclopedia of Apples*. He has contributed to several RHS publications, including the *Gardener's Encyclopedia of Plants and Flowers*, the *Encyclopedia of Gardening*, the *A–Z Encyclopedia of Garden Plants*, *Pruning and Training*, and *Propagating Plants*. Andrew teaches garden design and the RHS certificate at Warwickshire College, speaks to gardening clubs and societies throughout the UK and leads courses at Lamport Hall and Farncombe Estate, with occasional broadcasts for BBC Radio Northampton and Radio Leicester.